P9-DTA-021

French
phrase book

Berlitz Publishing Company, Inc.

Princeton   Mexico City   London   Eschborn   Singapore

ISBN 2-8315-6239-2
Ninth printing - September 2000
Printed in Spain

Developed and produced for Berlitz Publishing Company by:
G&W Publishing Services, Oxfordshire, U.K.

Contents

Pronunciation

This section is designed to make you familiar with the sounds of French using our simplified phonetic transcription. You'll find the pronunciation of the French letters and sounds explained below, together with their "imitated" equivalents. This system is used throughout the phrase book: simply read the pronunciation as if it were English, noting any special rules below.

The French language

French is spoken in a number of countries across the world, including various dependencies and former colonies of France. These are the countries where you can expect to hear French spoken (figures are approximate):

France **France**
French is spoken by the whole population (56 million). Other languages occasionally heard: Provençal (southeast France), Breton (Brittany), Alsatien (German dialect in Alsace and Lorraine), Corse (an Italian dialect in Corsica), and Catalan and Basque (along the border with Spain).

Belgique **Belgium**
French is one of the official languages; it is understood everywhere and has 3.5 million native speakers. Other languages: Flemish (4.5 million native speakers) with 1 million bilingual.

Luxembourg **Luxembourg**
French is the official language. Other languages: German and occasionally Luxembourgian.

Suisse **Switzerland**
French is one of the national languages; native tongue of 20% of the population (esp. in the west). Other languages: German (70% of population) in the north and east, Italian in the south, and the much rarer Romansh.

Canada **Canada**
French is one of the official languages, together with English. 7 million speakers, mainly in Quebec.

Afrique **Africa**
French is the official language (or one of them) in: Benin, Burkina Faso, Burundi, Cameroon, Central African Republic, Chad, Congo, Gabon, Guinea, Ivory Coast, Madagascar, Niger, Rwanda, Senegal, Togo and Zaïre. It is spoken to varying degrees, alongside native languages. Also heard in Algeria, Morocco and Tunisia.

Antilles françaises **French West Indies**
Consisting of the French Caribbean islands of Guadeloupe and Martinique. Other languages: French creole, English (in tourist areas). Also in the Caribbean, French is the official language in Haïti.

The French alphabet is the same as English, although the letter **w** appears only in foreign words. It also uses several accents: grave (`), acute (´), circumflex (^) and the cedilla (ç - only on the letter **c**).

Historical interaction between France and England has meant that many French words will be comprehensible to the English speaker.

But watch out for the "false friends" that don't mean what you might think: **la cave** (cellar, basement), **la conférence** (lecture), **la librairie** (bookstore), **le magasin** (store), **le médecin** (doctor), **la monnaie** (change/coins), **une prune** (plum), **un raisin** (grape), **sale** (dirty).

Consonants

Letter	Approximate pronunciation	Symbol	Example	
b, c, d, f, k, l, m, n, p, s, t, v, x, z	as in English			
ch	like *sh* in *sh*ut	sh	**chercher**	*shehrshay*
ç	like *s* in *s*it	s	**ça**	*sa*
g	1) before **e, i, y**, like *s* in plea*s*ure	zh	**manger**	*mangzhay*
	2) before **a, o, u**, like *g* in *g*o	g	**garçon**	*garsawng*
gn	like *ni* in o*ni*on	ñ	**ligne**	*leeñ*
h	always silent		**homme**	*om*
j	like *s* in plea*s*ure	zh	**jamais**	*zhamay*
qu	like *k* in *k*ill	k	**qui**	*kee*
r	rolled in the back of the mouth, rather like gargling	r	**rouge**	*roozh*
w	usually like *v* in *v*oice	v	**wagon**	*vagawng*

Vowels

Letter	Approximate pronunciation	Symbol	Example	
a, à or â	between the *a* in h*a*t and the *a* in f*a*ther	a/ah	**mari**	*maree*
é or ez	like *a* in l*a*te	ay	**été**	*aytay*
è, ê, e	like *e* in g*e*t	e/eh	**même**	*mem*
e	sometimes like *er* in oth*er*	er	**je**	*zher*
i	like *ee* in m*ee*t	ee	**il**	*eel*
o	generally like *o* in h*o*t but sometimes like *oa* in s*oa*r	o/ oa	**donner** **rose**	*donnay* *roaz*
ô	like *oa* in s*oa*r	oa	**Rhône**	*oan*
u	like *ew* in d*ew*	ew	**cru**	*krew*

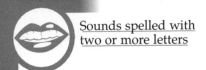

Sounds spelled with two or more letters

ai, ay,	can be pronounced	*ay*	**j'ai**	*zhay*
aient, ais,	like *a* in l*a*te or		**vais**	*vay*
ait, aî, ei	like *e* in g*e*t	*e/eh*	**chaîne**	*shen*
			peine	*pen*
(e)au	similar to *oa* in s*oa*r	*oa*	**chaud**	*shoa*
eu, eû,	like *ur* in f*ur*, but with	*ur*	**peu**	*pur*
œu	lips rounded, not spread			
euil, euille	like *uh* in h*uh*, but without	*uhy*	**feuille**	*fuhy*
	pronouncing the *h* and with			
	a *y* sound added			
ail, aille	like *ie* in t*ie*	*ie*	**taille**	*tie*
oi, oy	like *w* followed by	*wa*	**moi**	*mwa*
	the *a* in h*a*t			
ou, oû	like *o* in m*o*ve or *oo* in h*oo*t	*oo*	**nouveau**	*noovoa*
ui	approximately like	*wee*	**traduire**	*tradweer*
	wee in bet*wee*n			

Nasal sounds

French contains nasal vowels, which are transcribed with a vowel symbol plus *ng*. This *ng* should not be pronounced strongly but is included to show the nasal quality of the previous vowel. A nasal vowel is pronounced simultaneously through the mouth and the nose.

am, an	something like *arn* in t*arn*ish	*ahng*	**tante**	*tahngt*
em, en	generally like the previous sound	*ahng*	**entrée**	*ahngtray*
ien	sounds like *yan* in y*an*k	*yang*	**bien**	*byang*
im, in, **aim, ain,** **eim, ein**	approximately like *ang* in r*ang*	*ang*	**instant**	*angstahng*
om, on	approximately like *ong* in s*ong*	*awng*	**maison**	*mayzawng*
um, un	approximately like *ang* in r*ang*	*ang*	**brun**	*brang*

Liaison

Normally, final consonants of words are not pronounced in French. However, when a word ending in a consonant is followed by one beginning with a vowel, they are often run together, and the consonant is pronounced as if it began the following word. Examples:

| **nous** | *noo* | **nous avons un enfant** | *noo zavawng zang nahngfahng* |
| **comment** | *komahng* | **comment allez-vous?** | *komahng talay voo* |

Stress

All syllables in French are pronounced with more or less the same degree of stress (loudness). So stress has not been indicated in the phonetic transcription and each syllable should be pronounced with equal stress.

Pronunciation of the French alphabet

A	*ah*		**N**	*en*
B	*bay*		**O**	*oa*
C	*say*		**P**	*pay*
D	*day*		**Q**	*kew*
E	*er*		**R**	*ehr*
F	*ef*		**S**	*ess*
G	*zhay*		**T**	*tay*
H	*ahsh*		**U**	*ew*
I	*ee*		**V**	*vay*
J	*zhee*		**W**	*dooblervay*
K	*kah*		**X**	*eex*
L	*el*		**Y**	*ee grek*
M	*em*		**Z**	*zed*

Basic Expressions

ESSENTIAL

Yes.	**Oui.** *wee*
No.	**Non.** *nawng*
Okay.	**D'accord.** *dakor*
Please.	**S'il vous plaît.** *seel voo pleh*
Thank you (very much.)	**Merci (beaucoup).** *mehrsee (boakoo)*

Greetings/Apologies Salutations/Excuses

Hello!/Hi!	**Bonjour!/Salut!** *bawngzhoor/salew*
Good morning/afternoon.	**Bonjour.** *bawngzhoor*
Good evening.	**Bonsoir.** *bawngswar*
Good night.	**Bonne nuit.** *bon nwee*
Good-bye.	**Au revoir.** *oa rervwar*
Excuse me! (*getting attention*)	**Excusez-moi, (s'il vous plaît)!** *exkewzay mwa (seel voo pleh)*
Excuse me. (*may I get past?*)	**Excusez-moi!/Pardon!** *exkewzay mwa/pardawng*
Excuse me!/Sorry!	**Pardon!/Désolé(e)!** *pardawng/dayzolay*
It was an accident.	**Je ne l'ai pas fait exprès.** *zher ner lay pa feh expreh*
Don't mention it.	**Je vous en prie** *zher voo zahng pree*
Never mind.	**Ça ne fait rien.** *sa ner feh ryang*

Communication difficulties
Problèmes de communication

Do you speak English?	**Parlez-vous anglais?** *parlay voo ahnggleh*
Does anyone here speak English?	**Y a-t-il quelqu'un ici qui parle anglais?** *ee ateel kelkang eessee kee parl ahnggleh*
Could you speak more slowly?	**Pourriez-vous parler plus lentement?** *pooryay voo parlay plew lahngtmahng*
Could you repeat that?	**Pourriez-vous répéter ça?** *pooryay voo raypaytay sa*
Pardon?/What was that?	**Pardon?/Qu'avez-vous dit?** *pardawng/kavay voo dee*
Could you spell it?	**Pourriez-vous l'épeler?** *pooryay voo layplay*
Please write it down.	**Pourriez-vous l'écrire, s'il vous plaît?** *pooryay voo laykreer seel voo pleh*
Can you translate this for me?	**Pourriez-vous me traduire ça?** *pooryay voo mer tradweer sa*
What does this/that mean?	**Qu'est-ce que ça veut dire?** *kess ker sa vuh deer*
Please point to the phrase in the book.	**Pourriez-vous me montrer l'expression dans le livre?** *pooryay voo mer mawng tray lexpressyawng dahng ler leevr*
I (don't) understand.	**Je (ne) comprends (pas).** *zher ner kawngprahng pa*
Do you understand?	**(Est-ce que) vous comprenez?** *(ess ker) voo kawngprernay*

– *Ça fait cent trente-cinq francs.* (That's 135 francs.)
– *Pardon, je ne comprends pas.*
(Sorry, I don't understand.)
– *Ça fait cent trente-cinq francs.*
(That's 135 francs.)
– *Pouvez-vous l'écrire, s'il vous plaît?*
(Can you write it down, please?)
– *Ah. Cent trente-cinq francs.* (Ah, 135 francs.)

Questions Questions

GRAMMAR

Questions can be formed in French:

1. by inverting the subject and verb:
   Pouvez-vous m'aider?   Can you help me?
2. by using a question word (▶12–17) + the inverted order:
   Comment voulez-vous payer?   How do you want to pay?
3. by using "est-ce que" + the affirmative word order:
   Est-ce que vous comprenez?   Do you understand?
4. by a questioning intonation + the affirmative word order:
   Vous désirez?   Do you want (anything)?

Where? Où?

Where is it?	**Où est-ce?** *oo ess*
Where are you going?	**Où allez-vous?** *oo alay voo*
to the meeting place [point]	**au point de rendez-vous** *oa pwang der rahngday voo*
across the market	**en face du marché** *ahng fas dew marshay*
away from me	**loin de moi** *lwang der mwa*
downstairs	**en bas** *ahng ba*
from the U.S.	**des États-Unis** *day zayta zewnee*
here (to here)	**ici** *eessee*
in the car	**dans la voiture** *dahng la vwatewr*
in France	**en France** *ahng frahngs*
inside	**à l'intérieur** *a langtayryurr*
near the bank	**près de la banque** *preh der la bahngk*
next to the apples	**à côté des pommes** *a koatay day pom*
on the left/right	**à gauche/à droite** *a goash/a drwat*
there	**là-bas** *la ba*
to the hotel	**à l'hôtel** *a loatel*
toward Paris	**vers Paris** *ver paree*
outside the café	**devant le café** *devahng ler kafay*
up to the traffic light	**jusqu'aux feux** *zhewskoa fur*
upstairs	**en haut** *ahng oa*

When …? Quand …?

When does the museum open? **Quand le musée est-il ouvert?** *kahng ler mewzay ehteel oovehr*

When does the train arrive? **À quelle heure arrive le train?** *a kel urr areev ler trang*

after lunch	**après le déjeuner** *apreh ler dayzhurnay*
always	**toujours** *toozhoor*
around midnight	**vers minuit** *vehr meenwee*
at 7 o'clock	**à sept heures** *a set urr*
before Friday	**avant vendredi** *avahng vahngdrerdee*
by tomorrow	**pour demain** *poor dermang*
early	**tôt/de bonne heure** *toa/der bon urr*
every week	**chaque semaine** *shak sermayn*
for 2 hours	**pendant deux heures** *pahngdahng dur zurr*
from 9 a.m. to 6 p.m.	**de neuf heures à dix-huit heures** *der nurf urr a deezweet urr*
immediately	**tout de suite** *too der sweet*
in 20 minutes	**dans vingt minutes** *dahng vang meenewt*
never	**jamais** *zhameh*
not yet	**pas encore** *pa zahngkor*
now	**maintenant** *mangtnahng*
often	**souvent** *soovahng*
on March 8	**le huit mars** *ler weet mars*
on weekdays	**pendant la semaine** *pahngdahng la sermayn*
sometimes	**quelquefois** *kelkefwa*
soon	**bientôt** *byangtoa*
then	**alors/ensuite/puis** *alor/ahngsweet/pwee*
within 2 days	**en deux jours** *ahng dur zhoor*
10 minutes ago	**il y a dix minutes** *eel ee a dee meenewt*

What kind of …? Quelle sorte de …?

I'd like something …	**Je voudrais quelque chose de …** *zher voodrey kelker shoaz der*
It's …	**C'est …** *seh*
beautiful/ugly	**beau (belle)/laid(e)** *boa (bel)/lay(d)*
better/worse	**mieux/pire** *myur/peer*
big/small	**grand(e)/petit(e)** *grahng(d)/pertee(t)*
cheap/expensive	**bon marché/cher** *bawng marshay/shehr*
clean/dirty	**propre/sale** *propr/sal*
dark/light	**foncé/clair(e)** *fongsay/klehr*
delicious/revolting	**délicieux(-ieuse)/dégoûtant(e)** *dayleesyur(z)/daygootahng(t)*
easy/difficult	**facile/difficile** *fasseel/deefeesseel*
empty/full	**vide/plein** *veed/plang*
good/bad	**bon(ne)/mauvais(e)** *bawng (bon)/moavay(z)*
heavy/light	**lourd(e)/léger(-ère)** *loor(d)/layzhay (layzhehr)*
hot, warm/cold	**chaud(e)/froid(e)** *shoa(d)/frwa(d)*
modern/old-fashioned	**moderne/démodé(e)** *modern/daymoday*
narrow/wide	**étroit(e)/large** *aytrwa(t)/larzh*
old/new	**vieux (vieille)/neuf (neuve)** *vyur (vyay)/nurf (nurv)*
open/shut	**ouvert(e)/fermé(e)** *oovehr(t)/fehrmay*
pleasant, nice/unpleasant	**agréable, beau (belle)/désagréable** *agrayabl, boa (bel)/dayzagrayabl*
quick/slow	**rapide/lent(e)** *rapeed/lahng(t)*
quiet/noisy	**silencieux(-ieuse)/bruyant(e)** *seelahngsyur(z)/brewyahng(t)*
right/wrong	**juste/faux (fausse)** *zhewst/foa(ss)*
large/small	**grand(e)/petit(e)** *grahng(d)/pertee(t)*
vacant/occupied	**libre/occupé(e)** *leebr/okkewpay*
young/old	**jeune/vieux (vieille)** *zhurn/vyur (vyay)*

Nouns in French are either masculine or feminine; adjectives agree in gender and number (*singular* or *plural*) with the noun they describe. Most adjectives form the feminine (shown in parentheses) by adding **-e** to the masculine, unless the word already ends in **-e**. See page 169 for more explanation.

How much/many? Combien?

How much is that?	**C'est combien?** *seh kawnbyang*
How many are there?	**Combien y en a-t-il?** *kawnbyang ee ahng na teel*
1/2/3	**un/deux/trois** *ang/dur/trwa*
4/5	**quatre/cinq** *katr/sangk*
none	**aucun(e)** *oakang(-kewn)*
about 100 francs	**environ cent francs** *ahngveerawng sahng frahng*
a little	**un peu** *ang pur*
a lot of traffic	**beaucoup de circulation** *boakoo der seerkewlasyawng*
enough	**assez** *assay*
few/a few of them	**quelques/quelques-un(e)s** *kelker/kelker zung (zewn)*
more than that	**plus que ça** *plew ker sa*
less than that	**moins que ça** *mwang ker sa*
much more	**beaucoup plus** *boakoo plews*
nothing else	**rien d'autre** *ryang doatr*
too much	**trop** *tro*

Why? Pourquoi?

Why is that?	**Pourquoi?** *poorkwa*
Why not?	**Pourquoi pas?** *poorkwa pa*
because of the weather	**à cause du temps** *a koaz dew tahng*
because I'm in a hurry	**parce que je suis pressé(e)** *pars ker zher swee pressay*
I don't know why.	**Je ne sais pas pourquoi.** *zher ner say pa poorkwa*

NUMBERS ➤ 216

Who?/Which? Qui?/Lequel?

Who's there?	**Qui est là?**	*kee eh la*
It's me!	**C'est moi!**	*seh mwa*
It's us!	**C'est nous!**	*seh noo*
someone	**quelqu'un**	*kelkang*
no one	**personne**	*pehrson*
Which one do you want?	**Lequel voulez-vous?** *lerkel voolay voo*	
one like that	**un(e) comme ceci** *ang (ewn) kom sersee*	
that one/this one	**celui-là/celui-ci** *serlwee la/serlwee see*	
not that one	**pas celui-là** *pa serlwee la*	
something	**quelque chose** *kelker shoaz*	
nothing	**rien** *ryang*	
none	**aucun** *oakang*	

Whose? À qui?

Whose … is that?	**À qui est-ce?**	*a kee ess*
It's …	**C'est …** *seh*	
mine/ours/yours	**à moi /à nous/à vous** *a mwa/a noo/a voo*	
his/hers/theirs	**à lui/à elle/à eux** *a lwee/a ell/a ur*	
It's … turn.	**C'est … tour.** *seh … toor*	
my/our/your	**mon/notre/votre** *mawng/notr/votr*	
his/her/their	**son/son/leur** *sawng/ lurr*	

GRAMMAR

Possessive adjectives agree in number and gender with the noun they modify, i.e., with the thing possessed and not the possessor.

	masculine	feminine	plural
my	**mon**	**ma**	**mes**
your (fam. sing.)	**ton**	**ta**	**tes**
his/her/its	**son**	**sa**	**ses**
our	**notre**	**notre**	**nos**
your	**votre**	**votre**	**vos**
their	**leur**	**leur**	**leurs**

How? Comment?

How would you like to pay?	**Comment voulez-vous payer?** *kommahng voolay voo payay*
How are you getting here?	**Comment arrivez-vous?** *kommahng tarivay voo*
by car	**en voiture** *ahng vwatewr*
by credit card	**avec une carte de crédit** *avek ewn kart der kraydee*
by chance	**par hasard** *par azar*
equally	**également** *aygalmahng*
extremely	**extrêmement** *extremmahng*
on foot	**à pied** *a pyay*
quickly	**vite/rapidement** *veet/rapeedmahng*
slowly	**lentement** *lahngtmahng*
too fast	**trop vite** *tro veet*
totally	**totalement** *totalmahng*
very	**très** *treh*
with a friend	**avec un(e) ami(e)** *avek ang (ewn) namee*
without a passport	**sans passeport** *sahng passpor*

Is it …?/Are there …? C'est …?/Y a-t-il …?

Is it …?	**(Est-ce que) c'est …?** *(ess ker) seh*
Is it free?	**C'est libre?** *seh leebr*
It isn't ready.	**Ce n'est pas prêt.** *ser neh pa preh*
Is/Are there …?	**Y a-t-il …?** *ee a teel*
Are there buses going into town?	**Y a-t-il des bus pour aller en ville?** *ee a teel day bews poor alay ahng veel*
Here it is/they are.	**Le/Les voici.** *ler/ley vwasee*
There it is/they are.	**Le/Les voilà.** *ler/ley vwala*

Can/May? Pouvoir

Can I have ...?	**Est-ce que je peux avoir ...?** *ess ker zher pur zavwar*
Can we have ...?	**Est-ce que nous pouvons avoir ...?** *ess ker noo poovawng zavwar*
Can you tell me ...?	**Pouvez-vous me dire ...?** *poovay voo mer deer*
Can you help me?	**Pouvez-vous m'aider?** *poovay voo mayday*
Can I help you?	**Est-ce que je peux vous aider?** *ess ker zher pur voo zayday*
Can you direct me to ...?	**Pouvez-vous m'indiquer le chemin pour ...?** *poovay voo mangdeekay ler shermang poor*
I can't.	**Je ne peux pas.** *zher ner pur pa*

What do you want? Qu'est-ce que vous voulez?

I'd like ...	**Je voudrais ...** *zher voodray*
Could I have ...?	**Est-ce que je pourrais avoir ...?** *ess ker zher pooray zavwar*
We'd like ...	**Nous voudrions ...** *noo voodryawng*
Give me ...	**Donnez-moi ...** *donay mwa*
I'm looking for ...	**Je cherche ...** *zher shehrsh*
I need to ...	**Je dois ...** *zher dwa*
go ...	**aller ...** *alay*
find ...	**trouver ...** *troovay*
see ...	**voir ...** *vwar*
speak to ...	**parler à ...** *parlay a*

– Excusez-moi! (Excuse me.)
– *Oui? (Yes?)*
– Pouvez-vous m'aider? (Can you help me?)
– *Oui, bien sûr. (Yes, certainly.)*
– Je voudrais parler à monsieur Blanc.
(I would like to speak to Mr. Blanc.)
– *Un moment, s'il vous plaît. (One moment, please.)*

Other useful words
Autres mots utiles

fortunately	**heureusement** *urrurzmahng*
hopefully	**en esperant ...** *ahng espehrahng*
of course	**bien sûr** *byang sewr*
perhaps/possibly	**peut-être** *pur tetr*
probably	**probablement** *probablmahng*
unfortunately	**malheureusement** *malurrurzmahng*

Exclamations   Exclamations

At last!	**Enfin!** *ahngfang*
Carry on.	**Continuez.** *kawngteeneway*
Damn!	**Zut!** *zewt*
Good God!	**Mon Dieu!** *mawng dyur*
I don't mind.	**Ça ne me fait rien.** *sa ner mer feh ryang*
No way!	**Pas question!/Pas possible!** *pa kestyawng/pa posseebl*
Really?	**Ah bon?/Vraiment?** *a bawng/vremahng*
Nonsense.	**Quelle bêtise!** *kel beteez*
That's enough.	**Ça suffit!** *sa sewfee*
That's true.	**C'est vrai.** *seh vreh*
How are things?	**Comment ça va?** *kommahng sa va*
Fine, thank you.	**Bien, merci.** *byang mehrsee*
great/brilliant	**super** *sewpehr*
great	**formidable** *formeedabl*
fine	**très bien** *treh byang*
not bad	**pas mal** *pa mal*
okay	**ça va** *sa va*
not good	**pas bien** *pa byang*
fairly bad	**plutôt mal** *plewtoa mal*
terrible	**(ça ne va) pas du tout** *(sa ner va) pa dew too*

Accommodations

All types of accommodations, from hotels to campsites, can be found through the tourist information center (**Office du Tourisme** or **Syndicat d'initiative**).

Hôtels *oatel*

Usually called **hôtels** or **hôtels de tourisme**, hotels in France are officially classified into four categories, ranging from basic one-star accommodations to luxury four-star establishments. Room prices, fixed according to amenities, size and to the hotel's star rating, must be posted visibly at the reception desk or in the window and behind each room door. Most hotels offer breakfast (which is rarely included in the total price, unless specified) but not all will have a restaurant. **Hôtel garni** means bed and breakfast.

Châteaux-Hôtels de France *chatoa zoatel der frahngss*

Hotels belonging to this association are four-star establishments, usually converted **châteaux**. They tend to be expensive but offer very high quality service. They are listed in a directory available from tourist offices.

Logis de France *lozhee der frahngss*

This voluntary organization places the emphasis on a warm welcome, comfort, size and to the best value for money. These hotels are usually located outside towns and offer a relaxed atmosphere. They are classified into four levels, from one to four **cheminées** (chimneys). A directory can be obtained from the French national tourist office.

Auberges *oabehrzh*

These country inns tend to be small and offer simple, economical accommodations. Some have very good restaurants and they are often in pleasant locations.

Gîtes de France *zheet der frahngss*

Gîtes are furnished rented holiday cottages or apartments in rural areas.

Auberges de jeunesse *oaberzh der zhurness*

Youth hostels require you to show your membership card, but you'll usually be able to get one on the spot. Some local student associations operate dormitories during high season.

Reservations/Booking   Réservations

In advance À l'avance

Can you recommend a
hotel in …?

**Pouvez-vous me recom-
mander un hôtel à …?**
*poovay voo mer rerkommahng
day ang noatel a*

Is it near the center
of town?

Est-ce près du centre-ville?
ess preh dew sahngtr veel

How much is it per night?

C'est combien par nuit?
seh kawnbyang par nwee

Is there anything cheaper?

Y a-t-il quelque chose de moins cher?
ee ateel kelker shoaz der mwang shehr

Could you reserve me a
room there, please?

**Pourriez-vous m'y réserver une chambre,
s'il vous plaît?** *pooryay voo mee
rayzehrvay ewn shahngbr seel voo pleh*

At the hotel À l'hôtel

Do you have any vacancies?

Avez-vous des chambres libres?
avay voo day shahngbr leebr

I'm sorry, we're full.

Je regrette, l'hôtel est complet.
zher rergret loatel eh kawngpleh

Is there another hotel nearby?

Y a-t-il un autre hôtel près d'ici?
ee ateel ang noatr oatel preh deessee

I'd like a single/double room.

**Je voudrais une chambre à un
lit/chambre pour deux personnes.**
*zher voodray ewn shahngbr a ang
lee/shahngbr poor dur person*

I'd like a room with …

Je voudrais une chambre avec …
zher voodray ewn shahngbr avek

a bath/shower

salle de bains/douche
sal der bang/doosh

– Avez-vous des chambres libres?
Je voudrais une chambre pour deux personnes.
(Do you have any vacancies? I'd like a double room.)
–Je regrette, l'hôtel est complet. (Sorry, we're full.)
– Oh. Y a-t-il un autre hôtel près d'ici?
(Is there another hotel nearby?)
– Oui, madame. L'hôtel Royal est près d'ici.
(Yes, the Royal Hotel is nearby.)

Reception À la réception

I have a reservation. My name is …	**J'ai réservé. Je m'appelle …** *zhay rayzehrvay. zher mapell*
We've reserved a double and a single room.	**Nous avons réservé une chambre pour deux personnes et une chambre à un lit.** *noo zavawng rayzervay ewn shahngbr poor dur person ay ewn shahngbr a ang lee*
I confirmed my reservation by mail.	**J'ai confirmé par lettre.** *zhay kawngfeermay par letr*
Could we have adjoining rooms?	**Pourrions-nous avoir des chambres côte à côte?** *poorryawng noo zavwar day shahngbr koat a koat*

Amenities and facilities Équipement

Is there … in the room?	**Y a-t-il … dans la chambre?** *ee ateel … dahng la shahngbr*
air conditioning	**la climatisation** *la kleemateezasyawng*
TV/telephone/fax	**la télévision/le téléphone/le fax** *la taylayveezyawng/ler taylayfon/ler fax*
Does the hotel have (a) …?	**Y a-t-il … à l'hôtel?** *ee ateel … a loatel*
cable TV	**la télévision par câble** *la taylayveezyawng par kabl*
laundry service	**un service de nettoyage** *ang sehrvees der nettwahyazh*
solarium	**un solarium** *ang solaryom*
swimming pool	**une piscine** *ewn peesseen*
Could you put … in the room?	**Pourriez-vous mettre … dans la chambre?** *pooryay voo metr … dahng la shahngbr*
an extra bed	**un lit supplémentaire** *ang leet sewplaymahngtehr*
a crib [cot]	**un lit d'enfant** *ang lee dahngfahng*
Do you have facilities for children/the disabled?	**Y a-t-il des aménagements pour enfants/handicapés?** *ee ateel day zamaynazhmahng poor ahngfahng/ahngdeekapay*

How long? Combien de temps ?

We'll be staying …	**Nous resterons …** *noo restrawng*
overnight only	**une nuit seulement** *ewn nwee surlmahng*
a few days	**quelques jours** *kelker zhoor*
a week (at least)	**une semaine (au moins)** *ewn sermayn (oa mwang)*
I'd like to stay an extra night.	**Je voudrais rester une nuit supplémentaire.** *zher voodray restay ewn nwee sewplaymahngtehr*

> – Bonjour. Je m'appelle John Newton.
> (Hello. My name is John Newton.)
> – *Bonjour monsieur Newton. (Hello, Mr. Newton.)*
> – Je voudrais rester deux nuits.
> (I'd like to stay for two nights.)
> – *Ah oui. Pouvez-vous remplir cette fiche?*
> *(Oh yes. Please fill out this form.)*

Est-ce que je peux voir votre passeport, s'il vous plaît?	May I see your passport, please?
Pouvez-vous remplir cette fiche?	Please fill out this form.
Quel est votre numéro d'immatriculation?	What is your license plate number?

CHAMBRE SEULE … FF	room only FF…
PETIT DÉJEUNER COMPRIS	breakfast included
REPAS	meals available
NOM/PRÉNOM	name/first name
LIEU DE RÉSIDENCE/RUE/ NUMÉRO	home address/street/ number
NATIONALITÉ/PROFESSION	nationality/profession
DATE/LIEU DE NAISSANCE	date/place of birth
NUMÉRO DE PASSEPORT	passport number
NUMÉRO D'IMMATRICULATION DE LA VOITURE	license plate number
LIEU/DATE	place/date
SIGNATURE	signature

23

Price   Prix

How much is it …?	**Quel est le prix …?** *kel eh ler pree*
per night/week	**par nuit/semaine** *par nwee/sermayn*
for bed and breakfast	**pour la chambre et le petit déjeuner** *poor la shahngbr ay ler pertee dayzhurnay*
excluding meals	**sans les repas** *sahng lay repa*
for American Plan (A.P.) [full board]	**pour la pension complète** *poor la pahngsyawng kawngplet*
for Modified American Plan (M.A.P.) [half board]	**pour la demi-pension** *poor la dermee pahngsyawng*
Does the price include …?	**Est-ce-que cela comprend …?** *ess ker serla kawngprahng*
breakfast	**le petit déjeuner** *ler pertee dayzhurnay*
sales tax [VAT]	**la T.V.A.** *la tay vay ah*
Do I have to pay a deposit?	**Dois-je verser des arrhes?** *dwazh vehrsay day zar*
Is there a discount for children?	**Y a-t-il une réduction pour enfants?** *ee ateel ewn raydewksyawng poor ahngfahng*

Decision   Décision

May I see the room?	**Puis-je voir la chambre?** *pweezh vwar la shahngbr*
That's fine. I'll take it.	**C'est bien. Je la prends.** *seh byang. zher la prahng*
It's too …	**Elle est trop …** *el eh tro*
dark/small	**sombre/petite** *sawngbr/perteet*
noisy	**bruyante** *brewyahngt*
Do you have anything …?	**Avez-vous quelque chose de …?** *avay voo kelker shoaz der*
bigger/cheaper	**plus grand/moins cher** *plew grahng/mwang sher*
quieter/warmer	**plus calme/plus chaud** *plew kalm/plew shoa*
No, I won't take it.	**Non, je ne la prends pas.** *nawng zher ner la prahng pa*

Problems Problèmes

The ... doesn't work.
... ne marche pas.
ner marsh pa

air conditioning
La climatisation
la kleemateezassyawng

fan
Le ventilateur *ler vahngteelaturr*

heat [heating]
Le chauffage *ler shoafazh*

light
La lumière *la lewmyehr*

I can't turn the heat [heating] on/off.
Je ne peux pas allumer/éteindre le chauffage. *zher ner pur pa alewmay/aytangdr ler shoafazh*

There is no hot water/ toilet paper.
Il n'y a pas d'eau chaude/de papier toilette. *eel nee a pa doa shoad/der papyay twalett*

The faucet [tap] is dripping.
Le robinet fuit. *ler robeeneh fwee*

The sink/toilet is clogged.
Le lavabo est bouché./Les toilettes sont bouchées. *ler lavaboa eh booshay/lay twalett sawng booshay*

The window/door is jammed.
La fenêtre/porte est coincée. *la fernetr port eh kwangsay*

My room has not been made up.
Ma chambre n'a pas été faite. *ma shahngbr na pa zaytay fet*

The ... is broken.
... est cassé(e). *eh kassay*

blind
Le store *ler stor*

lock
La serrure *la sehrewr*

There are insects in our room.
Il y a des insectes dans notre chambre. *eel ee a day zangsekt dahng notr shahngbr*

Action Action

Could you have that taken care of?
Pourriez-vous vous en occuper? *pooryay voo voo zahng nokewpay*

I'd like to move to another room.
Je voudrais changer de chambre. *zher voodray shahngzhay der shahngbr*

I'd like to speak to the manager.
Je voudrais parler au directeur. *zher voodray parlay oa deerekturr*

Requirements Besoins généraux

The 220-volt, 50-cycle AC is now almost universal in France, Belgium and Switzerland, although 110 volts may still be encountered, especially in older buildings.

If you bring your own electrical appliances, buy a Continental adapter plug (round pins, not square) before leaving home. You may also need a transformer appropriate to the wattage of the appliance.

About the hotel À propos de l'hôtel

Where's the …?	**Où est …?** *oo eh*
bar	**le bar** *ler bar*
bathroom [toilet]	**la toilette** *la twalet*
parking lot [car park]	**le parking** *ler parking*
dining room	**la salle à manger** *la sal a mahngzhay*
elevator [lift]	**l'ascenseur** *lassahngsurr*
shower	**la douche** *la doosh*
swimming pool	**la piscine** *la peesseen*
tour operator's bulletin board	**le tableau d'affichage de l'agence de voyages** *ler tabloa dafeeshazh der lazhahngs der vwahyazh*
Where are the bathrooms?	**Où sont les toilettes?** *oo sawng lay twalett*
What time is the front door locked?	**À quelle heure fermez-vous la porte d'entrée?** *a kel urr fermay voo la port dahngtray*
What time is breakfast served?	**À quelle heure servez-vous le petit déjeuner?** *a kel urr servay voo ler pertee dayzhurnay*
Is there room service?	**Y a-t-il un service de chambre?** *ee ateel ang sehrvees der shahngbr*

COMPOSER LE … POUR L'EXTÉRIEUR	dial … for an outside line
NE PAS DÉRANGER	do not disturb
PORTE COUPE-FEU	fire door
PRISE POUR RASOIRS	shavers only
SORTIE DE SECOURS	emergency exit

Personal needs Besoins personnels

The key to room ..., please.	**La clé de la chambre ...,** **s'il vous plaît.** *la klay der la shahngbr ... seel voo pleh*
I've lost my key.	**J'ai perdu ma clé.** *zhay pehrdew ma klay*
I've locked myself out of my room.	**Je ne peux plus ouvrir la porte de ma chambre.** *zher ner pur plew oovreer la port der ma shahngbr*
Could you wake me at ...?	**Pourriez-vous me réveiller à ..., s'il vous plaît?** *pooryay voo mer rayvayay a ... seel voo pleh*
I'd like breakfast in my room.	**Je voudrais le petit déjeuner dans ma chambre, s'il vous plaît.** *zher voodray ler pertee dayzhurnay dahng ma shahngbr seel voo pleh*
Can I leave this in the safe?	**Puis-je laisser ceci dans le coffre-fort de l'hôtel?** *pweezh layssay sersee dahng ler kofr for der loatel*
Could I have my things from the safe?	**Puis-je prendre mes affaires dans le coffre-fort?** *pweezh prahngdr may zafer dahng ler kofr for*
Where is our tour representative?	**Où est le représentant de notre voyage organisé?** *oo eh ler reprayzahngtanf der notr vwahyazh orgahneezay*
the maid	**la femme de chambre** *la fam der shahngbr*
May I have a(n) (extra)...?	**Puis-je avoir ...(supplémentaire)?** *pweezh avvwar ...(sewplaymahngtehr)*
bath towel	**une serviette de bain** *ewn servyett der bang*
blanket	**une couverture** *ewn koovehrtewr*
hangers	**des cintres** *day sangtr*
pillow	**un oreiller** *ang norayay*
soap	**du savon** *dew savawng*
Is there any mail for me?	**Y a-t-il du courrier pour moi?** *ee ateel dew kooryay poor mwa*
Are there any messages for me?	**Y a-t-il des messages pour moi?** *ee ateel day messazh poor mwa*

BREAKFAST ➤ 43; CHANGING MONEY ➤ 138

Renting Location (de logement)

We've reserved an apartment/house in the name of …	**Nous avons réservé un appartement/une maison au nom de …** *noo zavawng rayzervay ang napartmahng/ewn mayzawng oa nawng der*
Where do we pick up the keys?	**Où devons-nous prendre les clés?** *oo dervawng noo prahngdr lay klay*
Where is the …?	**Où est …?** *oo eh*
electric meter	**le compteur électrique** *ler kawngturr aylektreek*
fuse box	**la boîte à fusibles** *la bwat a fewzeebl*
faucet [tap]	**le robinet d'arrêt** *ler robeeneh dareh*
water heater	**le chauffe-eau** *ler shoaf oa*
Are there any spare …?	**Y a-t-il des … de rechange?** *ee ateel day … der rershahngzh*
fuses	**fusibles** *fewzeebl*
gas bottles	**bouteilles de gaz** *bootayy der gaz*
sheets	**draps** *dra*
Which day does the housekeeper come?	**Quel jour vient la femme de ménage?** *kel zhoor vyang la fam der maynazh*
Where/When do I put out the trash [rubbish]?	**Où/Quand dois-je sortir les poubelles?** *oo/kahng dwazh sorteer lay poobell*

Problems? Problèmes?

Where can I contact you?	**Où est-ce que je peux vous contacter?** *oo ess ker zher pur voo kawngtaktay*
How does the water heater/stove [cooker] work?	**Comment fonctionne le chauffe-eau/la cuisinière?** *kommahng fawngksyon ler shoaf oa/la kweezeenyehr*
The … is/are dirty.	**… est sale/sont sales.** *eh sal/sawng sal*
The … has broken down.	**… est cassé(e).** *eh kassay*
We have accidentally broken/lost …	**Nous avons cassé/perdu …** *noo zavawng kassay/pehrdew*
That was already damaged when we arrived.	**C'était déjà abîmé quand nous sommes arrivés.** *sayteh dayzha abîmay kahng noo som zareevay*

HOUSEHOLD ARTICLES, CLEANING ITEMS ➤ 148

Useful terms Termes utiles

boiler	**la chaudière** *la shoadyehr*
freezer	**le congélateur** *ler kawngzhaylaturr*
frying pan	**la poêle** *la pwal*
kettle	**la bouilloire** *la booywar*
lamp	**la lampe** *la lahngp*
dishes [crockery]	**la vaisselle** *la vessell*
refrigerator	**le réfrigérateur/frigo** *ler raytreezhayraturr/freego*
saucepan	**la casserole** *la kasrol*
stove [cooker]	**la cuisinière** *la kweezeenyehr*
toilet paper	**le papier toilette/hygiénique** *ler papyay twalett/eezhyayneek*
utensils [cutlery]	**les couverts** *lay koovehr*
washing machine	**la machine à laver** *la masheen a lavay*

Rooms Chambres

balcony	**le balcon** *ler balkawng*
bathroom	**la salle de bains** *la sal der bang*
bedroom	**la chambre** *la shahngbr*
dining room	**la salle à manger** *la sal a mahngzhay*
kitchen	**la cuisine** *la kweezeen*
living room	**la salle de séjour/le salon** *la sal der sayzhoor/ler salawng*
bathroom [toilets]	**les toilettes/les WC** *lay twalett/lay doobl-vay say*

Youth hostel Auberge de jeunesse

Do you have any places left for tonight?	**Vous reste-t-il des places pour ce soir?** *voo rest teel day plass poor ser swar*
Do you rent bedding?	**Louez-vous des draps?** *looay voo day dra*
What time are the doors locked?	**À quelle heure les portes ferment-elles?** *a kel urr lay port ferm tell*
I have an International Student Card.	**J'ai une carte d'étudiant internationale.** *zhay ewn kart daytewdyahng angtehrnasyonal*

REQUIREMENTS ➤ 26; CAMPING ➤ 30

Camping Camping

Camping is very well organized in France and sites are classified from one to four stars, depending on their amenities. A **camping municipal** (public campsite) can be found in most towns, while tourist areas will also have other privately owned campsites. Ask the local tourist information office for a list of campsites in the area.

Checking in Arrivée

Is there a camp site near here?
Y a-t-il un camping près d'ici?
ee ateel ang kahngpeeng preh deessee

Do you have space for a tent/trailer [caravan]?
Avez-vous de la place pour une tente/une caravane? *avay voo der la plass poor ewn tahngt/ewn karavahn*

What is the charge …?
Quel est le tarif …? *kel eh ler tareef*

per day/week
par jour/semaine *par zhoor/sermayn*

for a tent/a car
pour une tente/voiture *poor ewn tahngt/vwatewr*

for a trailer/camper
pour une caravane *poor ewn karavahn*

Facilities Équipement

Are there cooking facilities on site?
Est-il possible de faire la cuisine sur le terrain? *eteel posseebl der fer la kweezeen sewr ler terang*

Are there any electric outlets [power points]?
Y a-t-il des branchements électriques? *ee ateel day brahngshmahng aylektreek*

Where is/are the …?
Où est/sont …? *oo eh/sawng*

drinking water
l'eau potable *loa potabl*

trashcans [dustbins]
les poubelles *lay poobell*

laundry facilities
les bacs à linge/les machines à laver *lay bak a langzh/lay masheen a lavay*

showers
les douches *lay doosh*

Where can I get some butane gas?
Où puis-je trouver du gaz butane? *oo pweezh troovay dew gaz bewtahn*

CAMPING INTERDIT	no camping
EAU POTABLE	drinking water
FEUX/BARBECUES INTERDITS	no fires/barbecues

RESERVATIONS ➤ 21; LENGTH OF STAY ➤ 23

Complaints Plaintes

It's too sunny/shady/ crowded here.
Il y a trop de soleil/ d'ombre/de gens ici.
eel ee a tro der solayy/ dawngbr/der zhahng eessee

The ground's too hard/uneven.
Le sol est trop dur/inégal.
ler sol eh trop dewr/eenaygal

Do you have a more level spot?
Avez-vous un emplacement plus plat?
avay voo ang nahngplasmahng plew pla

You can't camp here.
Vous ne pouvez pas camper ici.
voo ner poovay pa kahngpay eessee

Camping equipment Matériel de camping

butane gas	**du gaz butane** *dew gaz bewtahn*
campbed	**un lit de camp** *ang lee der kahng*
charcoal	**du charbon** *dew sharbawng*
hammer	**un marteau** *ang martoa*
mallet	**un maillet** *ang mieyeh*
matches	**des allumettes** *day zalewmet*
(air) mattress	**un matelas (pneumatique)** *ang matla (pnurmateek)*
kerosene [primus] stove	**un réchaud (de camping)** *ang rayshoa (der kahngpeeng)*
knapsack	**un sac à dos** *ang sak a doa*
rope	**une corde de tente** *ewn kord der tahngt*
sleeping bag	**un sac de couchage** *ang sak der kooshazh*
tarpaulin	**un tapis de sol** *ang tapee der sol*
tent	**une tente** *ewn tahngt*
tent pegs	**des piquets de tente** *day peekeh der tahngt*
tent pole	**un (grand) piquet de tente** *ang (grahng) peekeh der tahngt*
flashlight [torch]	**une lampe de poche/électrique** *ewn lahngp der posh/aylektreek*

Checking out Départ

What time do we need to vacate the room?	**À quelle heure devons-nous libérer la chambre?** *a kel urr dervawng noo leebayray la shahngbr*
Could we leave our baggage here until … p.m.?	**Pourrions-nous laisser nos bagages ici jusqu'à … heures du soir?** *pooryawng noo layssay no bagazh eessee zhewska … urr dew swar*
I'm leaving now.	**Je pars maintenant.** *zher par mangtnahng*
Could you call me a taxi, please?	**Pourriez-vous m'appeler un taxi, s'il vous plaît?** *pooryay voo maperlay ang taxee seel voo pleh*
It's been a very enjoyable stay.	**J'ai passé un très bon séjour.** *zhay passay ang treh bawng sayzhoor*

Paying Paiement

May I have my bill, please?	**Puis-je avoir ma note, s'il vous plaît?** *pweezh avwar ma not seel voo pleh*
I think there's a mistake in this bill.	**Je crois qu'il y a une erreur sur cette note.** *zher krwa keel ee a ewn erurr sewr set not*
I've made … telephone calls.	**J'ai passé … coups de téléphone.** *zhay passay … koo der taylayfon*
I've taken … from the minibar.	**J'ai pris … au mini-bar.** *zhay pree … oa meenee bar*
Can I have an itemized bill?	**Est-ce que je peux avoir une note détaillée?** *ess ker zher pur avwar ewn not daytieyay*
Could I have a receipt?	**Est-ce que je peux avoir un reçu?** *ess ker zher pur avwar ang rersew*

Tipping: a service charge is generally included in hotel and restaurant bills. However, if the service has been particularly good, you may want to leave an extra tip. The following chart is a guide:

	France	Belgium	Switzerland
Bellman [Porter]	5F	30F	1–2F
Hotel maid, per week	50–100F	100–150F	10F
Waiter	optional	optional	optional

32

Eating Out

Restaurants Restaurants

Auberge *oabehrzh*
An inn, often in the country; serves full meals and drinks.

Bar *bar*
Bar; can be found on virtually every street corner; coffee and drinks served, sometimes light meals, too.

Bistrot *beestroa*
Can vary from a café, selling mostly drinks and basic food (sandwiches, salads, snacks) to a more picturesque restaurant, with traditional French cuisine; usually not very expensive.

Brasserie *brasserree*
A large café serving good, simple food and drinks, very often offering a **plat du jour** (dish of the day).

Buffet *bewfeh*
A restaurant found in principal train stations; the food is generally good.

Café *kafay*
Come here for a croissant with your morning coffee; and now many cafés also offer snacks, salads and sandwiches. Beer, wine and liquor are served, but don't ask for any fancy cocktails or highballs.

Crêperie *krepehree*
Offers snacks of light pancakes with various fillings.

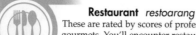

Restaurant   *restoarang*

These are rated by scores of professional and amateur gourmets. You'll encounter restaurants classified by stars, forks and knives and endorsed by everyone including travel agencies, automobile associations and gastronomic guilds. Bear in mind that any form of classification is relative.

Restoroute   *restoaroot*

A large restaurant just off a highway [motorway]; table and/or cafeteria service is available.

Rôtisserie   *roateesserree*

Very often linked with a **charcuterie** and specializes in meat products: roast chickens, quiches, sausages, ham, hors-d'œuvre, etc.

Routier   *rootyay*

Roughly equivalent to a roadside diner; the food is simple but can be surprisingly good if you happen to hit upon the right place.

Meal times Heures des repas

le petit déjeuner   *ler pertee dayzhurnay*

Breakfast: from 7-10 a.m. Traditionally just bread, butter, jam, a croissant and **un petit noir** (small black coffee), tea or hot chocolate; hotels are now offering more filling fare ➤ 43.

le déjeuner   *ler deayzhurnay*

Lunch: from noon until 2 p.m. If you haven't time for a leisurely meal, try a restaurant offering a **plat du jour** (single dish of the day) or light salad. In a hurry, go for fast-food outlets, pizzerias or crêperies, or just grab a baguette sandwich ➤ 40.

le dîner   *ler deenay*

Dinner is usually served late, from 8-10 p.m. The French are likely to linger over their meal, so service may seem on the slow side.

French cuisine Cuisine française

There are few countries where you can spend more delightful hours just eating. For, apart from the many regional specialties that do ample justice to the local produce, you can sample, among others, **haute cuisine** (sophisticated dishes made according to time-honored recipes) or **nouvelle cuisine** (a more refined preparation enhancing the delicate flavors of the food).

Most restaurants display a menu (**la carte**) outside. Besides ordering **à la carte**, you can order a fixed price menu – **le menu** (**à prix fixe**). Cheaper meals often run to three courses, with or without wine, but service is always included. More expensive menus stretch to four or even five courses, but hardly ever include wine.

ESSENTIAL

A table for 1/2/3/4	**Une table pour...** *ewn tabl poor* **un/deux/trois/quatre** *ang/dur/trwa/katr*
Thank you.	**Merci.** *mehrsee*
The check [bill], please.	**L'addition, s'il vous plaît.** *ladeesyawng seel voo pleh*

Finding a place to eat On cherche un restaurant

Can you recommend a good restaurant?	**Pouvez-vous nous recommander un bon restaurant?** *poovay voo noo rerkommahngday ang bawng restoarahng*
Is there a ... restaurant near here?	**Y a-t-il un restaurant ... près d'ici?** *ee ateel ang restoarahng ... preh deessee*
traditional local	**local traditionnel** *lokal tradeessyonell*
Chinese	**chinois** *sheenwa*
Greek	**grec** *grek*
Italian	**italien** *eetalyang*
French	**français** *frangsay*
inexpensive	**bon marché** *bawng marshay*
vegetarian	**végétarien** *vayzhaytaryang*
Where can I find a(n) ...?	**Où puis-je trouver ...?** *oo pweezh troovay*
burger stand	**un kiosque à hamburger** *ang keeosk a amburger*
café	**un café** *ang kafay*
restaurant/café with a beer garden	**un café/restaurant avec jardin/terrasse** *ang kafay/restoarahng avek zhardang/tehrass*
fast-food restaurant	**un fast-food** *ang fast food*
tea room	**un salon de thé** *ang salawng der tay*
pizzeria	**une pizzeria** *ewn peetzehreea*
steak house	**un restaurant-grill** *ang restoarahng greel*

Reservations Réservations

I'd like to reserve a table for 2.	**Je voudrais réserver une table pour deux personnes.** *zher voodray rayzehrvay ewn tabl poor dur pehrsonn*
For this evening/ tomorrow at …	**Pour ce soir/demain à … heures.** *poor ser swar/dermang a … urr*
We'll come at 8:00.	**Nous viendrons à huit heures.** *noo vyangdrawng a weet urr*
A table for 2, please.	**Une table pour deux, s'il vous plaît.** *ewn tabl poor dur seel voo pleh*
We have a reservation.	**Nous avons réservé.** *noo zavawng rayzehrvay*

C'est à quel nom, s'il vous plaît?	What's the name, please?
Je regrette. Il y a beaucoup de monde/nous sommes complets.	I'm sorry. We're very busy/full.
Nous aurons une table libre dans … minutes.	We'll have a free table in … minutes.
Revenez dans … minutes.	Please come back in … minutes.

Where to sit Où s'asseoir

Could we sit …?	**Pouvons-nous nous asseoir …?** *poovawng noo noo zaswar*
outside	**dehors** *der or*
in a non-smoking area	**dans une zone non-fumeur** *dahng zewn zon nawng fewmurr*
by the window	**près de la fenêtre** *preh der la fernetr*

> – Je voudrais réserver une table pour ce soir.
> (I'd like to reserve a table for this evening.)
> – Pour combien de personnes? (For how many people?)
> – Pour quatre. (For four.)
> – À quelle heure arriverez-vous?
> (What time are you coming?)
> – Nous arriverons à huit heures.
> (We'll come at 8 o'clock.)
> – Et c'est à quel nom, s'il vous plaît?
> (And what's the name, please?)
> – Peters. (Peters.)
> —Très bien, alors à ce soir. (Good. See you tonight.)

Ordering Commandes

Waiter!/Waitress!	**Garçon!/Mademoiselle!** *garsawng/madmwazel*
May I see the wine list, please?	**Puis-je avoir la carte des vins, s'il vous plaît?** *pweezh avwar la kart day vang seel voo pleh*
Do you have a set menu?	**Avez-vous un menu à prix fixe?** *avay voo zang mernew a pree feex*
Can you recommend some typical local dishes?	**Pouvez-vous recommander des spécialités régionales?** *poovay voo rerkommahngday day spaysyaleetay rayzhyonal*
Could you tell me what … is?	**Pourriez-vous me dire ce qu'est …?** *pooryay voo mer deer ser keh*
What's in it?	**Qu'y a-t-il dedans?** *kee ateel derdahng*
I'd like …	**Je voudrais …** *zher voodray*
a bottle/glass/carafe of …	**une bouteille/un verre/une carafe de …** *ewn bootay/ang verr/ewn karaf der*

Vous désirez commander?	Are you ready to order?
Qu'est-ce que vous prendrez?	What would you like?
Voulez-vous prendre un apéritif pour commencer?	Would you like to order drinks first?
Je vous recommande/conseille …	I recommend …
Nous n'avons pas de …	We haven't got …
Il faudra attendre … minutes.	That will take … minutes.
Bon appétit.	Enjoy your meal.

> – *Vous désirez commander?* (Are you ready to order?)
> – Pouvez-vous nous recommander des spécialités régionales?
> (Can you recommend some local dishes?)
> – *Oui. Je vous conseille le coq au vin.*
> (Yes, I recommend the "coq au vin".)
> – Bon, je le prends. (Good, I'll have that.)
> – *Et que voulez-vous boire?*
> (And what would you like to drink?)
> – Une carafe de vin rouge, s'il vous plaît.
> (A karafe of red wine, please.)
> – *Entendu.* (Certainly.)

DRINKS ➤ 49; MENU READER ➤ 52

Side dishes Accompagnements

Could I have ... without the ...?
Est-ce que je pourrais avoir ... sans ...?
ess ker zher pooray avvar ... sahng

With a side order of ...
Avec ... comme accompagnement.
avek ... kom akawngpañmahng

Could I have salad instead of vegetables, please?
Est-ce que je pourrais avoir une salade à la place des légumes?
ess ker zher pooray avvar ewn salad a la plass day laygewm

Does the meal come with vegetables/potatoes?
Le plat est-il servi avec des légumes/ pommes de terre? *ler pla eteel sehrvee avek day laygewm/pom der tehr*

Do you have any sauces?
Avez-vous des sauces?
avay voo day soass

Would you like ... with that?
Est-ce que vous voulez ... avec?
ess ker voo voolay ... avek

vegetables/salad
des légumes/de la salade
day laygewm/der la salahd

potatoes/French fries [chips]
des pommes de terre/des frites
day pom der tehr/day freet

sauce
de la sauce *der la soass*

ice
des glaçons *day glassawng*

May I have some ...?
Puis-je avoir ...? *pweezh avvar*

bread
du pain *dew pang*

butter
du beurre *dew burr*

lemon
du citron *dew seetrawng*

mustard
de la moutarde *der la mootard*

pepper
du poivre *dew pwavr*

salt
du sel *dew sel*

seasoning
de l'assaisonnement/de la vinaigrette
der lassayzonmahng/der la veenaygret

sugar
du sucre *dew sewkr*

(artificial) sweetener
de l'édulcorant *der laydewlkorahngt*

vinaigrette [French dressing]
de la vinaigrette *der la veenaygret*

General questions
Questions d'ordre général

Could I have a(n) (clean) …, please?	**Pourriez-vous m'apporter … (propre)?** *pooryay voo maportay … (propr)*
ashtray	**un cendrier** *ang sahngdryay*
cup/glass	**une tasse/un verre** *ewn tass/ang vehr*
fork/knife	**une fourchette/un couteau** *ewn foorshett/ang kootoa*
napkin	**une serviette** *ewn sehrvyett*
plate/spoon	**une assiette/une cuillère** *ewn assyett/ewn kweeyehr*
I'd like some more …, please.	**Je voudrais un peu plus de …** *zher voodray ang pur plews der*
Nothing more, thanks.	**Ça suffit, merci.** *sa sewfee mehrsee*
Where are the restrooms?	**Où sont les toilettes?** *oo sawng lay twalett*

Special requirements Régimes spéciaux

I mustn't eat food containing …	**Je ne dois pas manger de plats contenant …** *zher ner dwa pa mahngzhay der pla kawngtnahng*
salt/sugar	**du sel/du sucre** *dew sel/dew sewkr*
Do you have meals/ drinks for diabetics?	**Avez-vous des repas/boissons pour diabétiques?** *avay voo day rerpa/bwassawng poor dyabayteek*
Do you have vegetarian meals?	**Avez-vous des repas végétariens?** *avay voo day rerpa vayzhaytaryang*

For the children Pour les enfants

Do you have children's portions?	**Faites-vous des portions enfants?** *fet voo day porsyawng ahngfahng*
Could we have a child's seat, please?	**Pourrions-nous avoir une chaise haute (pour bébé)?** *pooryawng noo avvar ewn shez oat (poor baybay)*
Where can I feed/ change the baby?	**Où est-ce que je peux allaiter/ changer le bébé?** *oo ess ker zher pur aletay/shahngzhay ler baybay*

CHILDREN ➤ 113

Fast food/Café Fast food/Café

Something to drink Boissons

I'd like a cup of …	**Je voudrais une tasse de …**
	zher voodray ewn tass der
tea/coffee	**thé/café** *tay/kafay*
black/with milk	**noir/au lait** *nwar/oa leh*
I'd like a … of red/white wine.	**Je voudrais … de vin rouge/blanc.**
	zher voodray … der vang roozh/blahng
carafe/bottle/glass	**une carafe/une bouteille/un verre**
	ewn karaf/ewn bootay/ang vehr
Do you have … beer?	**Avez-vous de la bière …?**
	avay voo der la byehr
bottled/draft [draught]	**en bouteille/pression**
	ahng bootay/pressyawng

And to eat … Et nourriture …

A piece of …, please.	**Un morceau de …, s'il vous plaît.**
	ang morsoa der … seel voo pleh
I'd like two of those.	**J'en voudrais deux.**
	zhahng voodray dur
burger/fries	**un hamburger/des frites**
	ang amburger/ day freet
cake/sandwich	**un gâteau/un sandwich**
	ang gatoa/ang sahngdveesh

une glace *ewn glas*
ice cream: some common flavors are **à la vanille** (vanilla),
au chocolat (chocolate), **à la fraise** (strawberry).

une pizza *ang peetsa*
pizza: popular types include **marguerite** (cheese and tomato), **quatre saisons**
(four different toppings, usually ham, mushrooms, cheese and anchovy),
reine (ham and mushroom).

A … slice, please.	**Une …, s'il vous plaît.**
	ewn … seel voo pleh
small	**petite portion** *perteet porsyawng*
regular [medium]	**portion moyenne** *porsyawng mwahyenn*
large	**grosse portion** *gross porsyawng*
It's to go [take away].	**C'est pour emporter.**
	seh poor ahngportay
That's all, thanks.	**C'est tout, merci.** *seh too mehrsee*

> – *Vous désirez?* (What would you like?)
> – Deux cafés, s'il vous plaît.
> (Two coffees, please.)
> – *Noirs ou au lait?* (Black or with milk?)
> – Au lait, s'il vous plaît.
> (With milk, please.)
> – *Et quelque chose à manger?*
> (Anything to eat?)
> – Oui, deux gâteaux, s'il vous plaît.
> (Yes, two cakes, please.)
> – *Et avec ça?* (Anything else?)
> – C'est tout, merci. (That's all, thanks.)

Complaints Réclamations

I have no knife/fork/spoon.	**Je n'ai pas de couteau/fourchette/cuillère.** *zher nay pa der kootoa/foorshett/kweeyehr*
That's not what I ordered.	**Ce n'est pas ce que j'ai commandé.** *ser neh pa ser ker zhay kommahngday*
I asked for …	**J'ai demandé** … *zhay dermahngday*
The meat is …	**La viande est** … *la vyahngd eh*
overdone	**trop cuite** *tro kweet*
underdone	**pas assez cuite** *pa zassay kweet*
too tough	**trop dure** *tro dewr*
This is too …	**C'est trop** … *seh tro*
bitter/sour	**amer/acide** *amehr/asseed*
The food is cold.	**La nourriture est froide.** *la nooreetewr eh frwad*
How much longer will our food be?	**Il y en a encore pour combien de temps?** *eel yahng na ahngkor poor kawnbyang der tahng*
We can't wait any longer. We're leaving.	**Nous ne pouvons plus attendre. Nous partons.** *noo ner poovawng plew atahngdr. noo partawng*
This isn't clean.	**Ce n'est pas propre.** *ser neh pa propr*
I'd like to speak to the headwaiter/to the manager.	**Je voudrais parler au maître d'hôtel/au patron.** *zher voodray parlay oa metr doatel/oa patrawng*

41

Paying Paiement

Tipping: Service is generally included in the bill (15% in France), but if you are happy with the service, a personal tip for the waiter is appropriate and appreciated – round the bill up 5–10 francs.

The check [bill], please.	**L'addition, s'il vous plaît.** *ladeesyawng seel voo pleh*
We'd like to pay separately.	**Nous voudrions payer séparément.** *noo voodryawng payay sayparaymahng*
It's all together, please.	**Tous les repas ensemble, s'il vous plaît.** *too lay repa zahngsahngbl seel voo pleh*
I think there's a mistake in this bill.	**Je crois qu'il y a une erreur sur l'addition.** *zher krwa keel ee a ewn ehrurr sewr ladeesyawng*
What is this amount for?	**Que représente ce montant?** *ker reprayzahngt ser mawngtahng*
I didn't have that. I had …	**Je n'ai pas pris ça. J'ai pris …** *zher nay pa pree sa. zhay pree*
Is service included?	**Le service est-il compris?** *ler sehrveess eteel kawngpree*
Can I pay with this credit card?	**Puis-je payer avec cette carte de crédit?** *pweezh payay avek set kart der kraydee*
I've forgotten my wallet.	**J'ai oublié mon porte-monnaie.** *zhay oobleeay mawng port monnay*
I don't have enough money.	**Je n'ai pas assez d'argent.** *zher nay pa zassay darzhahng*
Could I have a receipt?	**Puis-je avoir un reçu?** *pweezh avwar ang rersew*
That was a very good meal.	**C'était un très bon repas.** *sayteh ang treh bawng repa*

– Garçon! L'addition, s'il vous plaît. (Waiter! The bill, please.)
  – Bien sûr. Voilà. (Certainly. Here you are.)
– Le service est-il compris? (Is service included?)
  – Oui. (Yes.)
– Est-ce que je peux payer avec cette carte de crédit?
  (Can I pay with this credit card?)
  – Bien sûr. (Certainly.)
– Merci. C'était un très bon repas.
  (Thank you. That was a very good meal.)

PAYING ➤ 32; NUMBERS ➤ 216

Course by Course Plats

Breakfast Petit déjeuner

The typical breakfast consists of coffee, rolls, croissants and jam.
Most of the larger hotels are used to providing an English or
American breakfast.

I'd like some …	**Je voudrais …** *zher voodray*
bread	**du pain** *dew pang*
butter	**du beurre** *dew burr*
eggs	**des œufs** *day zur*
fried eggs	**au plat** *oa plah*
scrambled eggs	**brouillés** *brooyay*
grapefruit juice	**un jus de pamplemousse** *ang zhew der pangplermoos*
honey	**du miel** *dew myel*
jelly/jam	**de la confiture** *der lah kawngfeetewr*
marmalade	**de la marmelade** *der lah marmerlad*
milk	**du lait** *dew lay*
orange juice	**un jus d'orange** *ang zhew dorahngzh*
rolls	**des petits pains** *day pertee pang*
toast	**du pain grillé** *dew pang greeyay*

Appetizers/Starters Hors-d'œuvre

andouille(tte) *angdooy(ett)*
seasoned, aromatic sausage made from tripe, served grilled or fried.

bouchée à la reine *booshay ah lah ren*
pastry shell usually filled with creamed sweetbreads and mushrooms.

pâté *patay*
liver purée that may be blended with other meat, such as **pâté de
campagne**; **pâté de foie gras** indicates a fine paste of duck or goose liver,
often with truffles (**truffé**); **pâté en croûte** is enveloped in a pastry crust.

quenelles *kernel*
light dumplings made of fish, fowl or meat, served with a velvety sauce;
the best known are **quenelles de brochet**, made of pike.

quiche *keesh*
a flan or open-faced tart with a rich, creamy filling of cheese, vegetables, meat or
seafood; **quiche lorraine**, the best known, is garnished with bacon.

Soups Potages et soupes

Soups appear on menus in various forms: **bouillon**, **consommé**, **crème**, **potage**, **soupe** and **velouté**. Look for these specialties:

aïgo bouïdo	aeegoa bweedoa	garlic soup (Provence)
bisque	beesk	seafood stew/chowder
bouillabaisse	booyabess	fish and seafood soup (Marseilles)
consommé	kawngssommay	clear, stock-based soup
à l'œuf	a lurf	with a raw egg
au porto	oa portoa	with port wine
Célestine	saylesteen	with chicken and noodles
Colbert	kolbehr	with poached eggs, spring vegetables
garbure	garbewr	cabbage soup, often with pork or goose
pot-au-feu	po toa fur	meat and vegetable stew
potage	potazh	soup
à l'ail	ah lay	garlic
au cresson	oa kressawn	watercress
bilibi	beeleebee	fish and oyster
bonne femme	bon fam	potato, leek and sometimes bacon
Condé	kawngday	mashed red beans
Crécy	krehsee	carrots and rice
du Barry	dew baree	cream of cauliflower
julienne	zhewlyen	shredded vegetables
Parmentier	parmahngtyay	potato
soupe	soop	soup
à la bière	a la byehr	beer with chicken stock and onions (Belgium)
à l'oignon	ah lonyawng	French onion
au pistou	oa peestoo	vegetable (Provence)
aux choux	oa shoo	cabbage
de Pélous	der payloo	crab with tomatoes
de poisson	der pwassawn	small fish, simmered and puréed
de volaille	der volay	chicken
velouté	verlootay	cream

Fish and seafood Poissons et fruits de mer

In coastal areas, take advantage of the wonderful variety of fresh fish and seafood. You'll recognize: **carpe**, **crabe**, **harengs**, **maquereau**, **perche**, **sardines**, **saumon**, **scampi**, **sole**, **turbot**.

cuisses de grenouilles	*kweess der grernooy*	frog's legs
escargots	*eskargoa*	snails
huîtres	*weetr*	oysters
morue	*morew*	cod
moules	*mool*	mussels
thon	*tawng*	tuna
truite	*trweet*	trout

bar aux herbes en chemise *bar oa erb ahng shermeez*
bass stuffed with spinach and herbs, wrapped in lettuce and poached in white wine.

cotriade *kotreeyad*
assorted fish soup/stew with shellfish, onion, carrots, potatoes, garlic, Calvados and white wine (Brittany).

homard à l'américaine *omar ah lamayreeken*
sautéed diced lobster, flamed in cognac and then simmered in wine, aromatic vegetables, herbs and tomatoes.

Meat Viandes

I'd like some …	**Je voudrais …** *zher voodreh*
bacon	**du lard** *dew lar*
beef	**du bœuf** *dew burf*
chicken	**du poulet** *dew pooleh*
duck	**du canard** *dew kanar*
goose	**de l'oie** *der lwah*
ham	**du jambon** *dew zhahngbawng*
lamb	**de l'agneau** *der lañoa*
pork	**du porc** *dew por*
rabbit	**du lapin** *dew lapang*
sausages	**des saucisses** *day soasseess*
steak	**du steak** *dew stek*
veal	**du veau** *dew voa*

Meat cuts Morceaux de viande

contre-filet	*kawngtre feeleh*	loin strip steak
côte de bœuf	*koat der burf*	T-bone steak
côtelettes	*koaterlet*	chops
entrecôte	*ahngtrerkoat*	rib or rib-eye steak
escalope	*eskaloap*	cutlet
filet	*feeleh*	fillet steak
gigot	*zheegoa*	leg
médaillon	*maydahyawng*	tenderloin steak
rognons	*roñawng*	kidneys
selle	*sel*	saddle
tournedos	*toornerdoa*	tenderloin of T-bone steak

Meat dishes Plats de viande

blanquette de veau *blawnket der voa*
veal stew in a white sauce (with eggs and cream), with onions and mushrooms.

bœuf bourguignon *burf boorgeeñawng*
a rich beef stew with vegetables, braised in red Burgundy wine.

canard à l'orange *kahnahr ah lorahngzh*
duck braised with oranges and orange liqueur.

cassoulet toulousain *kassoolay tooloozang*
a casserole of white beans, mutton or salt pork, sausages and preserved goose.

civet *seevay*
game stew, with wine, onions and blood sauce; e.g., **civet de lièvre** (jugged hare).

coq au vin *kok oa vang*
chicken stewed with onion, mushroom, bacon in a red wine sauce. Sometimes the menu will tell exactly what kind of wine was used, for instance, **coq au Chambertin**.

couscous *kooskoos*
Arab dish based on cracked wheat, eaten hot and topped with vegetables and meat.

lapin à la flamande *lahpang a la flamawnd*
marinated rabbit, braised potatoes, carrots, cabbage, turnip, bacon and sausage, simmered in beer (Belgium).

ragoût *ragoo*
meat stew, generally served in a delicate gravy with vegetables; for example **ragoût de bœuf** (beef stew).

Vegetables   Légumes

You'll recognize: **artichaut, carottes, concombre, lentilles, oignons, radis, tomates**.

haricots verts	*areekoa vehr*	French (green) beans
laitue	*lehtew*	lettuce
petits pois	*pertee pwah*	peas

champignons *shahngpeeñawng*
button mushrooms. Common wild varieties used in French cuisine include **bolets** (boletus), **cèpes** (flat), **chanterelle** (aromatic) and **morille** (sweet).

pommes (de terre) *pom (der tehr)*
potatoes; which may appear as: **allumettes** (matchsticks), **dauphine** (mashed and deep-fried), **duchesse** (mashed), **en robe des champs** (in their jackets), **frites** (fries), **gaufrettes** (waffles), **mignonettes** (fries), **paille** (straws), **pont-neuf** (straight cut).

truffes *trewf*
truffles: highly prized fungus with a heavy, musky flavor. The black truffle of Périgord is regarded as the supreme delicacy.

chou rouge à la flamande *shoo roozh ah lah flamangd*
red cabbage, cooked with apples, onions, red wine and vinegar (Belg.).

chou fassum *shoo fassang*
cabbage stuffed with rice, eggs, cheese and minced meat (Provence).

Salads   Salades

The French will save a side salad until the end of their main course.

salade au cabécou	*salad oa kabehkawng*	goat cheese (Dordogne)
salade composée	*salad kawngpoazay*	mixed salad
salade de foies de volaille	*salad der fwa der volay*	lettuce with chicken livers
salade russe	*salad rewss*	diced vegetables
salade de thon	*salad der tawng*	tuna salad
salade verte	*salad vehrt*	green salad

salade antiboise *salad awngteebwaz*
cooked diced fish, anchovy fillets, green peppers, beets, rice and capers in vinaigrette dressing.

salade niçoise *salad neeswaz*
a Riviera combination salad with tuna, anchovies, olives and vegetables.

Cheese Fromages

With almost 400 cheeses in France alone, there are plenty to suit any palate. Try goat's cheese (**fromage de chèvre**) for a distinctive sharp flavor.

mild	beaufort, beaumont, belle étoile, boursin, brie, cantal, comté, coulommiers, mimolette, petit-suisse, Port-Salut, reblochon, saint-paulin, tomme
sharp, tangy	bleu de Bresse, brousse, camembert, livarot, maroilles, munster, pont-l'évêque, roquefort, vacherin
goat's milk	bûcheron, cabécou, crottin de Chavignol, rocamadour, st-marcellin, valençay
Swiss cheeses	emmental, gruyère

croque-monsieur *krok mersyur*
toasted ham and cheese sandwich.

croûte au fromage *kroot oa fromazh*
hot, melted cheese served over a slice of toast, sometimes with ham and topped with a fried egg.

fromage blanc *fromazh blahng*
fresh white cheese to be eaten with sugar or with pepper and salt.

raclette *raklet*
a half round of a firm cheese grilled until the surface begins to melt; the melting cheese is then scraped off on to a warmed plate and eaten with cold meats, boiled potatoes, gherkins and pickled pearl onions.

Dessert Desserts

crêpe *krep*
Thin pancake; **à la confiture** (with jelly); **au sucre** (with sugar); **normande** (with Calvados and cream); **suzette** (simmered in orange juice and cream).

diplomate *deeplomat*
molded custard dessert with crystallized fruit and lined with sponge cake fingers steeped in liqueur.

sabayon *sabayawng*
creamy dessert of egg yolks, wine, sugar and flavoring.

tarte Tatin *tart tartang*
hot caramelized apples with crust on top and served with vanilla ice cream, **chantilly** or **crème anglaise** (custard).

Drinks Boissons

Beer Bières

Beer is to the Belgians what wine is to the French, and it is often served in its own type of glass. Look for the following types:

bière blanche (white beer): cloudy and honeyish e.g., *Hoegaarden, Kwak*
bière blonde (lager): light, Pilsener-style e.g., *Jupiler, Lamot, Stella Artois*
bière brune (red beer): refreshing and sour e.g., *Rodenbach*
bières trappistes (abbey beers): dark and full bodied e.g., *Chimay, Orval*
Gueuze (blended Lambic beers): e.g., *Kriek* (cherry), *Frambozen* (raspberries), *Faro* (sugar)
Lambic (wheat beer): fermented like wine with a sour, apple-like taste.

Elsewhere, popular brews include *Kronenbourg, Pelforth* and *Kanterbraü* (French) and *Cardinal* and *Hürlimann* (Swiss).

Wine Vins

French cuisine and wine are inseparable components that complement each other. Traditionally, white wine goes well with fish, fowl and light meats, while dark meats call for a red wine. A good rosé or dry champagne goes well with almost anything. The wine waiter (**le sommelier**) will be happy to offer advice – and a tip is appreciated for this service. The main grape varieties are:

red: Cabernet-Sauvignon, Carignan, Cinsaut, Gamay, Grenache, Merlot, Mourvedre, Pinot Noir, Syrah;

white: Chardonnay, Chenin Blanc, Gewurztraminer, Muscadet, Muscat, Riesling, Sauvignon Blanc, Sémillon.

Reading the label

AC (appellation contrôlée)/AOC
  highest quality wine; generally most expensive
blanc white
brut dry
cépage grape variety
château wine-making estate
côte/coteaux slope/hills
crémant sparkling
cru superior growth
demi-sec medium dry/sweet
doux sweet
millésime vintage
mis en bouteilles dans nos caves
  bottled in our cellars

mis en bouteilles par bottled by
mousseux sparkling/frothy
rosé rosé
rouge red
sec dry
VDQS regional wine of good quality
vignoble vineyard
vin de garde
  wine to lay down to mature
vin de pays
  local wine – less strict quality control than AC wines
vin de table
  table wine – variable quality
vin ordinaire table wine

Wine regions Régions et genres de vin

Alsace (almost only dry white wines) esp. Gewurztraminer, Riesling, Sylvaner

Bordeaux (major wine-growing area; red wine is known as Claret in the U.K.) esp. Entre-Deux-Mers, Graves, Médoc (red: Listrac, Margaux, Moulis, Pauillac, St-Estèphe, St-Julien), Pessac-Léognan, Pomerol (red: Château-Pétrus, Lalande-de-Pomerol, Néac), Sauternes (sweet: Château-d'Yquem, Barsac), Sainte-Croix-du-Mont (sweet), St-Émilion (Lussac, Montagne, Parsac, Puisseguin, St-Georges).

Bourgogne (Burgundy: major wine-growing area of 5 regions)
Beaujolais (red: Chiroubles, Fleurie, Juliénas, Moulin-à-Vent, Morgon, Régnié, St-Amour); Chablis (white); Côte Chalonnaise (Mercurey); Côte de Beaune (Aloxe-Corton, Beaune, Blagy, Chassagne-Montrachet, Chorley-lès-Beaune, Meursault, Pernand-Vergelesses, Pommard, Puligny-Montrachet, St-Romain, Santenay, Savigny-lès-Beaune, Volnay); Côte de Nuits (Chambolle-Musigny, Fixin, Gevrey-Chambertin, Marsannay, Morey-St-Denis, Nuits-St-Georges, Vosne-Romanée); Mâconnais (red: St-Véran).

Champagne (home of the world-famous sparkling wine)
e.g., Bollinger, Jacquart, Krug, Laurent Perrier, Merciet & Ruinart, Moët & Chandon, Mumm.

Côtes-du-Rhône (wide variety of white, red and rosé)
Northern Rhone (Cornas, Côte-Rôtie, Crozes-Hermitage, St-Joseph); Southern Rhone (Châteauneuf-du-Pape, Gigondas, Lirac, Muscat de Beaumes-de-Venise, Rasteau, Tavel-rosé, Vacqueyras); Côtes du Ventoux; Côtes du Lubéron.

Jura (small wine-growing area between Burgundy and Switzerland)
esp. Arbois, Château-Chalon, Côtes du Jura, l'Etoile.

Languedoc (largest wine-producing area in France, mostly table wine)
e.g., Blanquette de Limoux, Clairette de Bellegarde, Clairette du Languedoc, Corbières, Costières de Nîmes, Faugères, Fitou, Muscat (from Frontignan, Lunel, Minervois, Mireval, St-Jean-de-Minervois), St-Chinian.

Loire (regions providing much fine, underrated white, red and rosé)
Anjou (Coteaux-de-l'Aubance, Coteaux-du-Layon, Quarts-de-Chaume, Savennières); Berry and Nivernais (Menetou-Salon, Pouilly-Fumé, Quincy, Reuilly, Sancerre); Nantais (Muscadet); Saumur; Touraine (Bourgueil, Chinon, Montlouis, Vouvray).

Lorraine (minor wine-growing area)
e.g., Vins de la Moselle, Côtes-de-Toul.

Provence (wide range of red, white and rosé)
esp: Bandol, Bellet, Cassis, Coteaux-d'Aix-en-Provence, Côtes-de-Provence, Palette, Coteaux Varois.

Roussillon (produces 3/4 of France's sweet wine)
e.g., red: Côtes-du-Roussillon; sweet: Banyuls, Côtes-du-Haut-Roussillon, Grand-Roussillon, Muscat de Rivesaltes, Rivesaltes.

Savoie (bordering Switzerland – primarily dry white wines) e.g., Crépy, Seyssel.

Switzerland (produces primarily light, white wines)
esp. Neuchâtel (Auvernier, Cormondrèche, Cortaillod, Hauterive), Valais (Arvine, Dôle, Ermitage, Fendant, Johannisberg, Malvoisie), Vaud (Aigle, Dézaley, Mont-sur-Rolle, Lavaux, Yvorne).

Other drinks Autres boissons

Apéritifs are much more common than cocktails or highballs. Many are wine- and brandy-based with herbs and bit-
ters (e.g., *Amer Picon®, Byrrh®, Dubonnet®*); typically French is
the aniseed-based pastis (e.g., *Pernod®, Ricard®*). But you may
prefer a liqueur drink such as **blanc-cassis** or **kir** (chilled white
wine with black currant syrup). You'll recognize **un gin-tonic, un rhum, un
vermouth, une vodka, un whisky**.

After a meal, you may like to try a fruit-distilled brandy: **calvados** (apple),
kirsch (cherry), **marc** (grape), **poire William** (pear) or **quetsche** (plum). Other
popular liqueurs include the famous orange-flavored *Grand Marnier®* and
Cointreau®; and *Bénédictine®*– brandy-based with herbs.

Non-alcoholic drinks Boissons sans alcool

France offers a wide choice of mineral waters, such as *Badoit®, Evian®, Per-
rier®, Vichy®, Vittel®, Volvic®*. You'll also have no trouble finding your
favorite soft drinks or sodas, such as *Coca-Cola®, Fanta®, Pepsi®*.

I'd like …	**Je voudrais …** *zher voodray*
(hot) chocolate	**un chocolat (chaud)** *ang shokolah (shoa)*
coke/lemonade	**un coca/une limonade** *ang koka/ewn leemonad*
milkshake	**un frappé** *ang frapay*
mineral water	**de l'eau minérale** *der loa meenayral*
carbonated	**gazeuse** *gazurz*
non-carbonated/still	**non gazeuse** *nawng gazurz*
tonic water	**un Schweppes** *ang shweps*

un café *ang kafay*
Coffee can be served: **au lait** (with milk); **complet** (with bread, rolls, butter
and jam); **crème** (with cream); **décaféiné** (decaffeinated); **frappé** (shaken,
iced coffee); **noir** (black); **sans caféine** (decaffeinated); **soluble** (instant).

un jus de fruits *ang zhoo der frwee*
Common fruit juices are **jus d'orange** (orange), **jus de pamplemousse**
(grapefruit), **jus de poire** (pear), **jus de pomme** (apple), **jus de tomate**
(tomato); and ➤ 49 for others.

un thé *ang tay*
Tea can be drunk the British way, **au lait** (with milk), but it is more usual
to have it **au citron** (with lemon), **à la menthe** (mint tea), **glacé** (iced) or
nature (black). A **tisane** (herb tea) is also a popular alternative.

Menu Reader

à la vapeur	*a la vapurr*	steamed
au four	*oa foor*	baked
bouilli	*booyee*	boiled
braisé	*brezay*	braised
coupé en dés	*koopay ahng day*	diced
en ragoût	*ahng ragoo*	stewed
épicé	*aypeessay*	spicy
farci	*farsee*	stuffed
frit (dans la friture)	*free (dahng la freetewr)*	(deep) fried
fumé	*fewmay*	smoked
grillé	*greeyay*	grilled
mariné	*mareenay*	marinated
pané	*panay*	breaded
poché	*poshay*	poached
rôti	*roatee*	roasted / oven-browned
sauté	*soatay*	sautéed
velouté de ...	*velootay der*	creamed

very rare	**bleu** *blur*	
rare	**saignant** *señahng*	
medium	**à point** *a pwang*	
well-done	**bien cuit** *byang kwee*	

A à la, à l', au, aux in the manner of, as in, with
à l'étouffée stewed
à la croque au sel served raw with salt and French dressing
abricot apricot
agneau lamb
aiglefin (églefin) haddock
aïgo bouïdo garlic soup (*Prov.*)
aiguillettes de canard au vinaigre fillet of duck in raspberry vinegar (*Dord.*)
ail garlic

aïoli garlic mayonnaise
alose shad (fine textured fish with delicate flesh)
alouette lark
alouettes sans têtes stuffed small rolled veal cutlets
amandes almonds
américaine white wine, brandy, garlic, shallots, tomatoes, shrimp or lobster flavoring
amuse-gueule savory biscuits, crackers; appetizers
ananas pineapple
anchois anchovies

anchoïade purée of unsalted anchovies in olive oil (*Prov.*)

andouille(tte) tripe sausage ➤43

aneth dill

anglaise boiled or steamed vegetables; breaded and fried

anguille eel

anguille au vert eel flavored with sorrel, sage and parsley (*Belg.*)

anis aniseed

A.O.C. officially recognized wine

apéritifs aperitifs ➤51

artichaut artichoke

asperges asparagus

aspic (meat or fish in) aspic

assaisonnement seasoning

assiette anglaise assorted cold cuts

assiette de charcuterie selection of cold meats

attente: 15 min waiting time: 15 minutes

au bleu (especially for trout) poached when it's fresh

au choix choice of …

au citron with lemon

au four baked

au gril grilled

au lait with milk

aubergine eggplant/aubergine

avec de l'eau gazeuse with (seltzer) water

avec des glaçons on the rocks

B **baguette** long, thin loaf of French bread

ballon a glass

bananes Baronnet sliced bananas with lemon, cream and kirch

bar sea bass

bar aux herbes en chemise stuffed sea bass ➤45

barbue brill (fish like a turbot)

barquette small boat-shaped pastry shell garnished with fruit

basilic basil

bâtard small French bread stick

baudroie angler

bavarois Bavarian cream cakes

béarnaise creamy sauce of vinegar, egg, white wine, shallots, tarragon

bécasse woodcock

bécassine snipe

béchamel white sauce

beignet fritter, generally filled with fruit, vegetables or meat

betterave beet

beurre butter

beurre blanc butter, shallots, vinegar, white wine

beurre noir browned butter, vinegar and/or lemon juice

bien cuit well-done

bière beer ➤49

bière blonde/brune light/dark beer

bière en bouteilles bottled beer

bière sans alcool a non-alcoholic beer

bifteck beef steak

bigarade with oranges

bigorneaux periwinkels

biscuit de Savoie currant sponge cake

biscuits cookies/biscuits

biscuits apéritifs appetizers, snacks

biscuits salés crackers

bisque seafood chowder/stew

bisque d'écrevisses crayfish chowder/stew

bisque de homard lobster chowder/stew

blanc white (wine); breast (chicken)

blanchaille herring/whitebait

blanquette de veau veal in cream sauce ➤46

bleu very rare; blue (cheese); boiled fresh (fish)

bœuf beef

bœuf bourguignon rich beef stew ➤46

bœuf mode beef chunks with carrots and onions in red wine

bœuf salé corned beef

boissons drinks

boisson non alcoolisée soft drink/soda

bolets boletus mushrooms

bombe molded ice cream mousse

bordelaise sauce of mushrooms, red wine, shallots, beef marrow (*Bord.*)
bouchée à la reine sweetbreads in pastry ➤43
boudin blood sausage/black pudding
bouillabaisse fish and seafood soup (*Mar.*)
bouilleture d'anguilles eel cooked in cream (*Anjou*)
bouilli boiled; boiled beef
bouillon bouillon
bouillon de poulet chicken bouillon
boulettes (de viande) meatballs
bourguignonne red wine, herbs, button mushrooms, shallots
bourride fish chowder/stew (*Prov.*)
braisé braised
brandade de morue creamed salt cod
brème bream (fish)
brioche bun
brioche au sucre bun sprinkled with sugar
(à la) broche (on a) skewer
brochet pike
brochette skewered kebab
brugnon nectarine
brut very dry (wine)
bûche de Noël Christmas log
bulots large whelks (seafood)

C **cabillaud** (fresh) cod
cabri kid goat
cacahuètes peanuts
cade chickpea cake (*Riv.*)
café coffee ➤40
café au lait coffee with milk
café complet coffee with bread, rolls, butter and jam
café crème coffee with cream
café décaféiné decaffeinated coffee
café frappé shaked cold coffee
café noir black coffee
café sans caféine decaffeinated coffee
café soluble instant coffee
caille quail

calissons ground almonds and marzipan (*Aix*)
cal(a)mars squid
calvados apple brandy (*Norm.*)
canard (sauvage) (wild) duck
canard à l'orange duck in orange ➤46
canard laqué Peking duck
caneton duckling
caneton à la rouennaise duckling in red wine sauce (*Norm.*) ➤46
cannelle cinnamon
câpres capers
carafe carafe
carbonnade charcoal-grilled meat
carbon(n)ade flamande beef slices and onions in beer (*Belg.*)
caricoles sea snails (*Belg.*)
carottes carrots
carpe carp
carré d'agneau rack of lamb
carré braisé à la niçoise braised loin with vermouth and lemon peel
carrelet plaice (flat fish)
casse-croûte sandwich, snack
cassis black currants; black currant liqueur
cassoulet toulousain casserole ➤46
céleri(-rave) celeriac
cèpes flap mushrooms
céréales cereal
cerf venison (red deer)
cerfeuil chervil
cerises (noires) (black) cherries
cervelas type of sausage
cervelle brains
chabichou cheese of cow's and goat's milk
champignons (de Paris) mushrooms
chantilly whipped cream
chapon capon
charcuterie cold cuts; assorted pork products
charlotte fruit dessert in mold
Chartreuse herb liqueur ➤51
chasseur wine, mushrooms, onions, shallots, herbs

chateaubriand double fillet steak (tenderloin of porterhouse steak)

chaud hot

chaud-froid dressing containing gelatin

chaudrée fish and seafood stew

chausson aux pommes apple turnover

chevreuil venison/roe deer

chichifregi roll doughnuts, sold by the centimeter (Riv.)

chicorée endive/chicory

chips potato chips/crisps

chocolat (chaud) (hot) chocolate

chocolat froid cold chocolate

chocolatine chocolate puff pastry

chou (rouge) (red) cabbage

chou rouge à la flamande red cabbage in red wine (Belg.) ➤47

chou fassum stuffed cabbage (Prov.) ➤47

chou-fleur cauliflower

chou-fleur au gratin cauliflower cheese

choucroute sauerkraut

choucroute garnie sauerkraut, sausages and cured pork

choux de Bruxelles brussels sprouts

ciboulette chives

citron lemon

citron pressé lemon juice

citron vert lime

civet game stew ➤46

clafoutis fruit in pancake batter

clous de girofle clove

cochon de lait suckling pig

(en) cocotte pot-roasted

cœurs d'artichaut artichoke hearts

cognac brandy

colonel lemon (water ice) doused with vodka

communard red wine and black currant liqueur

compris(e) included

concombre cucumber

confit preserve

confiture jam

congolais coconut cake

consommé consommé ➤44

consommé à l'œuf consommé with a raw egg

consommé au porto consommé with port wine

consommé Célestine consommé with chicken and noodles

consommé Colbert consommé with poached eggs, spring vegetables

contre-filet loin strip steak

coq au vin chicken in red wine ➤46

coq de bruyère woodgrouse

coquelet à l'estragon spring chicken with tarragon sauce

coquilles St-Jacques scallops

coriandre coriander

cornichons pickles/gherkins

corsé full-bodied (wine)

côte rib

côte de bœuf T-bone steak

côtelettes chops

cotriade fish soup (Britt.) ➤45

cou d'oie farci stuffed goose neck (Dord.)

coulis soup; creamy sauce

coupe (glacée) ice cream dessert, sundae

courgette zucchini

couronne ring-shaped loaf

couscous Arab dish of cracked wheat with meat ➤46

couvert silverware

crabe crab

crème … cream of …

crème anglaise custard equivalent

crème brûlée custard with crispy caramel topping

crème caramel caramel pudding

crème Chantilly whipped cream

crème d'asperges cream of asparagus

crème de bolets cream of boletus mushrooms

crème de volaille cream of chicken

crème pâtissière cream with butter

crêpe pancake ➤48

crêpe à la confiture pancake with jam

crêpe au sucre pancake with sugar

crêpe dentelle thin biscuity pancake (*Britt.*)

crêpe normande pancake with Calvados and cream

crêpe suzette large, thin pancakes simmered in orange juice and flambéed with orange liqueur

crépinette flat seasoned sausage

cresson watercress

crevettes shrimp

croissants flaky crescent rolls

croquembouche caramel-coated pastry puff

croque-madame a croque-monsieur with an egg on top

croque-monsieur toasted ham and cheese sandwich

crottin de Chavignol goat's cheese

croustade filled pie/pastry shell

croûte au fromage melted cheese on toast, with ham and topped by a fried egg

cru raw; system of grading wine

crudités mixed raw vegetable salad

crustacés shellfish

cuisses de grenouilles frog's legs

cuit à la vapeur steamed

cuit au bleu poached when fresh (esp. trout)

cul de veau à l'angevine veal rump in rich sauce with vegetables (*Loire*)

cumin caraway

D **dartois** jam pastry

dattes dates

daube de bœuf beef stew with tomatoes and olives (*Prov.*)

daurade sea bream (fish)

décaféiné decaffeinated

délice dessert specialty of the chef

délimité de qualité supérieure superior quality (wine)

demi-bouteille a half bottle

demi-poulet grillé half a roasted chicken

dessert desserts ➤48

diable hot-pepper sauce

diabolo menthe mint cordial

dinde turkey

dinde aux marrons turkey, chestnuts and cranberry sauce

dindonneau young turkey (cock)

diplomate molded dessert ➤48

doux sweet (wine)

dur hard (egg)

duxelles with mushrooms

E **eau (chaude)** (hot) water

eau minérale mineral water ➤51

eau minérale gazeuse carbonated/mineral water

eau minérale non gazeuse non carbonated mineral water

échalote shallot

éclair au chocolat/café long cake filled with chocolate/coffee cream

écrevisses crayfish

émincé de bœuf aux morilles beef stew with morels

emporter, à to take out

en chemise baked in waxed paper

en saison in season

endives endive

entrecôte rib/rib-eye steak

entrées first course/appetizer

entremets small dish served before cheese; dessert

épaule shoulder

épaule braisée aux marrons braised shoulder stuffed with chestnuts

éperlans smelts/spaling (small fish)

épices spices

épinards spinach

escalope cutlet

escalope à la crème veal scallops cooked with cream

escalope viennoise breaded veal cutlet

escargots snails

espadon swordfish

estouffade de bœuf beef stew

estragon tarragon

expresso espresso coffee

F

faisan pheasant
far sweet batter pudding, often with dried fruit (*Britt.*)
farces stuffing, esp. liver and truffles
farci stuffed
faux-filet sirloin steak
fenouil fennel
féra lake salmon
fèves broad beans
ficelle thin bread stick
figues figs
filet fillet steak
filet mignon au poivre vert pork with green pepper sauce
financière Madeira wine, truffles, olives, mushrooms
fines herbes mixture of herbs; with herbs
flageolets small kidney beans
flamiche savory cheese pie with leeks or onions
flan custard tart
florentin thin crust of almonds and dark chocolate
(à la) florentine with spinach
foie liver
foie de veau grillé à la moutarde grilled calf's liver with mustard and breadcrumbs
foie gras goose or duck liver
fond d'artichaut artichoke heart
fondue melted cheese dip (*Switz.*)
fondue bourguignonne meat fondue with different sauces
fondue chinoise thinly sliced meat plunged into simmering stock
forestière with mushrooms, shallots and white wine
fougasse flat loaf with anchovies, olives, cheese (*Prov.*)
(au) four baked
fraises strawberries
framboises raspberries
frappé chilled, iced; milkshake
fricassée braised meat in a thick sauce

frigousse casserole of chicken, bacon and chestnuts (*Britt.*)
frisée curly lettuce
frit fried
frites French fries
friture de mer small fish, generally deep fried, eaten like chips (fries)
froid cold
fromage cheese
fromage blanc fresh white cheese to be eaten with sugar or with pepper and salt.
fromage blanc à la crème fresh white cheese served with cream
fromage de chèvre goat's cheese
fruits fruit
fruits confits candied fruit
fruits de mer seafood
fruits frais fresh fruits
fruits secs dried fruit
fumé smoked

G

galette flat, plain cake
galette complète crêpes filled with egg, fish or meat
ganses small fried cakes topped with sugar (*Prov.*)
garbure cabbage soup, with pork or goose
garniture au choix choice of vegetable accompaniment
gâteau cake
gâteau au chocolat chocolate cake
gâteau Bigarreau sponge cake with praline filling
gâteau breton rich Madeira cake
gâteau de riz rice pudding
gâteau de semoule semolina pudding
gâteau lyonnais chocolate and chestnut cake
gaufres waffles (*Belg.*)
(à la) gelée in aspic
génoise light cake
gibelotte de lapin rabbit stew in wine sauce
gibier game

gigot leg
gigot à la bretonne
  roast leg of lamb with
  dried beans
gin-tonic gin and tonic
gingembre ginger

glace ice cream
glace à la fraise/à la vanille
  strawberry/vanilla ice cream
glacé iced, glazed
goujon gudgeon
  (tiny freshwater fish)
grand veneur sauce for game
(au) gratin browned with breadcrumbs
  or cheese
gratin dauphinois sliced potatoes
  gratinéed with milk, cream and garlic
gratin de queues d'écrevisses
  baked crayfish tails
gratinée au four baked with cheese and
  ham
grattons grilled pork fat (*Lyon*)
grenadine red fruit syrup with
  lemonade
grenadine à l'eau red fruit syrup
  with water
grillades grilled meat
grillé grilled
grive thrush
grondin gurnard (firm fleshed fish)
groseilles red currants
groseilles à maquereau gooseberries

 hachis Parmentier shepherd's pie
harengs herring
haricots blancs haricot beans, white
  kidney beans
haricots verts French (green) beans
(aux) herbes with herbs
hollandaise egg yolks, butter, vinegar
homard lobster
homard à l'américaine
  sautéed lobster ➤45
homard thermidor
  lobster gratinéed with cheese
hors-d'œuvre appetizers
hors-d'œuvre variés assorted appetizers
huîtres oysters

 île flottante meringue in custard
(à l')indienne (in) curry sauce

 jambon ham
jambon de Bayonne raw,
  salty ham
jambon-beurre sandwich with ham
  and butter
jambonneau cured pig's knuckle
jardinière cooked assorted vegetables
jarret knuckle
Joconde almond sponge
julienne vegetables cut into fine strips
jus (fruit) juice ➤51
jus d'orange orange juice
jus de fruits fruit juice
jus de pamplemousse grapefruit juice
jus de poire pear juice
jus de pomme apple juice
jus de tomate tomato juice

 Kig-Ha-Farz mixture of pork,
  beef, vegetables and buckwheat
  (*Britt.*)
kir white wine with black currant
  liqueur
kir royal champagne and black currant
  liqueur
kirsch cherry liqueur
kouing-Aman crisp butter cakes (*Britt.*)

lait milk
laitue lettuce
lamproie lamprey
langouste spiny (rock) lobster
langoustines Dublin bay prawns,
  scampi
langue tongue
lapin rabbit
lapin à la flamande
  marinated rabbit (*Belg.*) ➤46
lard bacon
laurier bay leaf
léger light (wine)
légumes vegetables ➤47
lentilles lentils
lièvre wild hare

limonade lemonade; soft drink/soda
liqueur liqueur
(à la) lorraine braised in red wine with red cabbage
lotte burbot (firm white flesh fish)
lotte de mer anglerfish, monkfish (chewy, mild, sweet flesh)
loup sea bass
(à la) lyonnaise sautéed with onions

M **madère** with Madeira wine
magret de canard fillet breast of fattened duck (*Dord.*)
maïs corn
maison homemade
maître d'hôtel headwaiter (or maitre d')
mandarine tangerine
manons chocolate filled with fresh cream (*Belg.*)
maquereau mackerel
marc grape spirit
marcassin young wild boar
marchand de vin wine merchant
mariné marinated
marinière white wine, mussel broth thickened with egg yolks
marjolaine marjoram; layered nut cake
marrons chestnuts
matelote (d'anguilles) fish (esp. eel) stew with wine (*Tours, Anjou*)
médaillon tenderloin steak (lamb, pork or veal)
melon melon
menthe mint
menthe à l'eau mint cordial
menu à prix fixe set menu
menu gastronomique gourmet menu
menu touristique choice of dishes for each course, for a fixed price
meringue meringue
merlan whiting
méthode champenoise in the champagne style
meunière brown butter, parsley, lemon juice
miel honey

(à la) milanaise with Parmesan and noisette butter
milhassou sweet, cornmeal pudding
milkshake milkshake
mille-feuille flaky pastry with cream filling (napoleon)
(à la) mode in the style of, esp. local recipe
moelle bone marrow
mojhettes à la crème creamed green beans
molle soft (cheese)
mollet soft (egg)
mont-blanc chestnut dessert with whipped cream
morilles morels (mushrooms)
Mornay cheese sauce
mortadelle Bologna sausage
morue cod
moules mussels
moules marinière mussels simmering in white wine with shallots, thyme and parsley
mousse au chocolat chocolate mousse
mousse de foie light liver pâté
mousseline mayonnaise with cream; puréed raw fish with cream
mousseux sparkling (wine)
moutarde mustard; mustard sauce
mûres mulberries, blackberries
muscade nutmeg
myrtilles blueberries

N **nature** plain; black (tea)
navets turnips
nectar d'abricot apricot juice
(à la) niçoise with garlic, anchovies, olives, onions and tomatoes
Noilly Prat® a French vermouth
noir black (coffee/tea)
noisette hazelnut; boneless round piece of meat
noisette de porc aux pruneaux pork tenderloin/fillet with prunes and cream (*Loire*)

noix walnuts
noix de coco coconut
noix de muscade nutmeg
(à la) normande
  mushrooms, eggs and
  cream sauce
nouilles noodles

O **œufs** eggs
œuf à la coque boiled egg
œuf dur hard-boiled egg
œufs Argenteuil eggs on tartlet with asparagus and cream sauce
œufs à la Bruxelles eggs with braised chicory and cream sauce
œufs à la diable deviled eggs
œufs à la neige meringue on custard
œufs au bacon bacon and eggs
œufs au jambon ham and eggs
œufs au plat fried eggs
œufs brouillés scrambled eggs
œufs mimosa hard-boiled eggs served with mayonnaise
oie goose
oignons onions
olives olives
omble (chevalier) char (delicate, flavorful fish)
omelette (nature) (plain) omelet
omelette au fromage cheese omelet
omelette au jambon ham omelet
omelette aux champignons mushroom omelet
omelette aux fines herbes herb omelet
onglet prime cut of meat
opéra layered chocolate and nut cake
orange orange
orangeade orangeade
origan oregano
ormeaux abalones (chewy shellfish)
ortolan ortolan bunting

P **pain** bread
pain au chocolat flaky pastry lined with chocolate
pain au levain leaven bread
pain aux raisins snail-shaped bun with raisins

pain blanc/bis white/brown bread
pain complet/intégral
  whole-wheat/wholemeal bread
pain d'épices gingerbread (*Dijon*)
pain de seigle rye bread
pain de son bran bread
pain grillé toast
paillasson fried, sliced potatoes (*Lyon*)
palourdes clams
pamplemousse grapefruit
panaché selection; shandy
panbagna/pan bagnat
  tuna and salad sandwich (*Riv.*)
pannequet parcel shaped crêpe
(en) papillote baked in grease-proof paper
parfait glacé frozen dessert
Paris-Brest
  large pastry ring with cream
(à la) parisienne with mushrooms in white wine sauce
Parmentier with potatoes
pastèque watermelon
pastis aniseed-based drink (*Prov./Midi*) ➤51; flaky apple pie (*Dord.*)
pâté molded pastry case; liver purée ➤43
pâtes pasta
pâtes fraîches fresh pasta, noodles
pâtisseries pastries
paupiettes de veau Valentino
  veal "birds" stuffed with asparagus, with tomato sauce
(à la) paysanne containing vegetables
pêche peach
perche perch
perdreau young partridge
perdrix partridge
Périgueux with a goose – or duck – liver purée and truffles
Pernod® aniseed flavored aperitif
persil parsley
petit déjeuner breakfast ➤43
petit four small cake
petit noir espresso coffee
petit pain roll

petit pain au cumin
  roll with caraway seeds
petit pain aux pavots
  roll with poppy seeds
petit salé aux lentilles
  large pork sausage with lentils
petit-suisse thick fromage frais (fresh
  curd cheese)
petits pois peas
petits trianons chocolate fudge bars
pieds feet/trotters
pieds (et) paquets stuffed sheep's
  trotters (*Mar.*)
pigeon pigeon
pigeonneau squab
pignons buttery croissants with pine-
  nuts (*Prov.*)
pilaf rice boiled in a bouillon with
  onions
piment pimiento
pintade guinea fowl
pintadeau young guinea cock
pissaladière type of pizza made with
  onions and anchovies (*Prov.*)
pistou vegetable and pasta soup; garlic
  and fresh basil paste (*Riv.*)
plaque de chocolat chocolate bar (large)
plat (du jour) dish (of the day)
plateau plate
plat principal main course
plie plaice (flat fish)
poché poached
poire pear
poire à la Condé hot pear on bed of
  vanilla-flavored rice
poire Belle-Hélène pear with vanilla ice
  cream and chocolate sauce
poireaux leeks
pois mange-tout string-peas
poissons fish ➤45
poivrade pepper sauce
poivre pepper
poivrons sweet peppers
polenta polenta
pomme apple
pommes de terre potatoes ➤47
pommes allumettes potato matchsticks

pommes
  dauphine potato
  mashed in butter and
  egg yolks, mixed in
  seasoned flour and
  deep-fried
pommes duchesse potato
  mashed with butter and egg
  yolks
pommes en robe des champs
  potatoes in their jackets
pommes frites French fries
pommes mousseline mashed potato
pommes nature boiled, steamed potato
pommes nouvelles new potato
pommes vapeur steamed, boiled potato
pompes à l'huile cake flavored with
  orange flower water or aniseed (*Riv.*)
porc pork
porto port; with port wine
pot-au-feu beef stew with vegetables
potage soup ➤44
potage à l'ail garlic soup
potage au cresson watercress soup
potage bilibi fish and oyster soup
potage bonne femme potato, leek and
  sometimes bacon soup
potage Condé shredded vegetables
  soup
potage du Barry cream of cauliflower
potage julienne mashed red beans soup
potage Parmentier potato soup
potiron pumpkin
poularde fattened pullet
poule stewing fowl
poule au pot
  stewed chicken with vegetables
poulet chicken
poulet créole
  chicken in white sauce with rice
poulet Marengo
  chicken in white wine
poulet rôti roast chicken
poulette
  with butter, cream and egg yolks
poulpes octopus
pour deux personnes for two
poussin spring chicken

praires clams
pressé fresh (juice)
pression draft beer
profiterole filled choux pastry
(à la) provençale onions, tomatoes, garlic
pruneaux prunes
prunes plums
pudding à la Reine bread pudding with lemon, cream and apricot
puits d'amour pastry shell with liqueur-flavored custard
purée de pommes de terre mashed potatoes

Q **quatre-quarts** Madeira cake
quenelles dumplings ➤43
quiche flan or open-faced tart ➤43

R **raclette** melted cheese ➤48
radis radishes
ragoût meat stew ➤45
raie ray
raifort horseradish
raisin (blanc/noir) (white/black) grapes
raisins secs raisins
ramequin small cheese tart
râpé grated
rascasse fish used in bouillabaisse
ratatouille vegetable casserole
ravigote vinegar sauce with eggs, capers and herbs
religieuse au chocolat/café puff cake with chocolate/coffee filling
rémoulade sauce flavored with mustard and herbs
réserve du patron house wine
rhubarbe rhubarb
rhum rum
Ricard® aniseed-flavored aperitif
rillettes pâté, usually of duck
rillettes de porc minced pork served chilled in earthenware pots
rillons chunky pieces of pork hors-d'œuvre
ris de veau veal sweetbreads

riz rice
rognons kidneys
romarin rosemary
rosbif roast beef
rosé rosé (wine)
rosette dried sausage (*Lyon*)
rôti roast
rouge red (wine)
rouget red mullet
rouille pink, garlicky mayonnaise
rouilleuse white wine sauce, thickened with blood

S **sabayon** creamy dessert ➤48
sablé au beurre type of shortbread
sacristains pastry straws with sugar or cheese topping
safran saffron
saignant rare
saint-cyr baked meringue with frozen chocolate mousse
saint-honoré choux cake with cream
saint-pierre John Dory (nutty, sweet-flavored fish)
salade salad ➤47
salade composée mixed salad
salade au cabécou goat-cheese salad (*Dord.*)
salade chiffonnade shredded lettuce and sorrel in melted butter
salade de foies de volaille lettuce with chicken livers
salade de museau de bœuf marinated brawn (beef brains)
salade de thon tuna salad
salade niçoise a Riviera combination salad, which includes tuna, anchovies, black olives and tomatoes and rice
salade russe diced vegetable salad in mayonnaise
salade verte green salad
sandre pike perch, zander
sandwich sandwich
sandwich au fromage cheese sandwich
sandwich au jambon ham sandwich
sanglier wild boar
sans glaçon straight

sarcelle teal (a duck)

sardines sardines

sauces sauces

sauce bleue vinaigrette with blue cheese (roquefort type)

sauce diable sauce with cayenne, shallots, pepper

sauce Périgueux rich Madeira sauce with cognac and truffles

saucisse sausage

saucisse de Francfort frankfurter

saucisse de Morteau type of pork sausage to cook

saucisse de Strasbourg Strasbourg (pork) sausage, knackwurst

saucisson cold sausage

saucisson brioché large sausage in a bun (*Lyon*)

sauge sage

saumon salmon

sauté sautéed

savarin sponge cake in rum

scallopini breaded escalopes

scampi prawns (shrimp)

Schweppes® tonic water

sec dry (wine)

sel salt

selle saddle

selon arrivage when available

selon grosseur/grandeur (s.g.) price according to size

sirop syrup

socca chickpea cake, eaten hot (Nice)

sole sole

sorbet sherbet

soubise onion-cream sauce

soufflé light fluffy dish with browned egg whites

soufflé au Grand Marnier soufflé made of orange liqueur

soufflé Rothschild vanilla-flavored soufflé with candied fruit

soupe soup ➤44

soupe à la bière beer soup with chicken stock and onions (*Belg.*)

soupe à l'oignon French onion soup

soupe au pistou vegetable soup (*Prov.*)

soupe aux choux cabbage soup

soupe de Pélous crab soup with tomatoes, saffron and bread

soupe de poisson small fish, simmered with tomatoes and saffron, then puréed and sieved

soupe du jour soup of the day

spécialités locales local specialties

steak beef steak

steak au poivre steak with cracked black pepper

steak tartare raw minced fillet with egg, capers and parsely

steak-frites steak and French fries

sucre sugar

supplément/en sus extra charge

suprême thickened chicken broth

suprême de volaille chicken breast in cream sauce

sur commande made to order

T **tablier de sapeur** pig's feet/fried tripe in breadcrumbs

tajine lamb with almonds and sultanas

tapenade spicy mousse of olives and anchovies (*Prov.*)

tartare mayonnaise flavored with mustard and herbs

tarte à la brousse type of cheese cake (*Corsica*)

tarte à la cannelle blueberry-cinnamon flan

tarte au citron meringuée lemon meringue pie

tarte au fromage cheese tart

tarte aux pommes apple tart

tarte de blettes tart with minced beet leaves, cheese, dried currants

tarte frangipane almond cream tart

tarte Tatin apple tart ➤48

tartelette small tart

tartine buttered baguette with jam, marmelade or honey

tarte tropézienne rich cake filled with crème pâtissière

tasse de thé cup of tea
tellines small triangular shellfish seasoned with garlic and parsley (*Riv.*)
terrine sliced pâté
tête de nègre meringue cake covered with dark chocolate
thé tea
thé à la menthe mint tea
thé au citron tea with lemon
thé au lait tea with milk
thé glacé iced tea
thé nature black tea
thon tuna
thym thyme
tian de courgettes zucchini [courgette] custard (*Riv.*)
(en) timbale cooked in a pastry case or mold
tisane herb tea
tomates tomatoes
tomate aux crevettes tomato filled with shrimps and mayonnaise (*Belg.*)
tourain/tourin soup (*Dord.*)
tournedos tenderloin of T-bone steak
tournedos Rossini beef in Madeira wine sauce
tourte layer cake
tourteau fromager goat cheesecake
tranche slice
tripes à la mode de Caen baked tripe with Calvados
triple sec orange liqueur
truffes truffles
truite trout
truite saumonée salmon trout
turbot turbot

V **vacherin glacé** ice-cream cake
veau veal
velouté cream of ➤44
velouté de tomates cream of tomato
velouté de volaille cream of chicken
veloutée thickened chicken or meat stock
verre a glass
verre de lait a glass of milk

verte mayonnaise with spinach, watercress, herbs
viande meat ➤45
viande séchée des Grisons cured dried beef
vin wine ➤49
vinaigrette vinegar dressing
vin du pays local wine
vin ordinaire table wine
volaille fowl, poultry
V.S.O.P. cognac aged over 5 years

WX YZ **waterzooi de poulet** chicken in white wine (*Belg.*)
xérès sherry
yaourt/yoghourt yogurt

Travel

ESSENTIAL

1/2/3 for …	**Un/deux/trois pour …** _ang/dur/trwa poor_
To …, please.	**À…, s'il vous plaît.** _seel voo pleh_
one-way [single]	**aller-simple** _alay sangpl_
round-trip [return]	**aller-retour** _alay rertoor_
How much?	**C'est combien?** _seh kawnbyang_

Safety Sécurité

Would you accompany me …?	**Pourriez-vous m'accompagner …?** _pooryay voo makawngpañay_
to the bus stop	**jusqu'à l'arrêt d'autobus** _zhewska lareh doatobews_
to my hotel	**jusqu'à mon hôtel** _zhewska mawng noatel_
I don't want to … on my own.	**Je ne veux pas … tout(e) seul(e).** _zher ner vur pa … too(t) surl_
stay here	**rester ici** _restay eessee_
walk home	**rentrer chez moi à pied** _rahngtray shay mwa a pyay_
I don't feel safe here.	**Je ne me sens pas en sécurité ici.** _zher ner mer sahng pa zahng saykewreetay eessee_

Arrival Arrivée

Document Requirements

UK valid passport; visitors passport; or British Excursion document (valid 60 hours)

U.S./CAN valid passport

AUS visa required for France (check with embassy)

Duty Free Into:	Cigarettes	Cigars	Tobacco	Spirits	Wine
France/Belg.	200 or	50 or	250g	1L	2L
Switzerland 1)	200 or	50 or	250g	1L and	2L
2)	400 or	100 or	500g	1L and	2L
Canada	200 and	50 and	400g	1L or	1L
UK	200 or	50 or	250g	1L and	2L
U.S.	200 and	100 and	discretionary	1L or	1L

1) EU residents; 2) non-EU residents

Import restrictions between EU countries have been relaxed on items for personal use or consumption that are bought duty-paid within the EU. Suggested maximum: 90L wine or 60L sparkling wine, 20L fortified wine, 10L spirits and 110L beer.

If buying wine direct from a vineyard, check that the VAT has been paid (**capsule-congé** sticker on the bottle or case). Ask for a VAT receipt (**un reçu TVA**) if in doubt.

Passport control Contrôle des passeports

We have a joint passport.	**Nous avons un passeport joint.** *noo zavons ang passpor zhwang*
The children are on this passport.	**Les enfants sont sur ce passeport.** *lay zahngfahng sawng sewr ser passpor*
I'm here on vacation [holiday]/ business.	**Je suis ici en vacances/pour affaires.** *zher swee eessee ahng vakahngss/poor afehr*
I'm just passing through.	**Je suis en transit.** *zher swee zahng trahngzeet*
I'm going to ...	**Je vais à ...** *zher vay a*
I'm ...	**Je suis ...** *zher swee*
on my own	**tout(e) seul(e)** *too(t) surl*
with my family	**avec ma famille** *avek ma famee*
with a group	**avec un groupe** *avek ang groop*

Customs À la douane

I have only the normal allowances.	**Je n'ai que les quantités autorisées.** *zher nay ker lay kahngteetay oatoreezay*
It's a gift.	**C'est un cadeau.** *seh ang kadoa*
It's for my personal use.	**C'est pour mon usage personnel.** *seh poor mawng newzazh pehrsonell*

Avez-vous quelque chose à déclarer?	Do you have anything to declare?
Il y a des droits de douane à payer sur cet article.	You must pay duty on this.
Où avez-vous acheté ceci?	Where did you buy this?
Pouvez-vous ouvrir ce sac, SVP?	Please open this bag.
Avez-vous d'autres bagages?	Do you have any more luggage?

I would like to declare …	**Je voudrais déclarer …** *zher voodray dayklaray*
I don't understand.	**Je ne comprends pas.** *zher ner kawngprahng pa*
Does anyone here speak English?	**Y a-t-il quelqu'un ici qui parle anglais?** *ee a teel kelkang eessee kee parl ahnggleh*

CONTRÔLE DES PASSEPORTS	passport control
POSTE FRONTIÈRE	border crossing
DOUANE	customs
RIEN À DÉCLARER	nothing to declare
MARCHANDISES À DÉCLARER	goods to declare
MARCHANDISES HORS TAXE	duty-free goods

Duty-free shopping Marchandises hors taxe

What currency is this in?	**C'est en quelle monnaie?** *seh ahng kel monayy*
Can I pay in …?	**Est-ce que je peux payer en …?** *ess ker zher pur payay ahng*
dollars	**dollars** *dolar*
francs	**francs** *frahng*
pounds	**livres** *leevr*

Plane Avion

Air Inter, France's principal domestic airline, runs services between Paris and Bordeaux, Lyon, Marseilles, Montpellier, Mulhouse, Nantes, Nice, Strasbourg and Toulouse. Inquire about discounts based on day and time of flight.

Tickets and reservations Billets et réservations

When is the … flight to …?	**À quelle heure est le … vol pour …?** *a kel urr eh ler … vol poor*
first/next/last	**premier/prochain/dernier** *prermyay/proshang/dehrnyay*
I'd like 2 … tickets to …	**Je voudrais deux … pour …** *zher voodray dur … poor*
one-way [single]	**aller-simple** *alay sangpl*
round-trip [return]	**aller-retour** *alay rertoor*
first class	**première classe** *prermyehr klass*
business class	**classe affaires** *klass afehr*
economy class	**classe économique** *klass aykonomeek*
How much is a flight to …?	**Combien coûte un vol pour …?** *kawnbyang koot ang vol poor*
I'd like to … my reservation for flight number …	**Je voudrais … ma réservation pour le vol numéro …** *zher voodray … ma rayzehrvasyawng poor ler vol newmayroa*
cancel	**annuler** *anewlay*
change	**changer** *shahngzhay*
confirm	**confirmer** *kawngfeermay*

Inquiries about the flight Questions sur le vol

Are there any supplements/discounts?	**Y a-t-il des suppléments/réductions?** *ee a teel day sewplaymahng/ raydewksyawng*
What time does the plane leave?	**À quelle heure part l'avion?** *a kel urr par lavyawng*
What time will we arrive?	**À quelle heure arriverons-nous?** *a kel urr areevrawng noo*
What time do I have to check in?	**À quelle heure est l'enregistrement?** *a kel urr eh lahngrerzheestrermahng*

Checking in Enregistrement

Where is the check-in desk for flight …?	**Où est le bureau d'enregistrement pour le vol …?** *oo eh ler bewroa dahngr erzheestrermahng poor ler vol*
I have …	**J'ai …** *zhay*
3 suitcases to check in	**trois valises à faire enregistrer** *trwa valeez a fehr ahngrerzheestray*
2 pieces of hand luggage	**deux bagages à main** *dur bagazh a mang*

Votre billet/passeport, s'il vous plaît.	Your ticket/passport, please.
Voulez-vous un siège côté hublot ou côté couloir?	Would you like a window or an aisle seat?
Fumeur ou non-fumeur?	Smoking or non-smoking?
Veuillez vous rendre dans la salle de départ.	Please go through to the departure lounge.
Combien de bagages avez-vous?	How many pieces of luggage do you have?
Vos bagages sont trop lourds.	You have excess luggage.
Vous devrez payer un supplément de … F.	You'll have to pay a supplement of … F
Ceci est trop lourd/grand pour les bagages à main.	That's too heavy/large for hand luggage.
Avez-vous fait vos valises vous-même?	Did you pack these bags yourself?
Est-ce qu'ils contiennent des objets pointus ou électriques?	Do they contain any sharp or electrical items?

ARRIVÉES	arrivals
DÉPARTS	departures
CONTRÔLE DE SÉCURITÉ	security check
NE LAISSEZ PAS VOS BAGAGES SANS SURVEILLANCE	do not leave luggage unattended

LUGGAGE/BAGGAGE ➤ 71

Information Renseignements

Is there any delay
on flight ...?
Est-ce que le vol ... a du retard?
ess ker ler vol ... a dew rertar

How late will it be?
Il a combien de retard?
eel a kawnbyang der rertar

Has the flight from ... landed?
Est-ce que le vol de ... est arrivé?
ess ker ler vol der ... eh areevay

Which gate does flight ...
leave from?
De quelle porte part le vol ...?
der kel port par ler vol

Boarding/In-flight Embarquement/Vol aller

Your boarding pass, please.
Votre carte d'embarquement, s'il vous plaît. *votr kart dahngbarker mahng seel voo pleh*

Could I have a drink/
something to eat?
Est-ce que je pourrais avoir quelque chose à boire/à manger? *ess ker zher pooray avvar kelker shoaz a bwar/a mahngzhay*

Please wake me for the meal.
Pouvez-vous me réveiller pour le repas, s'il vous plaît? *poovay voo mer rayvayay poor ler rerpa seel voo pleh*

What time will we arrive?
À quelle heure arriverons-nous? *a kel urr areevrawng noo*

An airsick bag, please.
Un sac vomitoire, s'il vous plaît. *ang sak voameetwar seel voo pleh*

Arrival Arrivée

Where is/are ...?
Où est/sont ...? *oo eh/sawng*

currency exchange office
le bureau de change *ler bewroa der shahngzh*

buses
les autobus *lay oatobews*

car rental (office)
le bureau de location de voitures *ler bewroa der lokasyawng der vwatewr*

exit
la sortie *la sortee*

taxis
les taxis *lay taxee*

Is there a bus into town?
Est-ce qu'il y a un bus pour aller en ville? *ess keel ee a ang bewss poor alay ahng veel*

How do I get to the ... Hotel?
Comment est-ce que je peux me rendre à l'hôtel ...? *kommahng ess ker zher pur mer rahngdr a loatel*

Luggage/Baggage Bagages

Tipping: If you want to give a bellman [porter] a tip, the following amounts (per bag) are usual: France: 5F, Belgium: 30F, Switzerland: 1–2F.

Bellman [Porter]! Excuse me!	**Porteur! Excusez-moi!** *porturr. exkewzay mwa*
Could you take my luggage to …?	**Pourriez-vous emporter mes bagages à …?** *pooryay voo ahngportay meh bagazh a*
a taxi/bus	**jusqu'à un taxi/bus** *zhewska ang taxee/bewss*
Where is/are …?	**Où est/sont …?** *oo eh/sawng*
luggage carts [trolleys]	**les chariots à bagages** *lay sharyoa a bagazh*
luggage lockers	**la consigne automatique** *la kawngseeñ oatomateek*
baggage check [left-luggage office]	**la consigne** *la kawngseeñ*
Where is the luggage from flight …?	**Où sont les bagages du vol …?** *oo sawng laybagazh dew vol*

Loss, damage and theft Perte, dommages et vol

I've lost my baggage.	**J'ai perdu mes bagages.** *zhay pehrdew meh bagazh*
My baggage has been stolen.	**On m'a volé mes bagages.** *awng ma volay meh bagazh*
My suitcase was damaged.	**Ma valise a été abîmée.** *ma valeez a aytay abeemay*
Our baggage has not arrived.	**Nos bagages ne sont pas arrivés.** *no bagazh ner sawng pa areevay*

Comment sont vos bagages?	What does your baggage look like?
Avez-vous le ticket de consigne?	Do you have the claim ticket?
Vos bagages …	Your luggage …
ont peut-être été envoyés à …	may have been sent to …
arriveront peut-être dans la journée.	may arrive later today.
Veuillez revenir demain, SVP.	Please come back tomorrow.
Téléphonez à ce numéro pour savoir si vos bagages sont arrivés.	Call this number to check if your luggage has arrived.

POLICE ➤ 152; *COLORS* ➤ 143

Train   Train

TGV *tay zhay vay*

extra-high speed train (**Train à Grande Vitesse**); compulsory
reservation when you buy your ticket; a surcharge may be payable.

Eurostar/Le Shuttle *urroastar/ler shutel*

car and passenger Channel Tunnel link from London Waterloo to Paris and
Brussels (car from Folkstone to Calais only); no reservation necessary.

EuroCity	*urrosseettee*	international express train
Rapide	*rapeed*	long-distance express; luxury coaches (*Fr.*)
Intercity	*angtehrsseettee*	intercity express with few stops
Express	*express*	ordinary long-distance train (*Fr.*)
Direct	*deerekt*	ordinary long-distance train (*Bel., Sw.*)
Omnibus	*omneebewss*	local train (*Fr., Bel.*)
Train régional	*trang rayzhyonal*	local train (*Sw.*)
Autorail	*oatorighy*	small diesel used on short runs
RER (Réseau Express Régional)	*ehr er ehr*	Paris regional network, linked to the métro
Train-Auto-Couchette	*trang oato kooshett*	autotrain service; advance reservation required
wagon-restaurant	*vagawng restoarahng*	dining car
wagon-lit	*vagawng lee*	sleeping car with individual compartments and washing facilities
couchette	*kooshett*	berth with bedding; **supérieure** (upper) or **inférieure** (lower)

Check out the various discounts and travel passes available:
For children (**Carte Kiwi, Carte Jeune**); families (**Rail Europ F, Zoom**);
Senior Citizens (**Carte Vermeil, Rail Europ Senior**); under-26 (**Domino,
Eurail Youthpass; BIJ** [Belg.]; **InterRail**); couples (**Carte couple**); advance
bookings (**Joker**); Off-peak (**Carrissimo, billet séjour**).

Paris has several main stations – so don't go to the wrong one: gare du
Nord (north, incl. Eurostar, U.K.), gare de l'Est (east), gare d'Austerlitz
(southwest, Bordeaux, Spain), gare Saint-Lazare (Normandy, Dieppe),
Montparnasse (west, Brittany) and gare de Lyon (Riviera, Switzerland
and Italy).

To the station À la gare

How do I get to the (main) train station?	**Pour aller à la gare (principale)?** *poor alay a la gar (prangseepal)*
Do trains to ... leave from ... Station?	**Est-ce que les trains pour ... partent de la gare ...?** *ess ker lay trang poor ... part der la gar ...*
Is it far?	**(Est-ce que) c'est loin?** *(ess ker) seh lwang*
Can I leave my car there?	**Est-ce que je peux y laisser ma voiture?** *ess ker zher pur ee layssay ma vwatewr*

At the station À la gare

Where is/are the ...?	**Où est/sont ...?** *oo eh/sawng*
currency exchange office	**le bureau de change** *ler bewroa der shahngzh*
information desk	**le bureau des renseignements** *ler bewroa day rahngseñermahng*
baggage check [left-luggage office]	**la consigne** *la kawngseeñ*
lost-and-found [lost property office]	**le bureau des objets trouvés** *ler bewroa day zobzheh troovay*
luggage lockers	**la consigne automatique** *la kawngseeñ oatomateek*
platforms	**les quais** *lay kay*
snack bar	**le snack-bar/buffet** *ler snak bar/bewfeh*
ticket office	**le guichet** *ler geesheh*
waiting room	**la salle d'attente** *la sal datahngt*

ENTRÉE	entrance
SORTIE	exit
RÉSERVATIONS	reservations
RENSEIGNEMENTS	information
ACCÈS AUX QUAIS	to the platforms
ARRIVÉES	arrivals
DÉPARTS	departures

DIRECTIONS ➤ 94

Tickets Billets

Remember to validate your train ticket by inserting it in an orange validating machine (**machine à composter** or **composteur**) at the stations; otherwise the conductor (**contrôleur**) is entitled to fine you.

Where can I buy a ticket?	**Où puis-je acheter un billet?** *oo pweezh ashertay ang beeyeh*
I'd like a … ticket to …	**Je voudrais un billet … pour …** *zher voodray ang beeyeh … poor*
one-way [single]	**aller-simple** *alay sangpl*
round-trip [return]	**aller-retour** *alay rertoor*
first/second class	**de première/deuxième classe** *der prermyehr/durzyem klass*
reduced price	**à prix réduit** *a pree raydwee*
I'd like to reserve a seat.	**Je voudrais réserver une place.** *zher voodray rayzehrvay ewn plass*
aisle seat	**siège côté couloir** *syezh kotay coolwar*
window seat	**siège côté hublot** *syezh kotay ewblo*
Is there a sleeping car [sleeper]?	**Est-ce qu'il y a un wagon-lit?** *ess keel ee a ang vagawng lee*
I'd like a … berth.	**Je voudrais une couchette.** *zher voodray ewn kooshett*
upper/lower	**supérieure/inférieure** *sewpayryurr/angfayryurr*

Price Prix

How much is that?	**C'est combien?** *seh kawnbyang*
Is there a discount for …?	**Y a-t-il une réduction pour …?** *ee a teel ewn raydewksyawng poor*
children/families	**les enfants/les familles** *lay zahngfahng/lay famee*
senior citizens	**les personnes âgées** *lay pehrson azhay*
students	**les étudiants** *lay zaytewdyahng*
Do you offer a cheap same-day round-trip [return] ticket?	**Est-ce que vous offrez un aller-retour dans la même journée bon marché?** *ess ker voo zofray ang nalay rertoor dahng la mem zhoornay bawng marshay*

Queries Questions

Do I have to change trains?	**Est-ce que je dois changer de train?** *ess ker zher dwa shahngzhay der trang*
It's a direct train.	**C'est direct.** *seh deerekt*
You have to change at …	**Vous avez une correspondance à …** *voo zavay ewn korespawngdahngss a*
How long is this ticket valid for?	**Ce billet est valable pour combien de temps?** *ser beeyeh eh valabl poor kawnbyang der tahng*
Can I take my bicycle on the train?	**Est-ce que je peux emporter mon vélo dans le train?** *ess ker zher pur ahng portay mawng vaylo dahng ler trang*
Which car [coach] is my seat in?	**Dans quel wagon est mon siège?** *dahng kel vagawng eh mawng syezh*
Is there a dining car on the train?	**Est-ce qu'il y a un wagon-restaurant dans le train?** *ess keel ee a ang vagawng restoarahng dahng ler trang*

– Je voudrais un billet pour Versailles, s'il vous plaît.
(I'd like a ticket to Versailles, please.)
– Aller-simple ou aller-retour?
(One-way or round-trip?)
– Aller-retour, s'il vous plaît. (Round-trip, please.)
– Ça fait cinquante-six francs. (That's 56 francs.)
– Est-ce que je dois changer dè train?
(Do I have to change trains?)
– Oui, vous avez une correspondance à Issy.
(Yes, you have to change in Issy.)
– Merci, au revoir. (Thank you. Good-bye.)

Train timetable Horaires des trains

Could I have a timetable?	**Est-ce que je pourrais avoir un horaire?** *ess ker zher pooray avwar ang norehr*
When is the … train to …?	**À quelle heure est le … train pour …?** *a kel urr eh ler … trang poor*
first/next/last	**premier/prochain/dernier** *prermyay/proshang/dehrnyay*

How frequent are the trains to …?	**Combien de fois par jour (est-ce qu')il y a des trains pour …?** *kawnbyang der fwa par zhoor (ess k)eel ee a day trang poor*
once/twice a day	**une/deux fois par jour** *ewn/dur fwa par zhoor*
5 times a day	**cinq fois par jour** *sangk fwa par zhoor*
every hour	**toutes les heures** *toot lay zurr*
What time do they leave?	**À quelle heure partent-ils?** *a kel urr part teel*
on the hour	**toutes les heures/à l'heure juste** *toot lay zurr/a lurr zhewst*
20 minutes past the hour	**vingt minutes après l'heure** *vang meenewt apreh lurr*
What time does the train stop at …?	**À quelle heure le train s'arrête-t-il à …?** *a kel urr ler trang sarett teel a*
What time does the train arrive in …?	**À quelle heure le train arrive-t-il à …?** *a kel urr ler trang areev teel a*
How long is the trip [journey]?	**Combien de temps dure le voyage?** *kawnbyang der tahng dewr ler vwahyazh*
Is the train on time?	**Est-ce que le train est à l'heure?** *ess ker ler trang eh a lurr*

Departures Départs

Which platform does the train to … leave from?	**De quel quai part le train pour …?** *der kel kay par ler trang poor*
Where is platform 4?	**Où est le quai numéro 4?** *oo eh ler kay newmayroa katr*
over there	**là-bas** *la ba*
on the left/right	**à gauche/à droite** *a goash/a drwat*
Where do I change for …?	**Où est-ce que je dois changer pour …?** *oo ess ker zher dwa shahngzhay poor*
How long will I have to wait for a connection?	**Combien de temps dois-je attendre pour une correspondance?** *kawnbyang der tahng dwazh atahngdr poor ewn korespawngdahngss*

Boarding Embarquement

Is this the right platform for the train to …?
Est-ce bien le bon quai pour le train pour …?
ess byang ler bawng kay poor ler trang poor

Is this the train to …?
Est-ce que c'est bien le train pour …?
ess ker seh byang ler trang poor

Is this seat taken?
Est-ce que cette place est occupée/prise?
ess ker set plass eh okewpay/preez

I think that's my seat.
Je crois que c'est ma place.
zher krwa ker seh ma plass

Are there any availbable seats/ berths?
Est-ce qu'il y a des places/couchettes libres? *ess keel ee a day plass/ kooshett leebr*

Do you mind if …?
Est-ce que ça vous dérange si …?
ess ker sa voo dayrahngzh see

I sit here
je m'asseois ici *zher maswa eessee*

I open the window
j'ouvre la fenêtre *zhoovr la fernetr*

During the trip Pendant le voyage

How long are we stopping here?
Combien de temps est-ce que nous nous arrêtons ici? *kawnbyang der tahng ess ker noo noo aretawng eessee*

When do we get to …?
À quelle heure arrivons-nous à …?
a kel urr areevawng noo a

Have we passed …?
Est-ce que nous sommes passés à …?
ess ker noo som passay a

Where is the dining/sleeping car?
Où est le wagon-restaurant/ wagon-lit? *oo eh ler vagawng restoarahng/vagawng lee*

Where is my berth?
Où est ma couchette?
oo eh ma kooshett

I've lost my ticket.
J'ai perdu mon billet.
zhay pehrdew mawng beeyeh

ARRÊT D'URGENCE	emergency brake
SONNETTE D'ALARME	alarm
PORTES AUTOMATIQUES	automatic doors

TIME ➤ 220

Long-distance bus (Auto)car

Long-distance bus (**car/autocar**) services are efficient and relatively cheap. Find details at the bus terminal (**gare routière**), generally located near the railway station.

Where is the bus [coach] station?	**Où est la gare routière?** *oo eh la gar rootyehr*
When's the next bus [coach] to …?	**À quelle heure est le prochain car pour …?** *a kel urr eh ler proshang kar poor*
Which stop does it leave from?	**De quel arrêt part-il?** *der kel areh par teel*
Where are the bus [coach] stops?	**Où sont les arrêts de car?** *oo sawng lay areh der kar*
Does the bus [coach] stop at …?	**Est-ce que le car s'arrête à …?** *ess ker ler kar sarett a*
How long does the trip [journey] take?	**Combien de temps dure le voyage?** *kawnbyang der tahng dewr ler vwahyazh*

Bus Bus

Tickets can normally be purchased from the driver, but remember that you must always validate your ticket (**compostez votre billet**) in the machine.

Where is the bus station/terminal?	**Où est la gare routière?** *oo eh la gar rootyehr*
Where can I get a bus to …?	**Où est-ce que je peux prendre un bus pour …?** *oo ess ker zher pur prahngdr ang bewss poor*
What time is the … bus to …?	**À quelle heure part le … bus pour …?** *a kel urr par ler … bewss poor*

Il faut aller à cet arrêt là-bas/ un peu plus loin	You need that stop over there/ down the road.
Vous devez prendre le bus numéro …	You need bus number …
Vous devez changer de bus à …	You must change buses at …

ARRÊT D'AUTOBUS	bus stop
ARRÊT FACULTATIF	request stop
DÉFENSE DE FUMER	no smoking
SORTIE DE SECOURS	(emergency) exit

Buying tickets Pour acheter des billets

Where can I buy tickets? | **Où est-ce que je peux acheter des billets?** *oo ess ker zher pur ashertay day beeyeh*

A ... ticket to ..., please. | **Un billet ... pour ..., s'il vous plaît.** *ang beeyeh ... poor ... seel voo pleh*

one-way [single] | **aller** *alay*
round-trip [return] | **aller-retour** *alay rertoor*
A booklet of tickets, please. | **Un carnet de tickets, s'il vous plaît.** *ang karneh der teekeh seel voo pleh*

How much is the fare to ...? | **Combien coûte un ticket pour ...?** *kawnbyang koot ang teekeh poor*

Traveling Pour voyager

Is this the right bus/streetcar [tram] to ...? | **Est-ce que c'est bien le bon bus/tram pour ...?** *ess ker seh byang ler bawng bewss/tram poor*

Could you tell me when to get off? | **Pourriez-vous me dire quand il faut descendre?** *pooryay voo mer deer kahng eel foa dessahngdr*

Do I have to change buses? | **Est-ce que je dois changer de bus?** *ess ker zher dwa shahngzhay der bewss*

How many stops are there to ...? | **Combien d'arrêts est-ce qu'il y a jusqu'à ...?** *kawnbyang dareh ess keel ee a zhewska*

Next stop, please! | **Prochain arrêt, s'il vous plaît!** *proshang areh seel voo pleh*

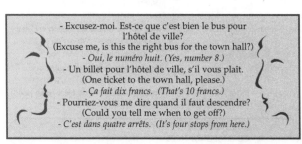

- Excusez-moi. Est-ce que c'est bien le bus pour l'hôtel de ville?
(Excuse me, is this the right bus for the town hall?)
- Oui, le numéro huit. (Yes, number 8.)
- Un billet pour l'hôtel de ville, s'il vous plaît.
(One ticket to the town hall, please.)
- Ça fait dix francs. (That's 10 francs.)
- Pourriez-vous me dire quand il faut descendre?
(Could you tell me when to get off?)
- C'est dans quatre arrêts. (It's four stops from here.)

NUMBERS ➤ 216; DIRECTIONS ➤ 94

Subway Métro

There are excellent subway systems in Paris, Brussels, Lille and Lyon. Big maps in each station make the systems easy to use. The fare is standard, irrespective of the distance you travel. Tickets can be bought cheaper in a book of ten (**un carnet**).

The Paris metro closes 12:50am – 5:30am.

General Inquiries Questions générales

Where's the nearest subway station?	**Où est la station de métro la plus proche?** *oo eh la stasyawng der maytroa la plew prosh*
Where can I buy a ticket?	**Où est-ce que je peux acheter un ticket?** *oo ess ker zher pur ashertay ang teekeh*
Could I have a map of the subway [metro]?	**Est-ce que je pourrais avoir un plan du métro?** *ess ker zher pooray avwar ang plahng dew maytroa*

Traveling En voyage

Which line should I take for …?	**Quelle ligne dois-je prendre pour …?** *kel leeñ dwazh prahngdr poor*
Is this the right train for …?	**Est-ce que c'est bien la bonne rame pour …?** *ess ker seh byang la bon ram poor*
Which stop is it for …?	**C'est quelle station pour …?** *seh kel stasyawng poor*
How many stops is it to …?	**Combien de stations est-ce qu'il y a jusqu'à …?** *kawnbyang der stasyawng ess keel ee a zhewska*
Is the next stop …?	**Est-ce que la prochaine station est bien …?** *ess ker la proshayn stasyawng eh byang*
Where are we?	**Où sommes-nous?** *oo som noo*
Where do I change for …?	**Où est-ce que je dois changer pour …?** *oo ess ker zher dwa shahngzhay poor*
What time is the last train to …?	**À quelle heure est la dernière rame pour …?** *a kel urr eh la dehrnyehr ram poor*

⊖	**AUTRES LIGNES/ CORRESPONDANCES**	to other lines ⊕

Ferry Ferry

Ferry companies operating services from the UK to the Continent include: Stena Sealink, Hoverspeed, Brittany Ferries, P&O, Sally Ferries, North Sea Ferries.

When is the … car ferry to …?	**À quelle heure est le … car-ferry pour …?** *a kel urr eh ler … kar fehrree poor*
first/next/last	**premier/prochain/dernier** *prermyay/proshang/dehrnyay*
hovercraft/ship	**l'hovercraft/le bateau** *lovehrkraft/ler batoa*
A round-trip [return] ticket for …	**Un billet aller et retour pour …** *ang beeyeh alay ay rertoor poor*
1 car and 1 trailer [caravan]	**une voiture et une caravane** *ewn vwatewr ay ewn karavahn*
2 adults and 3 children	**deux adultes et trois enfants** *dur zadewlt ay trwa zahngfahng*
I want to reserve a … cabin.	**Je voudrais réserver une cabine …** *zher voodray rayzehrvay ewn kabeen*
single/double	**pour une/deux personne(s)** *poor ewn/dur pehrson*

ACCÈS AUX GARAGES INTERDIT	no access to car decks
CANOT DE SAUVETAGE	life boat
GILETS DE SAUVETAGE	life belts
POINT DE RASSEMBLEMENT	meeting point

Boat trips Voyages en bateau

For a relaxing way to see Paris, take a cruise in a **bateau-mouche** or **vedette** along the Seine.

Is there a …?	**Est-ce qu'il y a …?** *ess keel ee a*
boat trip	**un voyage en bateau** *ang vwahyazh ahng batoa*
river cruise	**une croisière sur la rivière** *ewn krwazyehr sewr la reevyehr*
What time does it leave/return?	**À quelle heure part/revient le bateau?** *a kel urr par/rervyang ler batoa*
Where can we buy tickets?	**Où pouvons-nous acheter des billets?** *oo poovawng noo zashertay day beeyeh*

TIME ➤ 220; BUYING TICKETS ➤ 74, 79

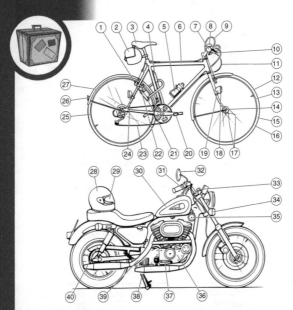

1 brake pad **plaquette de frein** f
2 bicycle bag **sacoche de bicyclette** f
3 saddle **selle** f
4 pump **pompe** f
5 water bottle **bidon d'eau** m
6 frame **cadre** m
7 handlebars **guidon** m
8 bell **sonnette** f
9 brake cable **câble de frein** m
10 gear/shift **levier de changement de vitesse** m
11 gear/control cable **câble de changement de vitesse** m
12 inner tube **chambre à air** f
13 front/back wheel **roue avant/arrière** f
14 axle **essieu** m
15 tire **pneu** m
16 wheel **roue** f
17 spokes **rayons** mpl
18 bulb **ampoule** f
19 headlamp **phare** m
20 pedal **pédale** f

21 lock **antivol** m
22 generator **dynamo** f
23 chain **chaîne** f
24 rear light **feu arrière** m
25 rim **jante** f
26 reflectors **réflecteurs** mpl
27 fender [mudguard] **garde-boue** m
28 helmet **casque** m
29 visor **visière** f
30 fuel tank **réservoir** m
31 clutch **embrayage** m
32 mirror **rétroviseur** m
33 ignition switch **contact** m
34 turn signal (indicator) **clignotant** m
35 horn **klaxon** m
36 engine **moteur** m
37 stick shift **levier de vitesse** m
38 kick stand **béquille** f
39 exhaust pipe **pot d'échappement** m
40 chain guard **couvre-chaîne** m

CAR REPAIRS ➤ 89

Bicycle/Motorbike Bicyclette/moto

Bicycle rental shops are plentiful; SNCF (French railways) operates a cycle rental service at railway stations (passport, deposit or credit card required). Many towns also have mopeds (**vélomoteurs**, **cyclomoteurs** or **mobylettes**) for rent.

In Belgium, it is compulsory to use low headlights on motorcycles at all times.

I'd like to rent a …	**Je voudrais louer …** *zher voodray looay*
3-/10-gear bicycle	**un vélo à trois/dix vitesses** *ang vaylo a trwa/dees veetess*
moped	**une mobylette** *ewn mobeelett*
motorbike	**une moto** *ewn moto*
How much does it cost per day/week?	**Ça coûte combien par jour/semaine?** *sa koot kawnbyang par zhoor/sermayn*
Do you require a deposit?	**Est-ce qu'il faut verser des arrhes?** *ess keel foa vehrsay day zarr*
The brakes don't work.	**Les freins ne marchent pas.** *lay frang ner marsh pa*
There are no lights.	**Il n'y a pas de feux.** *eel nee a pa der fur*
The front/rear tire [tyre] has a flat [puncture].	**Le pneu avant/arrière est crevé.** *ler pnur avahng/aryehr eh krervay*

Hitchhiking Auto-stop

Hitchhiking is permitted everywhere except on highways. Always take care before hitchhiking anywhere.

Where are you heading?	**Où allez-vous?** *oo alay voo*
I'm heading for …	**Je vais vers …** *zher vay vehr*
Is that on the way to …?	**Est-ce que c'est sur la route de …?** *ess ker seh sewr la root der*
Could you drop me off …?	**Est-ce que vous pourriez me déposer …?** *ess ker voo pooryay mer daypoazay*
here/at …	**ici/à …** *eessee/a*
at the … exit	**à la sortie …** *a la sortee*
in the center	**dans le centre** *dahng ler sahngtr*
Thanks for giving me a lift.	**Merci de m'avoir emmené.** *mehrsee der mavwar ahngmernay*

DIRECTIONS ➤ 94; NUMBERS ➤ 216

Taxi/Cab   Taxi

Many French taxis will only take 3 passengers; traveling in the front passenger seat is not usual. Taxis ordered by telephone will pick you up with the meter already running.

Tipping suggestions: France: 10–15%; Belgium: optional; Switzerland: 15% (sometimes included).

Where can I get a taxi?	**Où est-ce que je peux trouver un taxi?** *oo ess ker zher pur troovay ang taxee*
Do you have the number for a taxi?	**Avez-vous le numéro de téléphone pour appeler un taxi?** *avay voo ler newmay roa der taylayfon poor aperlay ang taxee*
I'd like a taxi ...	**Je voudrais un taxi ...** *zher voodray ang taxee*
now	**maintenant** *mangtnahng*
in an hour	**dans une heure** *dahng zewn urr*
tomorrow at 9:00	**demain à neuf heures** *dermang a nurf urr*
The address is ...	**L'adresse est ...** *ladress eh*
I'm going to ...	**Je vais à ...** ... *zher vay a*
Please take me to the ...	**Emmenez-moi à ..., s'il vous plaît.** *ahngmernay mwa a ... seel voo pleh*
airport	**l'aéroport** *la ayropor*
train station	**la gare** *la gar*
this address	**cette adresse** *set adress*
How much is that?	**C'est combien?** *seh kawnbyang*
You said ... Francs.	**Vous m'aviez dit ... francs.** *voo mavyay dee ... frahng*
On the meter it's ...	**Le compteur indique ...** *ler kawngturr angdeek*
Keep the change.	**Gardez la monnaie.** *garday la monay*

> - Emmenez-moi à la gare, s'il vous plaît.
> (Take me to the train station, please.)
> - *Bien sûr.* (Certainly.)
> - Combien est-ce que ça coûtera?
> (How much will it cost?)
> - *Soixante-cinq francs.* (65 francs, please.)
> - *Voilà, nous y sommes.* (Here we are.)
> - Merci. Gardez la monnaie. (Thank you. Keep the change.)

Car/Automobile Voiture

While driving, the following documents must be carried at all times: valid driver's license (**permis de conduire**), vehicle registration (**certificat d'immatriculation**) and insurance documentation (**certificat d'assurance**).

Insurance for minimum Third Party risks is compulsory in Europe. It is recommended that you take out International motor insurance (or a "Green Card") through your insurer.

Essential equipment: warning triangle and nationality plate; headlight beams must be adjusted for right-hand drive vehicles; wearing seat belts is compulsory.

Minimum driving age: 18; minimum rental age: 21 (25 with some firms).

Tolls are payable on many French autoroutes; usually pick up a ticket at point of entry and pay at the exit; Visa and Access (MasterCard) are accepted. Some barriers are operated automatically by depositing exact toll in coins.

For travel on Swiss highways/motorways, a pass/vignette is required – available from tourist offices, customs, post offices and garages. It is valid for 1 year, non-transferable and is to be attached to your windshield.

Traffic police can give on-the-spot fines (ask for a receipt).

Alcohol limit in blood: max. 80mg/100ml. Note that any alcohol may impair ability to drive safely.

Conversion Chart

km	1	10	20	30	40	50	60	70	80	90	100	110	120	130
miles	0.62	6	12	19	25	31	37	44	50	56	62	68	74	81

Road network

France	A (**autoroute**) - highway (blue sign; generally tolls); N (**route nationale**) - main road (green sign); D - secondary road (white sign); V - local road (white sign)
Belgium	A and E - highway (green signs, toll free); N - main road
Switzerland	A - highway (toll free); N - main road; E - secondary road

Speed limits *mph (km/ph)*	Built-up area	Outside built-up area	highway/ toll road
France	31 (50)	56 (90)	68 (110)/81 (130)
in bad weather		50 (80)	62 (100)/68 (110)
Belgium	31 (50)	56 (90)	74 (120)
Switzerland	31 (50)	50 (80)	62-74 (100-120)

Car rental Location de voitures

You will need to produce a valid driver's license (held for at least a year) and your passport. The minimum age ranges from 21 to 25, depending on the rental firm.

Many firms now require you to have a major credit card.

Where can I rent a car?	**Où est-ce que je peux louer une voiture?** *oo ess ker zher pur looay ewn vwatewr*
I'd like to rent a(n) …	**Je voudrais louer une …** *zher voodray looay ewn*
2-/4-door car	**voiture deux portes/quatre portes** *vwatewr dur port/katr port*
automatic	**voiture automatique** *vwatewr oatomateek*
car with air conditioning	**voiture avec climatisation** *vwatewr avek kleemateezassyawng*
I'd like it for a day/a week.	**Je la voudrais pour un jour/une semaine.** *zher la voodray poor ang zhoor/ ewn sermayn*
How much does it cost per day/week?	**Quel est le tarif par jour/semaine?** *keleh ler tareef par zhoor/sermayn*
Is mileage/insurance included?	**Est-ce-que le kilométrage/l'assurance est compris(e)?** *ess ker ler keelomaytrazh/ lassewrahngss eh kawngpree(z)*
Are there special weekend rates?	**Y a-t-il des tarifs spéciaux pour le week-end?** *ee a teel day tareef spaysyoa poor ler weekend*
Can I return the car at …?	**Est-ce que je peux rapporter la voiture à …?** *ess ker zher pur raportay la vwatewr a*
What kind of fuel does it take?	**Qu'est-ce qu'il faut mettre comme carburant?** *kess keel foa metr kom karbewrahng*
Where is the high/low [full/dipped] beam?	**Où sont les phares/les codes?** *oo sawng lay far/lay kod*
Could I have full insurance?	**Est-ce que je peux prendre une assurance tous risques?** *ess ker zher pur prahngdr ewn assewrahngss too reesk*

Gas [Petrol] station   Station-service

Where's the next gas [petrol] station?	**Où est la station-service la plus proche?**
	oo eh la stasyawng sehrveess la plew prosh
Is it self-service?	**Est-ce que c'est un self-service?**
	ess ker seh ang self sehrveess
Fill it up, please.	**Le plein, s'il vous plaît.**
	ler plang seel voo pleh
…liters of gasoline, please.	**… litres d'essence, s'il vous plaît.**
	leetr dessahngss seel voo pleh
premium [super]/regular	**super/ordinaire** *sewpehr/ordeenehr*
unleaded/diesel	**sans plomb/diesel** *sahng plawng/diaysel*
I'm pump number …	**Je suis à la pompe numéro …**
	zher swee za la pawngp newmayroa
Where is the air pump/water?	**Où est le compresseur pour l'air/l'eau?**
	oo eh ler kawngpressurr poor lehr/loa

PRIX AU LITRE   price per liter

Parking Stationnement

In Blue Zones, parking tokens/discs are required (available from police stations, tourist offices and some shops).

Unilateral parking on alternate days is marked by signs: **côté du stationnement**, **jours pairs** (even dates) and **jours impairs** (odd dates).

In one-way streets parking is permitted on the left-hand side only.

No parking where curbs are marked yellow or on Paris red routes (**axes rouges**).

Pull off the highway to park on roads outside towns.

Is there a parking lot [car park] nearby?	**Est-ce qu'il y a un parking près d'ici?**
	ess keel ee a ang parking preh deessee
What's the charge per hour/per day?	**Quel est le tarif par heure/jour?**
	kel eh ler tareef par urr/zhoor
Do you have some change for the parking meter?	**Avez-vous de la monnaie pour le parcmètre?** *avay voo der la mon nay poor ler parkmetr*
My car has been booted [clamped]. Who do I call?	**On a mis un sabot à ma voiture. À qui dois-je téléphoner?**
	awng a mee ang saboa a ma vwatewr. a kee dwazh taylayfonay

NUMBERS ➤ 216; DIRECTIONS ➤ 94

Breakdown Pannes

For help in the event of a breakdown:
refer to your breakdown assistance documents; or contact the nearest garage or agent for your type of car; or contact the police, who often have a list of 24-hour garages.

Orange emergency telephones can be found every 2km on highways and main roads.

Where is the nearest garage?	**Où se trouve le garage le plus proche?** *oo ser troov ler garazh ler plew prosh*
I've had a breakdown.	**Ma voiture est tombée en panne.** *ma vwatewr eh tawngbay ahng pan*
Can you send a mechanic/ tow [breakdown] truck?	**Pouvez-vous m'envoyer un mécanicien/ une dépanneuse?** *poovay voo mahngvwahyay ang maykaneesyang/ ewn daypanurz*
I belong to … road assistance service.	**Je suis membre du service d'assistance routière …** *zher swee mahngbr dew sehrveess dasseestahngss rootyehr*
My license plate number is …	**Mon numéro d'immatriculation est …** *mawng newmayroa deematreekewlasyawng eh*
The car is … on the highway [motorway] 2 km from …	**La voiture est …** *la vwatewr eh* **sur l'autoroute** *sewr loatoroot* **à deux kilomètres de …** *a dur keelometr der*
How long will you be?	**Combien de temps allez-vous mettre?** *kawnbyang der tahng alay voo metr*

What is wrong? Qu'est-ce qui ne va pas?

My car won't start.	**Ma voiture ne veut pas démarrer.** *ma vwatewr ner vur pa daymaray*
The battery is dead.	**La batterie est à plat.** *la batree eh a pla*
I've run out of gas [petrol].	**Je suis en panne d'essence.** *zher swee zahng pan dessahngss*
I have a flat [puncture].	**J'ai un pneu à plat.** *zhay ang pnur a pla*
There is something wrong with …	**J'ai un problème avec …** *zhay ang problemm avek*
I've locked the keys in the car.	**J'ai enfermé mes clés dans la voiture.** *zhay ahngfehrmay meh klay dahng la vwatewr*

Repairs Réparations

Do you do repairs?	**Faites-vous des réparations?** *fet voo day rayparasyawng*
Can you repair it (temporarily)?	**Est-ce que vous pouvez faire une réparation (temporaire)?** *ess ker voo poovay fehr ewn rayparasyawng (tahngporehr)*
Please make only essential repairs.	**Faites seulement les réparations essentielles.** *fett surlmahng lay ray parasyawng essahngsyell*
Can I wait for it?	**Est-ce que je peux attendre?** *ess ker zher pur atahngdr*
Can you repair it today?	**Est-ce que vous pouvez la réparer aujourd'hui?** *ess ker voo poovay la rayparay oazhoordwee*
When will it be ready?	**Quand est-ce qu'elle sera prête?** *kahng ess kel serra pret*
How much will it cost?	**Ça coûtera combien?** *sa kootra kawnbyang*
That's outrageous!	**C'est du vol!** *seh dew vol*
Can I have a receipt for the insurance?	**Est-ce que je peux avoir un reçu pour l'assurance?** *ess ker zher pur avwar ang rersew poor lassewrahngss*

... ne marche pas.	The ... isn't working.
Je n'ai pas les pièces nécessaires.	I don't have the necessary parts.
Il faut que je commande les pièces.	I will have to order the parts.
Je ne peux faire qu'une réparation temporaire.	I can only repair it temporarily.
Ça ne vaut pas la peine de la faire réparer	Your car is totaled/a write-off.
On ne peut pas la réparer.	It can't be repaired.
Elle sera prête ...	It will be ready ...
dans la journée	later today
demain	tomorrow
dans ... jours	in ... days

DAYS OF THE WEEK ➤ 218; *NUMBERS* ➤ 216

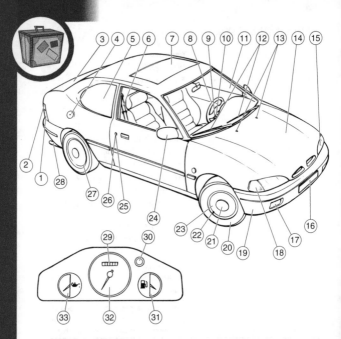

1 taillights [back lights] **feux arrière** mpl
2 brake lights **feux rouges (des freins)** mpl
3 trunk [boot] **coffre** m
4 gas tank door [petrol cap] **bouchon de réservoir (d'essence)** m
5 window **vitre** f
6 seat belt **ceinture de sécurité** f
7 sunroof **toit ouvrant** m
8 steering wheel **volant** m
9 ignition/starter **contact** m
10 ignition key **clé de contact** f
11 windshield [windscreen] **pare-brise** m
12 windshield [windscreen] wipers **essuie-glaces** mpl
13 windshield [windscreen] washer **jet lave-glace** m
14 hood [bonnet] **capot** m
15 headlights **phares** mpl

16 license [number] plate **plaque d'immatriculation** f
17 fog lamp **feu de brouillard** m
18 turn signals [indicators] **clignotants** mpl
19 bumper **pare-choc** m
20 tires **pneus** mpl
21 hubcap **enjoliveur** m
22 valve **valve** f
23 wheels **roues** fpl
24 outside [wing] mirror **rétroviseur extérieur** m
25 automatic locks [central locking] **fermeture centrale** f
26 lock **serrure** f
27 wheel rim **jante** f
28 exhaust pipe **pot d'échappement** m
29 odometer [milometer] **compteur kilomètrique** m

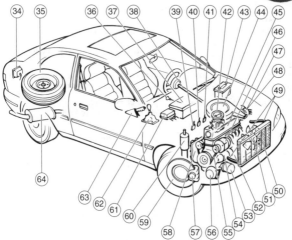

30 warning light **feu de détresse** m
31 fuel gauge **jauge de carburant** f
32 speedometer **compteur de vitesse** m
33 oil gauge **jauge à huile** f
34 backup [reversing] lights **feux de recul** mpl
35 spare tire [wheel] **roue de secours** f
36 choke **starter** m
37 heater **radiateur** m
38 steering column **colonne de direction** f
39 accelerator **accélérateur** m
40 pedal **pédale** f
41 clutch **embrayage** m
42 carburetor **carburateur** m
43 battery **batterie** f
44 alternator **alternateur** m
45 camshaft **arbre à cames** m
46 air filter **filtre à air** m
47 distributor **distributeur** m
48 points **vis platinées** fpl

49 radiator hose (top/bottom) **durite** f
50 radiator **radiateur** m
51 fan **ventilateur** m
52 engine **moteur** m
53 oil filter **filtre à huile** m
54 starter motor **démarreur** m
55 fan belt **courroie de ventilateur** f
56 horn **klaxon** m
57 brake pads **plaquettes de freins** fpl
58 transmission [gearbox] **boîte de
    vitesses** f
59 brakes **freins** mpl
60 shock absorbers **amortisseurs** mpl
61 fuses **fusibles** mpl
62 gear shift [lever] **levier de vitesses** m
63 emergency [hand] brake **frein à main** m
64 muffler [silencer] **silencieux** m

Accidents   Accidents

In the event of an accident:
1. report the accident to the police (compulsory if there is personal injury);
2. give your name, address, insurance company to the other party;
3. report it to the appropriate insurance company of the third party and your own company;
4. don't make any written statement without advice of a lawyer or automobile club official;
5. note all relevant details of the other party, any independent witnesses of the accident;
6. in France, get a police officer (**agent de police**) to make a report of major accidents in towns; on country roads send for the **gendarme**.

There has been an accident.	**Il y a un accident.** *eel ee a ang nakseedahng*
It's …	**Il est …** *eel eh*
on the highway [motorway]	**sur l'autoroute** *sewr loatoroot*
near …	**près de …** *preh der*
Where's the nearest telephone?	**Où est le téléphone le plus proche?** *oo eh ler taylayfon ler plew prosh*
Call …	**Téléphonez …** *taylayfonay*
an ambulance	**une ambulance** *ewn ambewlahngss*
a doctor	**un docteur** *ang dokturr*
the fire department [brigade]	**aux pompiers** *oa pawngpyay*
the police	**la police** *la poleess*
Can you help me please?	**Pourriez-vous m'aider, s'il vous plaît?** *pooryay voo mayday seel voo pleh*

Injuries   Blessures

There are people injured.	**Il y a des blessés.** *eel ee a day blessay*
No one is hurt.	**Personne n'est blessé.** *pehrson neh blessay*
He is seriously injured.	**Il est gravement blessé.** *eel eh gravmahng blessay*
She's unconscious.	**Elle a perdu connaissance.** *el a pehrdew konayssahngss*
He can't breathe/move.	**Il ne peut pas respirer/bouger.** *eel ner pur pa respeeray/boozhay*
Don't move him.	**Ne le déplacez pas.** *ner ler dayplassay pa*

INJURIES (DOCTOR) ➤ 162; DIRECTIONS ➤ 94

Legal matters Questions de droit

What's your insurance company?	**Quelle est votre compagnie d'assurance?** *kel eh votr kawngpañee dassewrahngss*
What's your name and address?	**Quels sont vos nom et adresse?** *kel sawng vo nawng ay adress*
He ran into me.	**Il m'est rentré dedans.** *eel meh rahngtray derdahng*
She was driving too fast/too close.	**Elle conduisait trop vite/trop près.** *el kawngdweezeh tro veet/tro preh*
I had the right of way.	**J'avais la priorité.** *zhaveh la preeoreetay*
I was (only) driving ... km/h.	**Je ne faisais que ... km à l'heure.** *zher ner ferzeh ker ... keelometr a lurr*
I'd like an interpreter.	**Je voudrais un interprète.** *zher voodray ang nangtehrpret*
I didn't see the sign.	**Je n'ai pas vu le panneau.** *zher nay pa vew la panoh*
He/She saw it happen.	**Il/Elle a vu ce qui s'est passé.** *eel/el a vew ser kee seh passay*
The license plate number was ...	**Le numéro d'immatriculation était ...** *ler newmayroa deematreekew-lasyawng ayteh*

Est-ce que je peux voir votre ...	Can I see your ...
permis de conduire	driver's license
certificat d'assurance	insurance certificate
carte grise	vehicle registration document
À quelle heure est-ce que ça s'est passé?	What time did it happen?
Où est-ce que ça s'est passé?	Where did it happen?
Est-ce qu'il y avait quelqu'un d'autre (impliqué)?	Was anyone else involved?
Est-ce qu'il y a des témoins?	Are there any witnesses?
Vous alliez trop vite.	You were speeding.
Vos feux ne marchent pas.	Your lights aren't working,
Vous devez payer une amende (sur place).	You'll have to pay a fine (on the spot).
Vous devez venir au commissariat pour faire une déposition.	You have to make a statement at the station.

TIME ➤ 220

Asking directions
Pour demander son chemin

Excuse me, please.
Excusez-moi, s'il vous plaît.
exkewzay mwa seel voo pleh

How do I get to ...?
Pour aller à ...? *poor alay a*

Where is ...?
Où est ...? *oo eh*

Can you show me on the map where I am?
Est-ce que vous pouvez me montrer où je suis sur la carte? *ess ker voo poovay mer mawngtray oo zher swee sewr la kart*

I've lost my way.
Je me suis perdu(e).
zher mer swee pehrdew

Can you repeat that?
Est-ce que vous pouvez répéter?
eh ser ker voo poovay raypaytay

Thanks for your help.
Merci pour votre aide.
mehrsee poor votr ayd

Traveling by car Voyage en voiture

Is this the right road for ...?
Est-ce que c'est bien la bonne route pour ...?
ess ker seh byang la bon root poor

How far is it to ... from here?
... est à combien de kilomètres d'ici?
eh a kawnbyang der keelometr deessee

How do I get onto the highway [motorway]?
Comment est-ce que je peux accéder à l'autoroute? *kommahng ess ker zher pur aksayday a loatoroot*

What's the next town called?
Comment s'appelle la prochaine ville?
kommahng sapell la proshayn veel

How long does it take by car?
Il faut combien de temps en voiture?
eel foa kawnbyang der tahng ahng vwatewr

- Excusez-moi, s'il vous plaît. Pour aller à la gare?
(Excuse me, please. How do I get to the train station?)

- Prenez la troisième route à droite et c'est tout droit.
(Take the third right and it's straight ahead.)

- La troisième à droite. C'est loin?
(The third right. Is it far?)

- C'est dix minutes, à pied. *(It's ten minutes, on foot.)*

- Merci pour votre aide. *(Thanks for your help.)*

- De rien. *(You're welcome.)*

Location Emplacement/situation

C'est ...	It's ...
tout droit	straight ahead
à gauche	on the left
à droite	on the right
de l'autre côté de la rue	on the other side of the street
au coin	on the corner
après le coin	round the corner
en direction de ...	in the direction of ...
en face de .../derrière ...	opposite .../behind ...
à côté de .../après ...	next to .../after ...
Descendez la	Go down the ...
rue transversale/rue principale	side street/main street
Traversez ...	Cross the ...
la place/le pont	square/bridge
Prenez la troisième route à droite.	Take the third turn on the right.
Tournez à gauche ...	Turn left ...
après les premiers feux (rouges)	after the first traffic light
au deuxième carrefour	at the second intersection [crossroad]

By car En voiture

C'est ... d'ici.	It's ... of here.
au nord/au sud	north/south
à l'est/à l'ouest	east/west
Prenez la route de ...	Take the road for ...
Vous êtes sur la mauvaise route.	You're on the wrong road.
Vous devez retourner à ...	You'll have to go back to ...
Suivez les panneaux vers ...	Follow the signs for ...

Is it far? C'est loin?

C'est ...	It's ...
près d'ici/loin	close/a long way
à cinq minutes à pied	5 minutes on foot
à dix minutes en voiture	10 minutes by car
à environ dix kilomètres	about 10 km away

TIME ➤ 220; NUMBERS ➤ 216

Road signs Panneaux

ALLUMEZ VOS PHARES	use headlights
BIS	alternative route
CÉDEZ LE PASSAGE	yield/give way
DÉVIATION	detour [diversion]
ÉCOLE	school
HAUTEUR LIMITÉE	low bridge
PRENEZ LA BONNE FILE	stay in lane/get in lane
ROUTE BARRÉE	road closed
SAUF RIVERAINS	local access only
SENS UNIQUE	one-way street

Town plans Plans de villes

aéroport	*a ayropor*	airport
arrêt d'autobus	*areh doatobews*	bus stop
bâtiment public	*bateemahng pewbleek*	public building
(bureau de) poste	*(bewroa der) post*	post office
cinéma	*seenayma*	movie theater [cinema]
commissariat	*komeessarya*	police station
église	*aygleez*	church
gare	*gar*	station
itinéraire des bus	*eeteenayrehr day bewss*	bus route
office du tourisme	*ofeess dew tooreezm*	information office
parc	*park*	park
parking	*parking*	parking lot [car park]
passage piétons	*passazh pyaytawng*	pedestrian crossing
passage souterrain	*passazh sootehrang*	underpass
rue principale	*rew prangseepal*	main [high] street
stade	*stad*	stadium
station de métro	*stasyawng der maytroa*	subway [metro] station
station de taxi	*stasyawng der taxee*	taxi stand [rank]
terrain de sports	*tehrrang der spor*	playing field [sports ground]
théâtre	*tayatr*	theater
vieille ville	*vyay veel*	old town
vous êtes ici	*voo zet eessee*	you are here
zone piétonnière	*zoan pyaytonyehr*	pedestrian zone [precinct]

DICTIONARY ➤ 169; SIGHTSEEING ➤ 97–107

Sightseeing

Tourist information Office du tourisme

Tourist information offices are often situated in the town center; look for
office du tourisme, **syndicat d'initiative** or simply **informations**.
Son et Lumière shows (telling the history of the town using special lighting
and sound effects), wine tastings and markets, along with many other
events, are advertised at the tourist information office.

Where's the tourist information office?	**Où est l'office du tourisme?** *oo eh loffeess dew tooreezm*
What are the main points of interest?	**Qu'est-ce qu'il y a d'intéressant à voir?** *kess keel ee a dangtayressahng a vwar*
We're here for …	**Nous restons …** *noo restawng*
only a few hours	**seulement quelques heures** *surlmahng kelker zurr*
a day	**une journée** *ewn zhoornay*
a week	**une semaine** *ewn sermayn*
Can you recommend …?	**Pouvez-vous recommander …?** *poovay voo rerkommahngday*
a sightseeing tour	**une visite touristique** *ewn veezeet tooreesteek*
an excursion	**une excursion** *ewn exkewrsyawng*
a boat trip	**une promenade en bateau** *ewn promnad ahng batoa*
Do you have any information on …?	**Avez-vous des renseignements sur …?** *avay voo day rahngsayñmahng sewr*
Are there any trips to …?	**Y a-t-il des voyages à …?** *ee ateel day vwahyazh a*

DAYS OF THE WEEK ➤ 218; DIRECTIONS ➤ 94

Reserving a tour
Pour réserver une excursion

How much does the tour cost?	**Combien coûte cette excursion?** *kawnbyang koot set exkewrsyawng*
Is lunch included?	**Le déjeuner est-il compris?** *ler dayzhurnay eteel kawngpree*
Where do we leave from?	**D'où partons-nous?** *doo partawng noo*
What time does the tour start?	**À quelle heure commence l'excursion?** *a kel urr kommahngss lexkewrsyawng*
What time do we get back?	**À quelle heure revenons-nous?** *a kel urr rervnawng noo*
Do we have free time in …?	**Est-ce que nous aurons du temps libre à …?** *ess ker noo zoarawng dew tahng leebr a*
Is there an English-speaking guide?	**Y a-t-il un guide qui parle anglais?** *ee ateel ang geed kee parl ahnggleh*

On tour En excursion

Are we going to see …?	**Est-ce que nous allons voir …?** *ess ker noo zalawng vwar*
We'd like to have a look at the …	**Nous aimerions voir …** *noo zaymryawng vwar*
Can we stop here …?	**Est-ce que nous pouvons nous arrêter ici …?** *ess ker noo poovawng noo zarettay eessee*
to take photographs	**pour prendre des photos** *poor prahngdr day foto*
to buy souvenirs	**pour acheter des souvenirs** *poor ashtay day soovneer*
to use the restrooms [toilets]	**pour aller aux toilettes** *poor alay oa twalett*
Would you take a photo of us, please?	**Pourriez-vous nous prendre en photo ici, s'il vous plaît?** *pooryay voo noo prahngdr ahng foto eessee seel voo pleh*
How long do we have here/in …?	**Combien de temps avons-nous ici/à …?** *kawnbyang der tahng avawng noo zeessee/a*
Wait! … isn't back yet.	**Attendez! … n'est pas encore là!** *atahngday … neh pa zahngkor la*

Sights Attractions touristiques

Town maps are displayed in major squares and streets and in the tourist information office.

Where is the …?	**Où est …?** *oo eh*
abbey	**l'abbaye** *labayee*
art gallery	**la galerie d' art** *la galree dar*
battleground	**le champ de bataille** *ler shahng der batie*
botanical garden	**le jardin botanique** *ler zhardang botahneek*
castle	**le château** *ler shatoa*
cathedral	**la cathédrale** *la kataydral*
cemetery	**le cimetière** *ler seemtyehr*
church	**l'église** *laygleez*
downtown area	**le centre-ville** *ler sahngtr veel*
fountain	**la fontaine** *la fawngtayn*
market	**le marché** *ler marshay*
(war) memorial	**le monument (aux morts)** *ler monewmahng (oa mor)*
monastery	**le monastère** *ler monastehr*
museum	**le musée** *ler mewzay*
old town	**la vieille ville** *la vyay veel*
opera house	**l'opéra** *lopayra*
palace	**le palais** *ler paleh*
park	**le parc** *ler park*
parliament building	**le parlement** *ler parlmahng*
ruins	**les ruines** *lay rween*
shopping area	**les rues commerçantes** *lay rew komehrsahngt*
statue	**la statue** *la statew*
theater	**le théâtre** *ler tayatr*
tower	**la tour** *la toor*
town hall	**l'hôtel de ville** *loatel der veel*
viewpoint	**le belvédère** *ler belvaydehr*
Can you show me on the map?	**Pouvez-vous me montrer sur la carte?** *poovay voo mer mawngtray sewr la kart*

DIRECTIONS ➤ 94

Admission Entrée

Museums are usually closed on Tuesdays and on important holidays (Christmas, New Year's Day, etc.).

Is the … open to the public?	**Est-ce que … est ouvert(e) au public?** *ess ker … eh oovehr(t) oa pewbleek*
Can we look around?	**Est-ce que nous pouvons regarder?** *ess ker noo poovawng regarday*
What are the hours?	**Quelles sont les heures d'ouverture?** *kel sawng lay zurr doovehrtewr*
When does it close?	**À quelle heure ferme-t-il?** *a kel urr fehrm teel*
Is … open on Sundays?	**Est-ce que … est ouvert(e) le dimanche?** *ess ker … eh oovehr(t) ler deemahngsh*
When's the next guided tour?	**À quelle heure est la prochaine visite guidée?** *a kel urr eh la proshayn veezeet geeday*
Do you have a guide book (in English)?	**Avez-vous un guide (en anglais)?** *avay voo ang geed (ahng nahngleh)*
Can I take photos?	**Est-ce que je peux prendre des photos?** *ess ker zher pur prahngdr day foto*
Is there access for the handicapped?	**Est-ce accessible aux handicapés?** *ess aksesseebl oa ahngdeekapay*
Is there an audio guide in English?	**Y a-t-il un guide audio en anglais?** *ee ateel ang geed oadyo ahng nahngleh*

Paying/Tickets Paiement/Billets

How much is the entrance fee?	**Combien coûte l'entrée?** *kawnbyang koot lahngtray*
Are there any discounts for …?	**Y a-t-il des réductions pour …?** *ee ateel day raydewksyawng poor*
children	**les enfants** *lay zahngfahng*
the handicapped	**les handicapés** *lay ahngdeekapay*
groups	**les groupes** *lay groop*
senior citizens	**les retraités** *lay rertretay*
students	**les étudiants** *lay zaytewdyahng*
1 adult and 2 children, please.	**Un adulte et deux enfants, s'il vous plaît.** *ang nadewlt ay dur zahngfahng seel voo pleh*
I've lost my ticket.	**J'ai perdu mon billet.** *zhay pehrdew mawng beeyeh*

OUVERT	open
FERMÉ	closed
MAGASIN DE SOUVENIRS	gift shop
DÉFENSE D'ENTRER	no entry
HEURES DES VISITES	visiting hours
ENTRÉE GRATUITE/LIBRE	admission free
PROCHAINE VISITE À … H	next tour at …
DERNIER BILLET À 17H	last entry at 5 p.m.
PHOTOS AU FLASH INTERDITES	no flash photography

– Cinq billets, s'il vous plaît.
Y a-t-il des réductions? (Five tickets, please.
Are there any discounts?)
– *Oui. Pour les enfants et les personnes
âgés, c'est quarante-cinq francs.
(Yes, for children and senior citizens it's 45 francs.)*
– Deux adultes et trois enfants, s'il vous plaît.
(Two adults and three children, please.)
– *Ça fait deux cent cinquante-cinq francs,
s'il vous plaît.
(That's 255 francs, please.)*

Impressions   Impressions

It's …	**C'est …** *seh*
amazing	**stupéfiant** *stewpayfyahng*
beautiful	**beau** *boa*
boring	**ennuyeux** *ahngnweeyur*
breathtaking	**époustouflant** *aypoostooflahng*
brilliant	**fantastique** *fahngtasteek*
interesting	**intéressant** *angtayressahng*
magnificent	**magnifique** *mañeefeek*
romantic	**romantique** *romahngteek*
stunning	**stupéfiant** *stewpayfyahng*
superb	**superbe** *sewpehrb*
ugly	**laid** *lay*
It's a good value.	**On en a pour son argent.** *awng ahng na poor sawng narzhahng*
It's a rip-off.	**C'est du vol.** *seh dew vol*
I (don't) like it.	**Ça (ne) me plaît (pas).** *sa (ner) mer pleh (pa)*

à chevrons herringbone
à colombages half-timbered
à l'échelle 1/100 scale 1:100
à poutres apparentes
 half-timbered
abside apse
aile (d'un bâtiment)
 wing (of building)
appartements royaux
 apartments (royal)
aquarelle watercolor
arc-boutant hanging buttress
argent silver
argenterie silverware
argile clay
arme weapon
arsenal armory
artisannat crafts
autel altar(piece)
bains baths
bâtiment building
beaux-arts fine arts
bibliothèque library
bijoux jewelry
bois wood
brique brick
cage d'escalier staircase
chaire pulpit
chef-d'œuvre masterpiece
chœur choir (stall)
cimetière churchyard
clef de voûte headstone
commandé par
 commissioned by
commencé en started in
complété en completed in
conception design
conçu par designed by
conférence lecture
construit en built in

contrefort buttress
cour courtyard
couronne crown
créneau battlement
dans le style de in the style of
découvert en discovered in
dessin drawing/design
dessiné par designed by
détail detail
détruit par destroyed by
doré à l'or fin gilded
douves moat
école de ... school of ...
émail enamel
en or gold(en)
en saillie overhanging
en surplomb overhanging
entrée doorway
érigé en erected in
escalier stairs
esquisse sketch
exposition display,
 exhibition
exposition temporaire
 temporary exhibit
fenêtre window
ferronnerie ironwork
flèche spire
fondé en founded in
fonts baptismaux font
fossé moat
fresque fresco
frise frieze
fronton pediment
fusain charcoal
gargouille gargoyle
grande salle de réception
 stateroom
gravure à l'eau-forte etching
gravure engraving

habitait lived
hall d'entrée foyer
hauteur height
horloge clock
image picture
impératrice empress
jardin à la française
 formal garden
joyaux jewelry
lambris paneling
légué par donated by
maître master
maquette model
marbre marble
meubles furniture
meurt died
moulures molding
mourut en died in
mur wall
nature morte still life
né en/à born in
nef nave
niveau 1 level 1
objet exposé exhibit
ombre shadow
orgue organ
œuvres works
panneau panel
par by (person)
paysage landscape/painting
paysage marin seascape
peint par painted by
peintre painter
peinture murale mural
peintures à l'huile oils
pendule clock
personnage en cire waxwork
pièce coin
pierre stone
pierre angulaire cornerstone
pierre précieuse gemstone

pierre tombale
 headstone
pignon gable
pilier pillar
plafond ceiling
pont-levis drawbridge
portail door, gate
porte doorway
poutre beam
prêté à on loan to
rebâti en rebuilt in
reconstruit en rebuilt in
reigne reign
reine queen
remparts battlement
renfoncement alcove
restauré en restored in
rinceau foliage
roi king
scène stage
sculpture carving, sculpture
siècle century
tableau painting
tableau vivant tableau
tapisserie tapestry
tenture hanging
terre cuite terracotta
thermes baths
toile canvas
toit roof
tombe grave/tomb
tombeau tomb
tour tower
tourelle turret
verrière (stained) glass
 window
vestibule foyer
vitrail (pl vitraux)
 stained glass window
vitrine display cabinet
voûte vault

Who/What/When? Qui/Quoi/Quand?

What's that building?	**Quel est ce bâtiment?** *kel eh ser bateemahng*
When was it built?	**Quand a-t-il été construit?** *kahng a teel aytay kawngstrwee*
Who was the …? architect/artist	**Qui était …?** *kee ayteh* **l'architecte/l'artiste** *larsheetekt/larteest*
What style is that?	**C'est quel style?** *seh kel steel*

Roman   ca. 11th–12th century
The romanesque style was characterized by simple lines and round arches; esp. religious architecture in Burgundy (e.g., Tournus and Cluny).

Gothique   ca. 12th–end 15th century
Very complex architectural forms, using pointed arches, rib vaults and flying buttresses; esp. cathedrals of Reims, Chartres, Strasbourg and Sainte-Chapelle in Paris.

Renaissance   ca. 15th–16th century
Cultural and artistic movement, derived from the Italian Renaissance that aimed to imitate the ancient Roman stability and poise, esp. châteaux of the Loire and at Fontainebleau.

Baroque   ca. 17th–18th century
Artistic movement; its music was finely polished, esp. Lully, Rameau and Couperin; its architectural style was large-scale and elaborately decorated, esp. many churches in the Savoie region.

Classicisme   ca. mid 18th–mid 19th century
The Classical movement brought about a return to classical values such as simplicity and methodical order, esp. the Louvre and its famous colonnade (by Perrault); artist: David.

Art nouveau   1880s–1910s
Simplified forms, ranging from the emulation of nature to abstract forms; esp. the use of undulating lines seen in glassware, jewelry and art.

Impressionnisme   1874–1886
Movement rejecting the true-to-life style of Réaliste art; moved toward a greater use of color and light to create an "impression"; esp. artists: Manet, Degas, Cézanne, Monet; composers: Debussy, Ravel.

Rulers Souverains

What period is that? **C'est quelle période?**
seh kel payryod

gallo-romain   59 BC–476 AD

Julius Caesar brought the whole of Gaul (now France, Belgium and Switzerland), under Roman rule. The western Roman Empire flourished, esp. in Lyon and Provence; on its collapse, Gaul was invaded by numerous barbarian tribes, including the Franks.

médiéval   476–1500

Dynasties and major figures of the Middle Ages include mérovingiens (486–751) – Clovis I; carolingiens (751–987) – Charlemagne; capétiens (987–1328) – Saint Louis; les Valois (1328–1589) – François I.

les Bourbons   1589–1793, 1815–1848

Dynasty founded by Henri IV; reached the pinnacle of power under Louis XIV (le Roi-Soleil – Sun King) with the magnificence of Versailles and Paris during le grand siècle (ca. 17th); ended with the execution of Louis XVI; briefly restored 1815-1848.

la Révolution   1789–1799

The French Revolution began with the storming of La Bastille prison (14 July 1789). Peasant uprisings (**la Grande Peur**) and Revolutionary wars follow. The Republic is declared, Louis XVI is executed and Robespierre leads a Reign of Terror (**la Terreur**).

l'Empire   1799–1814, 1852–1870

The Empire of Napoléon Bonaparte with its initial prosperity and military expansion across Europe crumbled with a disasterous campaign in Russia (1812) and final defeat at Waterloo. The Second Empire under Napoléon III saw Paris transformed by wide boulevards; but it also ended in defeat, followed by the Third Republic (1870–1940).

Churches Églises

France and Belgium are predominantly Roman Catholic, although places of worship for most faiths can be found, especially in large cities. Switzerland is equally divided between Roman Catholic and Protestant.

Catholic/Protestant church **une Église catholique/protestante**
ewn aygleez katoleek/protestahngt

mosque **une mosquée** *ewn moskay*

synagogue **une synagogue** *ewn seenagog*

What time is …? **À quelle heure est …?** *a kel urr eh*

mass/the service **la messe/le service**
la mess/ler sehrveess

In the countryside
À la campagne

I'd like a map of …	**Je voudrais une carte …** *zher voodray ewn kart*
this region	**de la région** *der la rayzhyawng*
walking routes	**des sentiers de randonnée** *day sahngtyay der rahngdonnay*
cycle routes	**des circuits cyclistes** *day seerkwee seekleest*
How far is it to …?	**Il y a combien de kilomètres jusqu'à …?** *eel ee a kawnbyang der keelometr zhewska*
Is there a right of way?	**Y a-t-il un droit de passage?** *ee ateel ang drwa der passazh*
Is there a trail/scenic route to …?	**Y a-t-il une route touristique pour aller à …?** *ee ateel ewn root tooreesteek poor alay a*
Can you show me on the map?	**Pouvez-vous me le montrer sur la carte?** *poovay voo mer ler mawngtray sewr la kart*
I'm lost.	**Je me suis perdu(e).** *zher mer swee pehrdew*

Guided tours Promenades organisées

When does the guided walk/hike start?	**À quelle heure commence la promenade?** *a kel urr kommahngss la promnahd*
When will we return?	**À quelle heure reviendrons-nous?** *a kel urr rervyangdrawng noo*
I'm exhausted.	**Je suis épuisé(e).** *zher swee zaypweezay*
What is the walk like?	**C'est quel genre de promenade?** *seh kel zhahngr der promnad*
gentle/medium/tough	**facile/moyenne/difficile** *fasseel/mwahyenn/deefeesseel*
What kind of … is that?	**C'est quel genre …?** *seh kel zhahngr*
animal/bird	**d'animal/d'oiseau** *dahneemal/dwazoa*
flower/tree	**de fleur/d'arbre** *der flurr/darbr*

HIKING GEAR ➤ 145

Geographic features
Caractéristiques géographiques

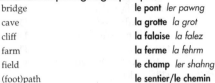

bridge	**le pont** *ler pawng*
cave	**la grotte** *la grot*
cliff	**la falaise** *la falez*
farm	**la ferme** *la fehrm*
field	**le champ** *ler shahng*
(foot)path	**le sentier/le chemin** *ler sahngtyay/ler shermang*
forest	**la forêt** *la foreh*
hill	**la colline** *la koleen*
lake	**le lac** *ler lak*
mountain	**la montagne** *la mawngtañ*
mountain pass	**le col (de montagne)** *ler kol (der mawngtañ)*
mountain range	**la chaîne de montagnes** *la shen der mawngtañ*
nature reserve	**le parc naturel** *ler park natewrel*
panorama	**le panorama** *ler pahnorama*
park	**le parc** *ler park*
peak	**le pic/le sommet** *ler peek/ler someh*
picnic area	**l'aire de pique-nique** *lehr der peek neek*
pond	**l'étang** *laytahng*
rapids	**les rapides** *lay rapeed*
river	**la rivière** *la reevyehr*
sea	**la mer** *la mehr*
stream	**le ruisseau** *ler rweessoa*
valley	**la vallée** *la valay*
viewpoint	**le point de vue/le belvédère** *ler pwang der vew/le belvaydehr*
village	**le village** *ler veelazh*
winery [vineyard]	**la vigne** *la veeñ*
waterfall	**la cascade** *la kaskad*
wood	**le bois** *ler bwa*

Leisure

What's on? Qu'y a-t-il à voir?

Local papers and, in large cities, weekly entertainment guides will tell you what's on. In Paris look for *L'Officiel des Spectacles* and *Pariscope*; in Brussels, *Le Bulletin*. You'll be spoiled for choice by the range of dance, music and theater offered.

Do you have a program of events?	**Avez-vous un programme des spectacles?** *avay voo ang program day spektakl*
Can you recommend a good …?	**Pouvez-vous me conseiller …?** *poovay voo mer kawngsayay*
Is there a … somewhere?	**Y a-t-il … quelque part?** *ee ateel … kelker par*
ballet/concert	**un ballet/un concert** *ang baleh/ang kawngsehr*
movie [film]	**un film** *ang feelm*
opera	**un opéra** *ang nopayra*

Availability Disponibilité

When does it start?	**À quelle heure commence-t-il?** *a kel urr kommahngss teel*
When does it end?	**À quelle heure finit-il?** *a kel urr feenee teel*
Are there any seats for tonight?	**Est-ce qu'il reste des places pour ce soir?** *ess keel rest day plass poor ser swar*
Where can I get tickets?	**Où est-ce que je peux me procurer des billets?** *oo ess ker zher pur mer prokewray day beeyeh*
There are … of us.	**Nous sommes …** *noo som*

Tickets Billets

How much are the seats?

Combien coûtent les places?
kawnbyang koot lay plass

Do you have anything cheaper?

Avez-vous quelque chose de moins cher? *avay voo kelker shoaz der mwang shehr*

I'd like to reserve …

Je voudrais réserver …
zher voodray rayzehrvay

3 for Sunday evening

trois places pour dimanche soir
trwa plass poor deemahngsh swar

1 for Friday matinee

une place pour vendredi en matinée
ewn plass poor vahngdrerdee ahng mateenay

Quel(le) est … de votre carte de crédit?	What's your credit card …?
le numéro/ le nom/ la date d'expiration	number/type/ expiration [expiry] date
Venez chercher les billets … avant … heures (du soir)	Please pick up the tickets … by … p.m.

May I have a program?

Est-ce que je peux avoir un programme?
ess ker zher pur avwar ang program

Where's the coat room?

Où est le vestiaire? *oo eh ler vestyehr*

– *Allô, le théâtre Molière.* (Hello, Molière Theater.)
– *Allô, je voudrais deux billets pour "Tartuffe" pour ce soir, s'il vous plaît.*
(I'd like two tickets for tonight's "Tartuffe", please.)
– *D'accord. Vous pouvez me donner le nom et le numéro de votre catre de crédit, s'il vous plaît?*
(Certainly. Could you give me the name and number of your credit card, please?)
– *Oui, c'est une Visa numéro zéro cinq zéro, trois six cinq, sept huit cinq quatre.*
(Yes, it's Visa number 050 365 7854.)

– *Et quelle est la date d'expiration, s'il vous plaît?*
(What's the expiration date, please?)
– *Sept quatre-vingt-dix-huit.* (July ninety-eight.)
– *Merci. Venez chercher vos billets au bureau de réservations.*
(Thank you. Please pick up the tickets at the reservations office.)

NUMBERS ➤ 216

Movies [Cinema]   Cinéma

For movies in their original English (with French subtitles),
look for those marked VO (**version originale**). However, you'll
find most American and British films are dubbed.

Tipping: Don't forget to tip the usherette: 2F in France
and 20F in Belgium is the norm.

Is there a movie theater [cinema] near here?	**Y a-t-il un cinéma près d'ici?** *ee ateel ang seenayma mewlteeplex preh deessee*
What's playing at the movie theater [cinema]?	**Qu'y a-t-il au cinéma ce soir?** *kee ateel oa seenayma ser swar*
Is the film dubbed/subtitled?	**Est-ce que le film est doublé/sous-titré?** *ess ker ler feelm eh dooblay/soo teetray*
Is the film in the original English?	**Est-ce que le film est en version originale (en anglais)?** *ess ker ler feelm eh ahng vehrsyawng oreezheenal (ahng ahngleh)*
A ..., please.	**..., s'il vous plaît.** *seel voo pleh*
box [carton] of popcorn	**une boîte de pop-corn** *ewn bwat der popkorn*
chocolate ice cream [choc-ice]	**une glace au chocolat** *ewn glass oa shokola*
hot dog	**une hot dog** *ang ot dog*
soft drink/soda	**une boisson gazeuse** *ewn bwassawng gazurz*
small/regular/large	**petit/moyen/grand** *pertee/mwahyang/grahng*

Theater   Théâtre

What's playing at the ... Theater?	**Qu'est-ce qu'on joue au théâtre ...?** *kess kawng zhoo oa tayatr*
Who's the playwright?	**Qui est l'auteur?** *kee eh loaturr*
Do you think I'd enjoy it?	**Pensez-vous que ça me plairait?** *pahngsay voo ker sa mer plehreh?*
I don't know much French.	**Je ne connais pas beaucoup de français.** *zher ner konneh pa boakoo der frahngseh*

Opera/Ballet/Dance
Opéra/Ballet/Danse

Where's the opera house?

Où est l'opéra?
oo eh lopayra

Who's the composer/soloist?

Qui est le compositeur/soliste?
kee eh ler kawngpozeeturr/soleest

Is formal dress required?

Faut-il être en tenue de soirée?
foa teel etr ahng tenew der swaray

Who's dancing?

Qui est-ce qui danse?
kee ess kee dahngss

I'm interested in
contemporary dance.

Je m'intéresse à la danse contemporaine.
*zher mangtayress a la dahngss
kawngtahngporayn*

Music/Concerts   Musique/Concerts

Where's the concert hall?

Où est la salle de concerts?
oo eh la sal der kawngsehr

Which orchestra/ band
is playing?

Quel orchestre/groupe joue?
kel orkestr/groop zhoo

What are they playing?

Qu'est-ce qu'ils jouent? *kess keel zhoo*

Who is the conductor/soloist?

Qui est le chef d'orchestre/le soliste?
kee eh ler shef dorkestr/ler soleest

Who is the support band?

Qui est le groupe en première partie?
kee eh ler groop ahng prermyehr partee

I really like …

J'aime beaucoup … *zhem boakoo*

country music

la musique country *la mewzeek country*

folk music

la musique folk *la mewzeek folk*

jazz

le jazz *ler dzhazz*

music of the '60s

la musique des années soixante
la mewzeek day zahnay swassahngt

pop

la musique pop *la mewzeek pop*

rock music

la musique rock *la mewzeek rok*

soul music

la musique soul *la mewzeek soul*

Have you ever heard of
her/him?

**Est-ce que vous en avez déjà
entendu parler?** *ess ker voo zahng
navay dayzha ahngtahngdew parlay*

Are they popular?

Est-ce qu'ils sont connus?
ess keel sawng konnew

Nightlife Vie nocturne

What is there to do in the evenings?	**Qu'est-ce qu'il y a à à faire le soir?** *kess keel ee a a fehr ler swar*
Can you recommend a …?	**Pouvez-vous me recommander un(e) …?** *poovay voo mer rekommahngday ang (ewn)*
Is there a … in town?	**Est-ce qu'il y a … en ville?** *ess keel ee a … ahng veel*
bar	**un bar** *ang bar*
casino	**un casino** *ang kazeeno*
discotheque	**une discothèque/une boîte (de nuit)** *ewn deeskotek/ewn bwat (der nwee)*
gay club	**un club gay** *ang klurb gay*
nightclub	**un night-club** *ang naytklurb*
restaurant	**un restaurant** *ang restoarahng*
What type of music do they play?	**Quel genre de musique jouent-ils?** *kel zhahngr der mewzeek zhoo teel*
How do I get there?	**Comment est-ce que je peux m'y rendre?** *kommahng ess ker zher pur mee rahngdr*

Admission Entrée

What time does the show start?	**À quelle heure commence le spectacle?** *a kel urr kommahngss ler spektakl*
Is evening dress required?	**Faut-il être en tenue de soirée?** *foa teel etr ahng ternew der swaray*
Is there a cover charge?	**Faut-il payer pour rentrer?** *foa teel payay poor rahngtray*
Is a reservation necessary?	**Faut-il réserver?** *foa teel rayzehrvay*
Do we need to be members?	**Faut-il être membre?** *foa teel etr mahngbr*
How long will we have to stand in line [queue]?	**Combien de temps devrons-nous faire la queue?** *kawnbyang der tahng dervrawng noo fehr la kur*
I'd like a good table.	**Je voudrais une bonne table.** *zher voodray ewn bon tabl*

UNE BOISSON GRATUITE COMPRISE	includes 1 complimentary drink

TIME ➤ 220; TAXI ➤ 84

Children Enfants

Can you recommend something for the children?
Pouvez-vous recommander quelque chose pour les enfants? *poovay voo rerkommahngday kelker shoaz poor lay zahngfahng*

Are there changing facilities here for infants?
Y a-t-il une salle de change pour bébé ici? *ee ateel ewn sal der shahngzh poor baybay eessee*

Where are the restrooms [toilets]?
Où sont les toilettes? *oo sawng lay twalett*

game/amusement arcade
la salle de jeux *la sal der zhur*

fairground
la fête foraine *la fet forayn*

kiddie [paddling] pool
le petit bassin *ler pertee bassang*

playground
la cour de récréation *la koor der raykrayasyawng*

playgroup/nursery school
la garderie/l'école maternelle *la garderree/laykol matehrnel*

zoo
le zoo *ler zoa*

Baby-sitting Garde d'enfants

Can you recommend a reliable baby-sitter?
Pouvez-vous recommander une gardienne d'enfants sérieuse? *poovay voo rerkommahngday ewn gardyenn dahngfahng sayryurz*

Is there constant supervision?
Sont-ils surveillés tout le temps? *sawng teel sewrvayay too ler tahng*

Are the helpers properly trained?
Le personnel est-il qualifié? *ler pehrsonel eteel kaleefyay*

When can I drop them off?
À quelle heure est-ce que je peux les amener? *a kel urr ess ker zher pur lay zamnay*

I'll pick them up at …
Je viendrai les chercher à … *zher vyangdray lay shehrshay a*

We'll be back by …
Nous reviendrons à … *noo rervyangdrawng a*

She's 3 and he's 18 months.
Elle a trois ans et il a dix-huit mois. *el a trwa zahng ay eel a deezwee mwa*

Sports   Sports

Soccer, tennis and racing (bicycles, cars and horses) are popular spectator sports in France. You'll also find plenty of opportunity yourself for sailing, fishing, horseback riding, golf, tennis, hiking, cycling, swimming and skiing (➤ 117).

Spectator Sports En spectateurs

Is there a soccer game [football match] this Saturday?	**Y a-t-il un match de football samedi?** *ee ateel ang match der footbal samdee*
Which teams are playing?	**Quelles sont les équipes?** *kel sawng lay zaykeep*
Can you get me a ticket?	**Pouvez-vous me procurer un ticket?** *poovay voo mer prokewray ang teekeh*
What's the admission charge?	**Combien coûtent les places?** *kawnbyang koot lay plass*
Where's the racetrack [race course]?	**Où est l'hippodrome?** *oo eh leepodrom*
Where can I place a bet?	**Où est-ce que je peux faire un pari?** *oo ess ker zher pur fehr ang paree*
What are the odds on …?	**Quelle est la cote de …?** *kel eh la kott der*
athletics	**athlétisme** *atlayteezm*
basketball	**basket(ball)** *basket(bal)*
cycling	**cyclisme** *seekleezm*
soccer [football]	**football** *footbal*
golf	**golf** *golf*
horseracing	**courses de chevaux** *koorss der shervoa*
swimming	**natation** *natasyawng*
tennis	**tennis** *teneess*
volleyball	**volley(ball)** *voleh(bal)*

la pétanque   *la paytawnk*
Provençal name for **boules**, in which metal balls/boules are thrown at the wooden jack (**cochonnet**); the game is played throughout France, wherever there is an available piece of gravel.

le Tour de France   *ler toor der frawns*
world's most prestigious cycle tour (June-July annually) winds a demanding route around France, with the **maillot vert** (green jersey) for the King of the Mountains (Pyrenees and Alps), and the award of the prized **maillot jaune** (yellow jersey) to the winner back in Paris.

Participating Pour les sportifs

Where's the nearest …?	**Où est … le plus proche?** *oo eh … ler plew prosh*
golf course	**le terrain de golf** *ler tehrang der golf*
sports club	**le club sportif** *ler klurb sporteef*
Where are the tennis courts?	**Où sont les courts de tennis?** *oo sawng lay koor der tenneess*
What's the charge per …?	**Combien ça coûte par …?** *kawnbyang sa koot par*
day/round/hour	**jour/partie/heure** *zhoor/partee/urr*
Do I need to be a member?	**Faut-il être membre du club?** *foa teel etr mahngbr dew klurb*
Where can I rent …?	**Où est-ce que je peux louer …?** *oo ess ker zher pur looay*
boots	**des chaussures** *day shoassewr*
clubs	**des clubs (de golf)** *day klurb (der golf)*
equipment	**du matériel** *dew matayryell*
racket	**une raquette** *ewn rakett*
Can I take lessons?	**Est-ce que je peux prendre des leçons?** *ess ker zher pur prahngdr day lerssawng*
Do you have a fitness center?	**Avez-vous une salle de musculation?** *avay voo ewn sal der mewskewlasyawng*
Can I join in?	**Est-ce que je peux vous tenir compagnie?** *ess ker zher pur voo terneer kawngpañee*

Je regrette, nous sommes complets.	I'm sorry, we're booked.
Il faut verser … francs de caution/d'arrhes.	There is a deposit of …
Quelle pointure faites-vous?	What size are you?
Il vous faut une photo d'identité.	You need a passport-size photo.

⊘	PÊCHE INTERDITE	no fishing	⊘
	PERMIS OBLIGATOIRE	permit holders only	
⓪	VESTIAIRES	locker rooms	⓪

At the beach À la plage

Most beaches are supervised (**plage/baignade surveillée**) by lifeguards unless specified **non surveillée**.

Always follow the flags regarding swimming safety: *green* – no danger; *orange* – danger, be cautious; *black* – no bathing.

Topless bathing is accepted on most French beaches, although in some places it may be frowned upon: be wise and do what other people do.

Is the beach …?	**Est-ce que c'est une plage …?** *ess ker seh tewn plazh*
pebbly/sandy	**de galets/de sable** *der galeh/der sabl*
Is there a … here?	**Y a-t-il … ici?** *ee ateel … eessee*
children's pool	**une piscine pour enfants** *ewn peesseen poor ahngfahng*
swimming pool	**une piscine …** *ewn peesseen*
indoor/outdoor	**couverte/en plein air** *koovehrt/ahng plang ehr*
Is it safe to swim/dive here?	**Est-ce qu'on peut se baigner/plonger ici sans danger?** *ess kawng pur ser bayñay/ plawngzhay eessee sahng dahngzhay*
Is it safe for children?	**Est-ce que c'est sans danger pour les enfants?** *ess ker seh sahng dahngzhay poor lay zahngfahng*
Is there a lifeguard?	**Y a-t-il un maître-nageur?** *ee ateel ang metr nazhurr*
I want to rent a/some …	**Je voudrais louer …** *zher voodray looay*
deck chair	**une chaise longue** *ewn shez lawngg*
jet ski	**un scooter des mers** *ang skooturr day mehr*
motorboat	**un canot automobile** *ang kahnoa oatomobeel*
skin-diving equipment	**un équipement de plongée (sous-marine)** *ang naykeepmahng der plawngzhay (soo mareen)*
umbrella [sunshade]	**un parasol** *ang parassol*
surfboard	**une planche de surf** *ewn plahngsh der surrf*
waterskis	**des skis nautiques** *day skee noateek*
For … hours.	**Pendant … heures.** *pahngdahng … urr*

Skiing   Ski

Generally speaking, the Alps are the best for downhill skiing (**descente**) and the Pyrenees for cross-country (**ski de fond**). French resorts tend to be modern and efficient; in Switzerland the emphasis is more on tradition and character. However, excellent skiing is to be found in both countries.

Is there much snow?	**Est-ce qu'il y a beaucoup de neige?** *ess keel ee a boakoo der nayzh*
What's the snow like?	**Comment est la neige?** *kommahng eh la nayzh*
heavy/icy	**lourde/gelée (verglacée)** *loord/zherlay (vehrglassay)*
powdery/wet	**poudreuse/mouillée** *poodrurz/ mooyay*
I'd like to rent some …	**Je voudrais louer …** *zher voodray looay*
poles	**des bâtons** *day batawng*
skates	**des patins** *day patang*
ski boots	**des chaussures de ski** *day shoassewr der skee*
skis	**des skis** *day skee*
These are too …	**Ils sont trop …** *eel sawng tro*
big/small	**grands/petits** *grahng/pertee*
They're uncomfortable.	**Ils ne sont pas confortables.** *eel ner sawng pa kawngfortabl*
A lift pass for a day/5 days, please.	**Un forfait pour une journée/cinq jours, s'il vous plaît.** *ang forfeh poor ewn zhoornay/sangk zhoor seel voo pleh*
I'd like to join the ski school.	**Je voudrais prendre des leçons à l'école de ski.** *zher voodray prahngdr day lerssawng a laykol der skee*
I'm a beginner.	**Je suis débutant.** *zher swee daybewtahng*
I'm experienced.	**J'ai déjà de l'expérience.** *zhay dayzha der lexpayryahngss*

REMONTE-PENTE/TIRE-FESSES	ski lift
TÉLÉPHÉRIQUE/ŒUFS	cable car/gondolas
TÉLÉSIÈGE	chair lift

Making Friends

Introductions Présentations

Greetings vary according to how well you know someone.

It's polite to shake hands, both when you meet and say good-bye to a French person, especially when it is for the first time.

The titles **monsieur, madame, mademoiselle** (sir, madam, miss) are used in French much more than in English and do not sound as formal. In fact, it is polite to add them after **bonjour**, especially when addressing someone you do not know.

In French, there are two forms for "you" (taking different verb forms):
tu (informal/familiar) is used when talking to relatives, close friends and children (and between young people);
vous (formal) is used in all other cases, and is also the plural form of **tu**.

Hello, I don't think we've met.	**Bonjour, nous ne nous connaissons pas, je crois?** *bawngzhoor noo ner noo konessawng pa zher krwa*
My name is …	**Je m'appelle …** *zher mappell*
May I introduce …?	**Puis-je vous présenter …?** *pweezh voo prayzahngtay*
Pleased to meet you.	**Enchanté.** *ahngshahngtay*
What's your name?	**Comment vous appelez-vous?** *kommahng voo zaplay voo*
How are you?	**Comment allez-vous?** *kommahng talay voo*
Fine, thanks. And you?	**Très bien, merci. Et vous [toi]?** *treh byang mehrsee et voo [twa]*

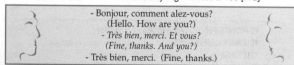

- Bonjour, comment alez-vous?
(Hello. How are you?)
- *Très bien, merci. Et vous?*
(Fine, thanks. And you?)
- Très bien, merci. (Fine, thanks.)

Where are you from?
D'où êtes-vous ?

Where do you come from?	**D'où venez-vous ?** *doo vernay voo*
Where were you born?	**Où êtes-vous né(e)?** *oo ayt voo nay*
I'm from ...	**Je viens ...** *zher vyang*
Australia	**d'Australie** *doastralee*
Britain	**de Grande-Bretagne** *der grahngd brertañ*
Canada	**du Canada** *dew kahnada*
England	**d'Angleterre** *dahnglertehr*
Ireland	**d'Irlande** *deerlahngd*
Scotland	**d'Écosse** *daykoss*
U.S.	**des États-Unis** *day zayta zewnee*
Wales	**du Pays de Galles** *dew payee der gal*
Where do you live?	**Où habitez-vous?** *oo abeetay voo*
What part of ... are you from?	**Vous êtes de quelle région de ...** *voo zayt der kel rayzhyawng der*
Belgium	**Belgique** *belzheek*
France	**France** *frahngss*
Switzerland	**Suisse** *sweess*
We come here every year.	**Nous venons ici tous les ans.** *noo vernawng eessee too lay zahng*
It's my/our first visit.	**C'est la première fois que je viens/ nous venons.** *seh la prermyehr fwa ker zher vyang/noo vernawng*
Have you ever been to ...?	**Est-ce que vous êtes déjà allés ... ?** *ess ker voo zayt dayzha alay*
Britain/the U.S.	**en Grande-Bretagne/aux États-Unis** *ahng grahngd brertañ/oa zayta zewnee*
Do you like it here?	**Ça vous plaît ici?** *sa voo pleh eessee*
What do you think of the ...?	**Que pensez-vous de ...?** *ker pahngsay voo der*
I love the ... here.	**J'adore ... ici.** *zhador ... eessee*
I don't really like the ... here.	**Je n'aime pas beaucoup ... ici.** *zher naym pa boakoo ... eessee*
food/people	**la cuisine/les gens** *la kweezeen/lay zhang*

119

Who are you with?
Avec qui êtes-vous?

Who are you with?	**Avec qui êtes-vous?** *avek kee ayt voo*
I'm on my own.	**Je suis tout(e) seul(e).** *zher swee too(t) surl*
I'm with a friend.	**Je suis avec un(e) ami(e).** *zher swee zavek ang (ewn) amee*
I'm with my …	**Je suis avec …** *zher swee zavek*
wife	**ma femme** *ma fam*
husband	**mon mari** *mawng maree*
family	**ma famille** *ma famee*
children	**mes enfants** *may zahngfahng*
parents	**mes parents** *may parahng*
boyfriend/girlfriend	**mon copain/ma copine** *mawng kopang/ma kopeen*
father/son	**mon père/fils** *mawng pehr/feess*
mother/daughter	**ma mère/fille** *ma mehr/fee*
brother/uncle	**mon frère/oncle** *mawng frehr/awngkl*
sister/aunt	**ma sœur/tante** *ma surr/tahng*
What's your son's/wife's name?	**Comment s'appelle votre fils/femme?** *kommahng sappell votr feess/fam*
Are you married?	**Êtes-vous marié(e)?** *ayt voo maryay*
I'm …	**Je suis …** *zher swee*
married/single	**marié(e)/célibataire** *maryay/sayleebatehr*
divorced/separated	**divorcé(e)/séparé(e)** *deevorsay/separay*
engaged	**fiancé(e)** *feeahngsay*
We live together.	**Nous vivons ensemble.** *noo veevawng zahngsahngbl*
Do you have any children?	**Avez-vous des enfants?** *avay voo day zahngfahng*
2 boys and a girl.	**Deux garçons et une fille.** *dur garsawng ay ewn fee*
How old are they?	**Quel âge ont-ils?** *kel azh awng teel*
They're ten and twelve.	**Ils ont dix et douze ans.** *eel zawng dees ay dooz ahng*

PIER C SIMPLY BOOKS
SAN FRANCISCO INTL AIRPORT
SAN FRANCISCO. CALIFORNIA

2085 MARIA

TRN 9183 JUL27'01 11:09AM

9782831562391

1 *BOOKS GENERC   7.95

Subtotal   7.95
Tax   0.64
Amt Paid   8.59
Cash   8.59

THANK YOU. PLEASE COME AGAIN

What do you do?
Qu'est-ce que vous faites?

What do you do?	**Qu'est-ce que vous faites dans la vie/comme travail?** *kess ker voo fet dahng la vee/ kom travie*
What line are you in?	**Dans quelle branche êtes-vous?** *dahng kel brahngsh ayt voo*
What are you studying?	**Qu'est-ce que vous étudiez?** *kess ker voo zaytewdyay*
I'm studying …	**J'étudie …** *zhaytewdee*
I'm in …	**Je suis dans …** *zher swee dahng*
business	**le commerce** *ler komehrss*
engineering	**l'ingénierie** *langzhaynyeree*
retail	**la vente au détail** *la vahngt oa daytay*
sales	**la vente** *la vahngt*
Who do you work for …?	**Pour qui travaillez-vous …?** *poor kee travieyay voo*
I work for …	**Je travaille pour …** *zher traviey poor*
I'm a(n) …	**Je suis …** *zher swee*
accountant	**comptable** *kawngptabl*
housewife	**femme au foyer** *fam oa fwayay*
student	**étudiant(e)** *aytewdyahng(t)*
retired	**retraité(e)** *rertretay*
self-employed	**à mon compte** *a mawng kawngt*
unemployed	**au chômage** *oa shoamazh*
What are your interests/ hobbies?	**Quels sont vos intérêts/hobbies?** *kel sawng vo zangtayreh/obbee*
I like …	**J'aime …** *zhaym*
music	**la musique** *la mewzeek*
reading	**la lecture** *la lektewr*
sports	**le sport** *ler spor*
I play …	**Je joue …** *zher zhoo*
Would you like to play …?	**Voulez-vous/(veux-tu) jouer …?** *voolay voo/(vur tew) zhooay*
cards	**aux cartes** *oa kart*
chess	**aux échecs** *oa zayshek*

What weather! Quel temps!

What a lovely day!	**Quelle belle journée!**	*kel bell zhoornay*
What awful weather!	**Quel temps horrible!**	*kel tahng zoreebl*
Isn't it cold/hot today!	**Qu'est-ce qu'il fait froid/chaud aujourd'hui!**	*kess keel feh frwa/shoa oazhoordwee*
Is it usually as warm as this?	**Est-ce qu'il fait aussi chaud d'habitude?**	*ess keel feh oassee shoa dabeetewd*
Do you think it's going to ... tomorrow?	**Croyez-vous qu'il va ... demain?**	*krwahyay voo keel va ... dermang*
be a nice day	**faire beau**	*fehr boa*
rain	**pleuvoir**	*plurvwar*
snow	**neiger**	*nayzhay*
What is the weather forecast?	**Que dit la météo pour demain?**	*ker dee la maytayo poor dermang*
It's ...	**Il y a ...**	*eel ee a*
cloudy	**des nuages**	*day newazh*
foggy	**du brouillard**	*dew brooyar*
frosty	**du givre**	*dew zheevr*
icy	**du verglas**	*dew vehrgla*
thundering	**du tonnerre**	*dew tonehr*
windy	**du vent**	*dew vahng*
It's raining.	**Il pleut.**	*eel plur*
It's snowing.	**Il neige.**	*eel nayzh*
It's sunny.	**Il fait du soleil.**	*eel feh dew solayy*
Has the weather been like this for long?	**Il fait ce temps-là depuis longtemps?**	*eel feh ser tahng la derpwee lawnggtahng*
What's the pollen count?	**Quel est le taux de pollen?**	*kel eh ler toa der pollenn*
high/medium/low	**élevé/moyen/bas**	*aylervay/mwahyang/ba*
What's the forecast for skiing?	**Quelle est la météo pour le ski?**	*kel eh la maytayo poor ler skee*

PRÉVISIONS MÉTÉOROLOGIQUES	weather forecast

Enjoying your trip?
Vous passez de bonnes vacances?

Est-ce que vous êtes en vacances?	Are you on vacation?
Comment êtes-vous venu(s) ici?	How did you travel here?
Où logez-vous?	Where are you staying?
Depuis combien de temps êtes-vous ici?	How long have you been here?
Combien de temps restez-vous?	How long are you staying?
Qu'est-ce que vous avez fait jusqu'à présent?	What have you done so far?
Où allez vous ensuite?	Where are you going next?
Est-ce que vous profitez bien de vos vacances?	Are you enjoying your vacation?

I'm here on … **Je suis ici en …** *zher swee zeessee ahng*
a business trip **voyage d'affaires** *vwahyazh dafehr*
vacation [holiday] **vacances** *vakahngss*

We came … **Nous sommes venus …** *noo som vernew*
by train/by bus/by plane **en train/en bus/par avion**
ahng trang/ahng bews/par avyawng

by car/by ferry **en voiture/par le ferry**
ahng vwatewr/par ler fehree

I have a rented car. **J'ai une voiture de location.**
zhay ewn vwatewr der lokasyawng

We're staying … **Nous logeons …** *noo lozhawng*
in an apartment **dans un appartement**
dahng zang napartmahng

at a hotel/campsite **à l'hôtel/dans un camping**
a loatel/dahng zang kahngpeeng

with friends **chez des amis** *shay day zamee*
Can you suggest …? **Pouvez-vous nous conseiller …?**
poovay voo noo kawngsayay

things to do **quelque chose à faire**
kelker shoaz a fehr

places to eat **des endroits pour manger**
day zahngdrwa poor mahngzhay

places to visit **des endroits à visiter**
day zahngdrwa a veezeetay

We're having a great/ **Nous passons un très bon/**
an awful time. **très mauvais séjour.** *noo passawng*
ang treh bawng/treh moaveh sayzhoor

Invitations Invitations

Would you like to have dinner with us on …?	**Voulez-vous venir dîner avec nous …?** *voolay voo verneer deenay avek noo*
May I invite you to lunch?	**Est-ce que je peux vous inviter à déjeuner?** *ess ker zher pur voo zangveetay a dayzhurnay*
Can you come for a drink this evening?	**Est-ce que vous pouvez venir prendre un verre ce soir?** *ess ker voo poovay verneer prahngdr ang vehr ser swar*
We are having a party. Can you come?	**Nous donnons une soirée. Pouvez-vous venir?** *noo donawng ewn swaray. poovay voo verneer*
May we join you?	**Est-ce que nous pouvons nous joindre à vous?** *ess ker noo poovawng noo zhwangdr a voo*
Would you like to join us?	**Voulez-vous vous joindre à nous?** *voolay voo voo zhwangdr a noo*

Going out Sorties

What are your plans for …?	**Qu'avez-vous de prévu pour …?** *kavay voo der prayvew poor*
today/tonight	**aujourd'hui/ce soir** *oazhoordwee/ser swar*
tomorrow	**demain** *dermang*
Are you free this evening?	**Est-ce que vous êtes libre ce soir?** *ess ker voo zayt leebr ser swar*
Would you like to …?	**Est-ce que vous aimeriez …?** *ess ker voo aymeryay*
go dancing	**aller danser** *alay dahngsay*
go for a drink	**aller prendre un verre** *alay prahngdr ang vehr*
go out for a meal	**aller manger** *alay mahngzhay*
go for a walk	**faire une promenade** *fehr ewn promnahd*
go shopping	**aller faire des courses** *alay fehr day koorss*
I'd like to go to …	**J'aimerais aller à …** *zhaymray alay a*
I'd like to see …	**J'aimerais voir …** *zhaymray vwar*
Do you enjoy …?	**Aimez-vous …?** *aymay voo*

Accepting or declining
Pour accepter ou décliner

Great. I'd love to.
Avec plaisir.
avek playzeer

Thank you, but I'm busy.
Merci mais j'ai à faire.
mehrsee meh zhay a fehr

May I bring a friend?
Est-ce que je peux amener un(e) ami(e)?
ess ker zher pur amnay ang namee (ewn amee)

Where shall we meet?
Où nous retrouvons-nous?
oo noo rertroovawng noo

I'll meet you …
Je vous [te] retrouverai …
zher voo [ter] rertroovray

in front of your hotel
devant votre [ton] hôtel
devahngt votr [tawngn] oatel

I'll pick you up at 8.
Je passerai vous [te] chercher à huit heures.
zher passray voo [ter] shehrshay a weet urr

Could we make it a bit later/earlier?
Un peu plus tard/tôt si c'est possible?
ang pur plew tar/toa see seh posseebl

How about another day?
Peut-être un autre jour?
pur tetr ang noatr zhoor

That will be fine.
D'accord. *dakor*

Dining out/in   Dîner

The French don't tend to "go dutch" in restaurants. The person who has invited usually pays – with the others offering to return the favor next time.

If you are invited home for a meal, always take a gift – a box of chocolates, a nice bouquet of flowers or possibly a good wine (but not a **vin de table**).

Let me buy you a drink.
Permettez-moi de vous offrir quelque chose à boire.
pehrmettay mwa der voo zofreer kelker shoaz a bwar

Do you like …?
Aimez-vous [aimes-tu] …?
aymay voo [aym tew]

What are you going to have?
Qu'est-ce que vous prenez [tu prends]?
kess ker voo prenay [tew prahng]

That was a lovely meal.
C'était un très bon repas.
sayteh ang treh bawng repa

Encounters Rencontres

Do you mind if …?	**Ça vous dérange si …?** *sa voo dayrahngzh see*
I sit here/I smoke	**je m'asseois ici/je fume** *zher masswa eessee/zher fewm*
Can I get you a drink?	**Puis-je vous offrir quelque chose à boire?** *pweezh voo zofreer kelker shoaz a bwar*
I'd love to have some company.	**J'aimerais bien que vous veniez me tenir compagnie.** *zhaymray byang ker voo vernyay mer teneer kawngpañee*
Why are you laughing?	**Pourquoi riez-vous [ris-tu]?** *poorkwa reeay voo [ree tew]*
Is my French that bad?	**Est-ce que mon français est si mauvais que ça?** *ess ker mawng frahngseh eh see moaveh ker sa*
Shall we go somewhere quieter?	**Si on allait dans un endroit un peu plus calme?** *see awng aleh dahng zang nahngdrwa ang pur plew kalm*
Leave me alone, please!	**Laissez-moi tranquille, s'il vous plaît!** *layssay mwa trahngkee seel voo pleh*
You look great!	**Tu es très beau (belle)!** *tew eh treh boa (bell)*
Would you like to come home with me?	**Est-ce que tu veux venir finir la soirée chez moi?** *ess ker tew vur verneer feeneer la swaray shay mwa*
May I kiss you?	**Est-ce que je peux t'embrasser?** *ess ker zher pur tahngbrassay*
I'm not ready for that.	**C'est encore trop tôt.** *set ahngkor tro toa*
Thanks for the evening.	**Merci pour cette bonne soirée.** *mehrsee poor set bon swaray*
I'm afraid we've got to leave now.	**Il faut que nous partions maintenant.** *eel foa ker noo partyawng mangtnahng*
Can I see you again tomorrow?	**Est-ce que je peux vous [te] revoir demain?** *ess ker zher pur voo [ter] revwar dermang*
See you soon.	**À bientôt.** *a byangtoa*
Can I have your address?	**Est-ce que je peux avoir votre [ton] adresse?** *ess ker zher pur zavwar votr [tawngn] adress*

Telephoning   Téléphone

It's now almost impossible in France to phone using coins, except in rural areas or some cafés. Public telephone booths take phonecards, available at the post office or wherever you see the **Télécarte** sign. Simply lift the receiver, wait for dial tone, insert card and dial.

To phone home from French-speaking countries, dial 00 followed by: Australia 61; Canada 1; Ireland 353; New Zealand 64; UK 44; USA 1. Note that you will usually have to omit the initial 0 of the area code.

Can I have your telephone number?	**Pouvez-vous me donner votre numéro de téléphone?** *poovay voo mer donnay votr newmayroa der taylayfon*
Here's my number.	**Voilà mon numéro.** *vwala mawng newmayroa*
Please call me.	**Appelez-moi.** *applay mwa*
I'll give you a call.	**Je vous appellerai.** *zher vooz appellray*
Where's the nearest telephone booth?	**Où est la cabine téléphonique la plus proche?** *oo eh la kabeen taylayfoneek la plew prosh*
May I use your phone?	**Est-ce que je peux me servir de votre téléphone?** *ess ker zher pur mer sehrveer der votr taylayfon*
It's an emergency.	**C'est urgent.** *set ewrzhahng*
I'd like to call someone in England.	**Je voudrais téléphoner en Angleterre.** *zher voodray taylayfonay ahng nahnglertehr*
What's the area [dialling] code for …?	**Quel est le code pour …?** *kel eh ler kod poor*
I'd like a phone card, please.	**Je voudrais une Télécarte, s'il vous plaît.** *zher voodray ewn taylaykart seel voo pleh*
What's the number for Information [Directory Enquiries]?	**Quel est le numéro des Renseignements?** *kel eh ler newmayroa day rahngssayñmahng*
I'd like the number for …	**Je voudrais le numéro de …** *zher voodray ler newmayroa der*
I'd like to call collect [reverse the charges].	**Je voudrais faire un appel en P.C.V.** *zher voodray fehr ang nappell ahng pay say vay*

On the phone Parler au téléphone

Hello. This is …	**Allô. C'est …** *aloa. seh*
I'd like to speak to …	**Je voudrais parler à …** *zher voodray parlay a*
Extension …	**Poste …** *posst*
Speak louder/more slowly, please.	**Pouvez-vous parler plus fort/plus lentement, s'il vous plaît.** *poovay voo parlay plew for/plew lahngtmahng seel voo pleh*
Could you repeat that, please?	**Pouvez-vous répéter, s'il vous plaît?** *poovay voo raypaytay seel voo pleh*
I'm afraid he/she's not in.	**Je regrette, il/elle n'est pas là.** *zher rergrett eel/el neh pa la*
You have the wrong number.	**Vous avez fait un faux numéro.** *voo zavay feh ang foa newmayroa*
Just a moment.	**Un instant, s'il vous plaît.** *ang nangstahng seel voo pleh*
Hold on, please.	**Ne raccrochez pas, s'il vous plaît.** *ner rakroshay pa seel voo pleh*
When will he/she be back?	**Quand reviendra-t-il/elle?** *kahng rervyangdra teel/tel*
Will you tell him/her that I called?	**Pouvez-vous lui dire que j'ai appelé?** *poovay voo lwee deer ker zhay applay*
My name is …	**Je m'appelle …** *zher mapl*
Would you ask him/her to phone me?	**Pouvez-vous lui demander de me rappeler?** *poovay voo lwee dermahng-day der mer rapplay*
I must go now.	**Il faut que je vous quitte, maintenant.** *eel foa ker zher voo keet mangtnahng*
Nice to speak to you.	**J'ai été content(e) de vous parler.** *zhay aytay kawngtahng(t) der voo parlay*
I'll be in touch.	**Je vous [te] téléphonerai.** *zher voo [ter] taylayfonray*
Bye.	**Au revoir.** *oa rervwar*

Stores & Services

France still places the emphasis on small, traditional specialty stores, offering a more personal experience, although modern shopping malls are to be found in most town centers.

There are department stores. Common chains include **Galeries Lafayette, Printemps** and **Nouvelles Galeries.**

Local markets can be found everywhere, from big cities to the smallest regional towns. Flea markets (**marchés aux puces**) are also common, as are **brocantes** (secondhand/junk shops).

ESSENTIAL

I'd like …	**Je voudrais …** *zher voodray*
Do you have …?	**Avez-vous …?** *avay voo*
How much is that?	**C'est combien?** *seh kawnbyang*
Thank you.	**Merci**. *mehrsee*

OUVERT	open
FERMÉ	closed

Stores and services
Magasins et services

Where is ...? Où est ...?

Where's the nearest ...?	**Où est … le/la plus proche?** *oo eh … ler/la plew prosh*
Where's there a good ...?	**Où y a-t-il un(e) bon(ne) …?** *oo ee ateel ang (ewn) bawng (bon)*
Where's the main mall [shopping centre]?	**Où est le centre commercial principal?** *oo eh ler sahngtr komehrsyal prangseepal*
Is it far from here?	**Est-ce loin d'ici?** *ess lwang deessee*
How do I get there?	**Comment puis-je y aller?** *kommahng pweezh ee alay*

Stores Magasins

antiques shop	**l'antiquaire** *lahngteekehr*
bakery	**la boulangerie** *la boolahngzhree*
bank	**la banque** *la bahngk*
bookstore [shop]	**la librairie** *la leebrehree*
butcher shop	**la boucherie** *la boosheree*
camera shop	**le magasin de photos** *ler magazang der foto*
cigarette kiosk [tobacconist]	**le (bureau de) tabac** *ler (bewroa der) taba*
clothing store [clothes shop]	**le magasin de vêtements** *ler magazang der vetmahng*
delicatessen	**le charcutier/le traiteur** *ler sharkewtyay/ler treturr*
department store	**le grand magasin** *ler grahng magazang*
drugstore	**la droguerie** *la drogree*
fish store [fishmonger]	**la poissonnerie** *la pwassonree*
florist	**le fleuriste** *ler flurreest*
gift shop	**le magasin de cadeaux** *ler magazang der kadoa*
greengrocer	**le marchand de fruits et légumes** *ler marshahng der frwee ay laygewm*
grocery store/grocer	**l'épicerie** *laypeesree*
health food store	**le magasin de diététique** *ler magazang der dyaytayteek*

jewelry store [jeweller]	**la bijouterie**
	la beezhootree
market	**le marché** *ler marshay*
newsstand [newsagent]	**le kiosque à journaux**
	ler keeosk a zhoornoa
pastry shop	**la pâtisserie** *la pateesree*
pharmacy [chemist]	**la pharmacie** *la farmassee*
record/music store	**le magasin de disques**
	ler magazang der deesk
shoe store	**le magasin de chaussures**
	ler magazang der shoassewr
shopping mall [centre]	**le centre commercial**
	ler sahngtr komehrsyal
souvenir store	**le magasin de souvenirs**
	ler magazang der soovneer
sporting goods store	**le magasin d'articles de sport**
	ler magazang darteekl der spor
supermarket	**le supermarché** *ler sewpehrmarshay*
toy and game store	**le magasin de jouets**
	ler magazang der zhooeh
liquor store [off-licence]	**le marchand de vin**
	ler marshahng der vang

Services Services

dentist	**le dentiste** *ler dahngteest*
doctor	**le médecin** *ler maydsang*
dry cleaner	**le pressing/nettoyage à sec**
	ler presseeng/netwahyazh a sek
hairdresser (ladies/men)	**le coiffeur (femmes/hommes)**
	ler kwafurr (fam/om)
hospital	**l'hôpital** *loapeetal*
laundromat	**la laverie automatique**
	la lavree oatomateek
library	**la bibliothèque** *la beebleeotek*
optician	**l'opticien** *lopteesyang*
police station	**le commissariat (de police)**
	ler komeessarya (der poleess)
post office	**la poste** *la posst*
travel agency	**l'agence de voyages**
	lazhahngss der vwahyazh

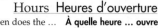

Hours Heures d'ouverture

When does the … open/close? **À quelle heure … ouvre-t-il/ferme-t-il?** *a kel urr … oovr teel/fehrm teel*

Are you open in the evening? **Êtes-vous ouverts le soir?** *ayt voo oovehr ler swahr*

Do you close for lunch? **Fermez-vous pour le déjeuner?** *fehrmay voo poor ler dayzhurnay*

General times in France, (Belgium) and [Switzerland].				
General times for:	Opening	Closing	Lunch break	Closed
stores	9/8	5.30-7 (6) [6.30]	12-2	Sun, Mon (a.m.)
department stores	9/9.30	7/7.30	none	Sun, Mon (a.m.)
supermarkets	9	9/10	none	Sun, Mon (a.m)
post office	8 (7.30) [9]	6.30/7 (6.30) [6]	12-2 12-2 [1.45]	Sat p.m., Sun weekend
banks	8.30/9 (9) [8.30]	4.30/5 (3.30/4) [4.30–5.30]	12-1.30 12.30–1.30	weekend weekend

Where is the …? **Où est …?** *oo eh*

cashier [cash desk] **la caisse** *la kess*

escalator **l'escalier roulant** *leskalyay roolahng*

elevator [lift] **l'ascenseur** *lassahngsurr*

store guide **le plan du magasin** *ler plahng dew magazang*

first [ground] floor **rez-de-chaussée** *ray der shoassay*

second [first] floor **premier étage** *prermyay aytazh*

Where's the … department? **Où est le rayon des …?** *oo eh ler rayawng deh*

HEURES D'OUVERTURE	business hours
FERMÉ POUR LE DÉJEUNER	closed for lunch
OUVERT TOUTE LA JOURNÉE	open all day
SORTIE	exit
SORTIE DE SECOURS	emergency/fire exit
ENTRÉE	entrance
ESCALIERS	stairs
ESCALIER ROULANT	escalator
ASCENSEUR	elevator

Service   Service

Can you help me?	**Pouvez-vous m'aider?** *poovay voo mayday*
I'm looking for …	**Je cherche …** *zher shehrsh*
I'm just browsing.	**Je regarde seulement.** *zher rergard surlmahng*
It's my turn.	**C'est à moi.** *set a mwa*
Do you have any …?	**Avez vous …?** *avay voo*
I'd like to buy …	**Je voudrais acheter …** *zher voodray ashtay*
Could you show me …?	**Pouvez-vous me montrer …?** *poovay voo mer mawngtray*
How much is this/that?	**Combien coûte ceci/celà?** *kawnbyang koot sersee/serla*
That's all, thanks.	**C'est tout, merci.** *seh too mehrsee*

Bonjour, madame/monsieur.	Good morning/afternoon, madam/sir.
Je peux vous aider?	Can I help you?
Vous désirez?/Qu'est-ce que vous voulez?	What would you like?
Je vais vérifier.	I'll just check that for you.
Ce sera tout?	Is that everything?
Et avec ça?/Il vous faut autre chose?	Anything else?

– *Je peux vous aider?* (Can I help you?)
– Non, merci. Je regarde seulement.
  (No, thanks. I'm just browsing.)
    – D'accord. (Fine.)
– Excusez-moi. (Excuse me.)
– *Oui, je peux vous aider?* (Yes, can I help you?)
– C'est combien? (How much is that?)
– *Hmm, je vais vérifier … C'est quatre-vingt-dix-huit francs.*
  (Hm, I'll just check that for you … It's 98 francs.)

ACCUEIL	reception
SOLDES	sale

Choices Préférence

I want something …	**Je voudrais quelque chose de …** *zher voodray kelker shoaz der*
It must be …	**Ça doit être …** *sa dwa tetr*
large/small	**grand/petit** *grahng/pertee*
cheap/expensive	**bon marché/cher** *bawng marshay/shehr*
dark/light	**foncé/clair** *fawngsay/klehr*
light/heavy	**léger/lourd** *layzhay/loor*
oval/round/square	**ovale/rond/carré** *ovahl/rawng/karay*
genuine/imitation	**un original/d'imitation** *ang oreezheenal/deemeetasyawng*
I don't want anything too expensive.	**Je ne veux pas quelque chose de trop cher.** *zher ner vur pa kelker shoaz der tro shehr*
About … francs.	**Dans les … francs environ.** *dawng lay … frahng ahngveerawng*

Quel(le) … voulez vous?	What … would you like?
couleur/forme	color/shape
qualité/quantité	quality/quantity
Quel genre voulez-vous?	What kind would you like?
Dans quel ordre de prix cherchez-vous?	What price range are you thinking of?

Do you have anything …?	**Avez-vous quelque chose de …?** *avay voo kelker shoaz der*
larger	**plus grand** *plew grahng*
better quality	**meilleure qualité** *mayurr kaleetay*
cheaper	**moins cher** *mwang shehr*
smaller	**plus petit** *plew pertee*
Can you show me …?	**Pouvez-vous me montrer …?** *poovay voo mer mawngtray*
that/this one	**celui-là (celle-là)/celui-ci (celle-ci)** *serlwee la (sel la)/serlwee see (sel see)*
these/those	**ceux-ci (celles-ci)/ceux-là (celles-là)** *sur see (sel see)/sur la (sel la)*
the one in the window/display case	**celui en vitrine** *serlwee ahng veetreen*
some others	**d'autres** *doatr*

COLORS ➤ 143

Conditions of purchase
Conditions d'achat

Is there a guarantee?

Y a-t-il une garantie?
ee ateel ewn garahngtee

Are there any instructions with it?

Est-ce qu'il y a des instructions?
ess keel ee a day zangstrewksyawng

Out of stock Épuisé

Je regrette, nous n'en avons plus.	I'm sorry, we don't have any.
L'article/Le stock est épuisé.	We're out of stock.
Est-ce que je peux vous montrer quelque chose d'autre?	Can I show you something else?
Voulez-vous que nous le commandions?	Shall we order it for you?

Can you order it for me?

Pouvez-vous me le commander?
poovay voo mer ler kommahngday

How long will it take?

Il faudra combien de temps?
eel foadra kawnbyang der tahng

Where else could I get …?

Où est-ce que je pourrais trouver …?
oo ess ker zher pooray troovay

Decision Décision

That's not quite what I want.

Ce n'est pas vraiment ce que je veux.
ser neh pa vraymahng ser ker zher vur

That's too expensive.

C'est trop cher. *seh tro shehr*

I'll take it.

Je le prends. *zher ler prahng*

– Bonjour madame. Je voudrais un sweat-shirt.
(Hello. I'd like a sweatshirt.)
– *Quel genre voulez-vous?*
(What kind would you like?)
– Orange, s'il vous plaît.
Et je voudrais quelque chose de grand.
(Orange, please. And I'd like something large.)
– *Voilà. C'est cinq cent francs.*
(Here you are. It's 500 francs.)
– Hmm, ce n'est pas vraiment ce que je cherche. Merci.
(Hm, that's not quite what I want. Thank you.)

Paying Paiement

Sales tax (**TVA**) is imposed on almost all goods and services; this is included in the TTC (**toutes taxes comprises**) price. Tax can be reclaimed on larger purchases when returning home (outside the EU).

Where do I pay?	**Où dois-je payer?** *oo dwazh payay*
How much is that?	**C'est combien?** *seh kawnbyang*
Could you write it down, please?	**Pourriez-vous me l'écrire, s'il vous plaît?** *pooryay voo mer laykreer seel voo pleh*
Do you accept traveler's checks [cheques]?	**Acceptez-vous les chèques de voyage?** *akseptay voo lay shek der vwahyazh*
I'll pay …	**Je paie …** *zher payy*
by cash	**en liquide** *ahng leekeed*
by credit card	**avec une carte de crédit** *avek ewn kart der kraydee*
I don't have any small change.	**Je n'ai pas de monnaie.** *zher nay pa der monayy*
Sorry, I don't have enough money.	**Je regrette, je n'ai pas assez d'argent.** *zher rergret, zher nay pa zassay darzhahng*

Comment payez-vous?	How are you paying?
Cette transaction n'a pas été approuvée/acceptée.	This transaction has not been approved/accepted.
Cette carte n'est pas valide.	This card is not valid.
Avez-vous une pièce d'identité?	May I have further identification?
Avez-vous de la monnaie?	Have you got any small change?

Could I have a receipt please?	**Est-ce que je peux avoir un ticket de caisse?** *ess ker zher pur avwar ang teekeh der kess*
I think you've given me the wrong change.	**Je crois que vous vous êtes trompé en me rendant la monnaie.** *zher krwa ker voo voo zayt trawngpay ahng mer rahngdahng la monayy*

PAYEZ ICI	please pay here
LES VOLEURS SERONT POURSUIVIS (EN JUSTICE)	shoplifters will be prosecuted

Complaints Plaintes

This doesn't work.	**Il y a un défaut.** *eel ee a ang dayfoa*
Can you exchange this, please?	**Pouvez-vous échanger ceci, s'il vous plaît?** *poovay voo zayshah- ngzhay sersee seel voo pleh*
I'd like a refund.	**Je voudrais être remboursé(e).** *zher voodray etr rahngboorsay*
Here's the receipt.	**Voici le ticket de caisse.** *vwasee ler teekeh der kess*
I don't have the receipt.	**Je n'ai pas le ticket de caisse.** *zher nay pa ler teekeh der kess*
I'd like to see the manager.	**Je voudrais voir le directeur du magasin** *zher voodray vwar ler deerekturr dew magazang*

Repairs/Cleaning Réparations

A **teinturerie** or a **pressing** is a dry cleaner, sometimes combined with a laundry (**blanchisserie**). If you want a self-service laundromat, look for **laverie automatique.**

This is broken. Can you repair it?	**C'est cassé. Pouvez-vous le réparer?** *seh kassay. poovay voo ler rayparay*
Do you have ... for this?	**Avez-vous ... pour ceci?** *avay voo ... poor sersee*
a battery	**une pile** *ewn peel*
replacement parts	**des pièces de rechange** *day pyes der rershahngzh*
There's something wrong with ...	**Quelque chose ne marche pas dans ...** *kelker shoaz ner marsh pa dahng*
Can you ... this?	**Pouvez-vous le ...?** *poovay voo ler*
clean	**nettoyer** *netwahyay*
press	**repasser** *rerpassay*
patch	**raccommoder** *rakomoday*
Could you alter this?	**Pouvez-vous y faire des retouches?** *poovay voo zy fehr day rertoosh*
When will it be ready?	**Quand sera-t-il prêt?** *kahng sera teel preh*
This isn't mine.	**Ce n'est pas à moi.** *ser neh pa za mwa*
There's ... missing.	**Il manque ...** *eel mahngk*

TIME ➤ 220; DATE ➤ 218

Bank/Currency exchange office
Banque/Bureau de change

Cash can be obtained from ATMs [cash machines] with Visa, Eurocard, American Express and many other international cards.

Remember your passport when you want to change money.

Not all banks provide currency exchange services – hotels will sometimes provide an exchange facility, but only to their guests.

Where's the nearest …?	**Où est … le/la plus proche?** *oo eh … ler/la plew prosh*
bank	**la banque** *la bahngk*
currency exchange office [bureau de change]	**le bureau de change** *ler bewroa der shahngz*

OUVERT/FERMÉ	open/closed
POUSSEZ/TIREZ/APPUYEZ	push/pull/press
CAISSES	cashiers
TOUTES TRANSACTIONS	all transactions

Changing money Pour changer de l'argent

Can I exchange foreign currency here?	**Est-ce que je peux changer des devises étrangères ici?** *ess ker zher pur shahngzhay day derveez aytrahngzhehr eessee*
I'd like to change some dollars/pounds into francs.	**Je voudrais changer des dollars/livres en francs.** *zher voodray shahngzhay day dolar/leevr ahng frahng*
I want to cash some traveler's checks.	**Je voudrais encaisser des chèques de voyage.** *zher voodray ahngkessay day shek der vwahyazh*
What's the exchange rate?	**Quel est le taux (de change)?** *kel eh ler toa (der shahngz)*
How much commission do you charge?	**Quelle commission prenez-vous?** *kel komeesyawng prernay voo*
Could I have some small change?	**Est-ce que je pourrais avoir de la petite monnaie?** *ess kerzher pooray avwar der la perteet monayy*
I've lost my traveler's checks [cheques]. These are the numbers.	**J'ai perdu mes chèques de voyage. Voici les numéros.** *zhay pehrdew may shek der vwahyazh. vwasee lay newmayroa*

Security Sécurité

Est-ce que je peux voir…?	Could I see …?
votre passeport	your passport
une pièce d'identité	some identification
votre carte bancaire	your bank card
Quelle est votre adresse?	What's your address?
Où logez-vous?	Where are you staying?
Pouvez-vous remplir cette fiche, s'il vous plaît.	Fill in this form, please.
Signez ici, s'il vous plaît.	Please sign here.

ATMs [Cash machines] Distributeur automatique

Can I withdraw money on my credit card here?
Est-ce que je peux retirer de l'argent avec ma carte de crédit ici? *ess ker zher pur rerteeray der larzhahng avek ma kart der kraydee eessee*

Where are the ATMs [cash machines]?
Où sont les distributeurs automatiques? *oo sawng lay deestreebewturr oatomateek*

Can I use my … card in the ATM [cash machine]?
Est-ce que je peux me servir de ma carte … dans ce distributeur? *ess ker zher pur mer sehrveer der ma kart … dahng ser deestreebewturr*

The machine has eaten my card.
Le distributeur a avalé ma carte. *ler deestreebewturr a avalay ma kart*

DISTRIBUTEUR AUTOMATIQUE	automated teller/ cash machine

Currency	100 centimes (ct.) = 1 franc (F, FF, FB, Fr.)
France	*Coins:* 5, 10, 20, 50 ct.; 1, 2, 5, 10, 20 FF
	Notes: 20, 50, 100, 200, 500 FF
Belgium	*Coins:* 50ct; 1, 5, 20, 50 FB
	Notes: 100, 500, 1000, 2000, 5000 FB
Switzerland	*Coins:* 5, 10, 20, 50 ct.; 1, 2, 5 Fr.
	Notes: 10, 20, 50, 100, 500, 1000 Fr.

Pharmacy   Pharmacie

Pharmacies are easily recognized by their sign: a green cross, usually lit up.

If you are looking for a pharmacy at night or during weekends, you'll find a list of **pharmacies de garde** (emergency pharmacies) in the window of any pharmacy or in the local newspaper.

In addition to pharmaceutical products, pharmacies in France also sell toiletries and cosmetics. A **parfumerie** or **grand magasin** (department store) will usually have a more extensive range of perfumes and cosmetics, while a **droguerie** generally sells toiletries and household products only.

Where's the nearest (all-night) pharmacy?	**Où est la pharmacie (de garde) la plus proche?** *oo eh la farmassee (der gard) la plew prosh*
What time does the pharmacy open/close?	**À quelle heure ouvre/ferme la pharmacie?** *a kel urr oovr/fehrm la farmassee*
Can you make up this prescription for me?	**Pouvez-vous me préparer cette ordonnance?** *poovay voo mer prayparay set ordonahngss*
Shall I wait?	**Est-ce que je dois attendre?** *ess ker zher dwa atahngdr*
I'll come back for it.	**Je reviendrai la chercher.** *zher rvyangdray la shehrshay*

Dosage instructions Posologie

How much should I take?	**Combien dois-je en prendre?** *kawnbyang dwazh ahng prahngdr*
How often should I take it?	**Combien de fois dois-je le prendre?** *kawnbyang der fwa dwazh ler prahngdr*
Is it suitable for children?	**Est-ce que ça convient aux enfants?** *ess ker sa kawngvyang oa zahngfahng*

Prenez ... comprimés/ cuillerées à café ...	Take ... tablets/... teaspoons ...
avant/après les repas	before/after meals
avec un verre d'eau	with water
entier (sans croquer)	whole (without chewing)
le matin/le soir	in the morning/at night
pendant ... jours	for ... days

DOCTOR ➤ 161

Asking advice Pour demander conseil

What would you recommend for …?	**Qu'est-ce que vous me recommandez pour …?** *kess ker voo mer rerkommahngday poor*
a cold	**le rhume** *ler rewm*
a cough	**la toux** *la too*
diarrhea	**la diarrhée** *la deearay*
a hangover	**la gueule de bois** *la gurl der bwa*
hay fever	**le rhume des foins** *ler rewm day fwang*
insect bites	**les piqûres d'insectes** *lay peekewr dangsekt*
a sore throat	**le mal de gorge** *ler mal der gorzh*
sunburn	**les coups de soleil** *lay koo der solayy*
motion [travel] sickness	**le mal des transports** *ler mal day trahngspor*
an upset stomach	**le mal de ventre** *ler mal der vahngtr*
Can I get it without a prescription?	**Puis-je l'obtenir sans ordonnance?** *pweezh lobterneer sahng zordonahngss*

Over-the-counter treatment
Médicaments délivrés sans ordonnance

Can I have …?	**Pouvez-vous me donner …?** *poovay voo mer donay*
antiseptic cream	**une crème antiseptique** *ewn la krem ahngteessepteek*
(soluble) aspirin	**de l'aspirine (soluble)** *der laspeereen (solewbl)*
gauze [bandage]	**un bandage** *ang bahngdazh*
condoms	**des préservatifs** *day prayzehrvateef*
cotton [cotton wool]	**du coton (hydrophile)** *dew kotawng (ydrofeel)*
insect repellent	**une crème/lotion contre les insectes** *ewn krem/losyawng kawngtr lay zangsekt*
pain killers	**des analgésiques** *day zanalzhayzeek*
vitamin pills	**des vitamines** *day veetameen*

Toiletries Articles de toilette

	I'd like …	**Je voudrais …** *zher voodray*
	aftershave	**de la lotion après-rasage** *der la losyawng apreh razazh*
	after-sun lotion	**de la lotion après-soleil** *der la losyawng apreh solayy*
deodorant		**un déodorant** *ang dayodorahng*
moisturizing cream		**de la crème hydratante** *der la krem ydratahngt*
razor blades		**des lames de rasoir** *day lam der razwar*
sanitary napkins [towels]		**des serviettes hygiéniques** *day sehrvyet yzhyayneek*
soap		**du savon** *dew savawng*
sun block		**de l'écran total** *der laykrahng total*
suntan lotion		**de la crème solaire** *der la krem solehr*
factor …		**facteur …** *fakturr*
tampons		**des tampons** *day tahngpawng*
tissues		**des mouchoirs en papier** *day mooshwar ahng papyay*
toilet paper		**du papier toilette/hygiénique** *dew papyay twalet/yzhyayneek*
toothpaste		**du dentifrice** *dew dahngteefreess*

Hair care Soins des cheveux

comb	**un peigne** *ang payñ*
conditioner	**de l'après-shampooing** *der lapreh shahngpwang*
hair mousse	**de la mousse pour cheveux** *der la mooss poor shervur*
hair spray	**de la laque** *der la lak*
shampoo	**du shampooing** *dew shahngpwang*

For the baby Pour le bébé

baby food	**des aliments pour bébé** *day zaleemahng poor baybay*
baby wipes	**des lingettes** *day langzhet*
diapers [nappies]	**des couches** *day koosh*
sterilizing solution	**de la solution de stérilisation** *der la solewsyawng der stayreeleezasyawng*

Clothing Habillement

Paris is renowned for its haute couture houses and their prêt-à-porter boutiques, for example: **Dior, Givenchy, Lanvin, Saint-Laurent, Ungaro, Féraud, Gaultier, Yamamoto, Hermès.**

You'll find that airport boutiques offering tax-free shopping may have cheaper prices but less selection.

General   Généralités

I'd like …	**Je voudrais …** *zher voodray*
Do you have any …?	**Avez-vous des …?** *avay voo deh*

VÊTEMENTS FEMMES	ladies wear
VÊTEMENTS HOMMES	menswear
VÊTEMENTS ENFANTS	childrens' wear

Color   Couleur

I'm looking for something in …	**Je cherche quelque chose en …** *zher shehrsh kelker shoaz ahng*
beige	**beige** *bayzh*
black	**noir** *nwar*
blue	**bleu** *blur*
brown	**marron** *marawng*
green	**vert** *vehr*
gray	**gris** *gree*
orange	**orange** *orahngzh*
pink	**rose** *roz*
purple	**violet** *veeoleh*
red	**rouge** *roozh*
white	**blanc** *blahng*
yellow	**jaune** *zhoan*
light …	**… clair** *klehr*
dark …	**… foncé** *fawngsay*
I want a darker/lighter shade.	**Je veux une teinte plus foncée/claire.** *zher vur ewn tangt plew fawngsay/klehr*
Do you have the same in …?	**Avez-vous le même en …?** *avay voo ler mem ahng*

Clothes and accessories
Vêtements et accessoires

belt	**une ceinture** *ewn sangtewr*
bikini	**un bikini** *ang beekeenee*
blouse	**un chemisier** *ang shermeezyay*
bra	**un soutien-gorge** *ang sootyang gorzh*
shorts/briefs	**une culotte** *ewn kewlot*
cap	**une casquette** *ewn kasket*
coat	**un manteau** *ang mahngtoa*
dress	**une robe** *ewn rob*
handbag	**un sac à main** *ang sak a mang*
hat	**un chapeau** *ang shapoa*
jacket	**une veste** *ewn vest*
jeans	**un jean** *ang dzheen*
leggings	**un legging** *ang legging*
pants	**un pantalon** *ang pahngtalawng*
pantyhose [tights]	**un collant** *ang kolahng*
pullover	**un pull-over/pull** *ang pewlovehr/pewl*
raincoat	**un imperméable** *ang nangpehrmayabl*
scarf	**une écharpe** *ewn aysharp*
shirt	**une chemise** *ewn shermeez*
shorts	**un short** *ang short*
skirt	**une jupe** *ewn zhewp*
socks	**des chaussettes** *day shoasset*
stockings	**des bas** *day ba*
suit	**un costume** *ang kostewm*
sweatshirt	**un sweat-shirt** *ang sweatshirt*
swimming trunks	**un slip de bain** *ang sleep der bang*
swimsuit	**un maillot de bain** *ang mahyo der bang*
T-shirt	**un T-shirt** *ang T-shirt*
tie	**une cravate** *ewn kravat*
underpants	**un slip** *ang sleep*
with long/short sleeves	**à manches longues/courtes** *a mahngsh lawngg/koort*
with V-/round neck	**à encolure en V/ronde** *a ahngkolewr ahng v/rawng*

Shoes Chaussures

A pair of ...	**Une paire de ...** *ewn pehr der*
boots	**bottes** *bott*
flip-flops	**tongs** *tawng*
sandals	**sandales** *sahngdal*
shoes	**chaussures** *shoassewr*
slippers	**pantoufles** *pahngtoofl*
trainers	**chaussures de sport** *shoassewr der spor*

Hiking/walking gear Équipement pour la marche

windbreaker	**un coupe-vent** *ang koop vahng*
knapsack	**un sac à dos** *ang sak a doa*
walking boots	**des chaussures de marche** *day shoassewr der marsh*
waterproof jacket	**un blouson imperméable** *ang bloozawng angpehrmayabl*

Fabric Tissu

I want something in ...	**Je veux quelque chose en ...** *zher vur kelker shoaz ahng*
cotton	**coton** *kotawng*
denim	**jean** *dzheen*
lace	**dentelle** *dahngtel*
leather	**cuir** *kweer*
linen	**lin** *lang*
wool	**laine** *layn*
Is this ...?	**Est-ce ...?** *ess*
pure cotton	**pur coton** *pewr kotawng*
synthetic	**en synthétique** *ahng sangtayteek*
Is it hand washable/ machine washable?	**Est-ce lavable à la main/lavable en machine?** *ess lavabl a la mang/ lavabl ahng masheen*

GRAND TEINT/NE DÉTEINT PAS	colorfast
LAVAGE MAIN SEULEMENT	handwash only
NE PAS REPASSER	do not iron
NETTOYAGE À SEC SEULEMENT	dry clean only

Does it fit? Ça va?

Can I try this on?	**Est-ce que je peux essayer ça?** *ess ker zher pur essayay sa*
Where's the fitting room?	**Où sont les cabines d'essayage?** *oo sawng lay kabeen dessayazh*
It fits well. I'll take it.	**Ça va bien. Je le prends.** *sa va byang. zher ler prahng*
It doesn't fit.	**Ça ne va pas.** *sa ner va pa*
It's too ...	**C'est trop ...** *seh tro*
short/long	**court/long** *koort/lawng*
tight/loose	**étroit/ample** *aytrwa/ahngpl*
Do you have this in size ...?	**Est-ce que vous avez ceci en taille ...?** *ess ker voo zavay sersee ahng tie*
What size is this?	**C'est quelle taille?** *seh kel tie*
Could you measure me, please?	**Pouvez-vous prendre mes mesures?** *poovay voo prahngdr may mezuwr*
I don't know French sizes.	**Je ne connais pas les tailles françaises.** *zher ner koneh pa lay tie frahngsayz*

Size Taille

Note that in French, clothes size is **la taille**, shoe (and glove) size is **la pointure**.

	Dresses/Suits						Women's shoes			
American	8	10	12	14	16	18	6	7	8	9
British	10	12	14	16	18	20	$4^{1/2}$	$5^{1/2}$	$6^{1/2}$	$7^{1/2}$
Continental	36	38	40	42	44	46	37	38	40	41

	Shirts				Men's shoes							
American } **British**	15	16	17	18	5	6	7	8	$8^{1/2}$ 9	$9^{1/2}$ 10	11	
Continental	38	41	43	45	38	39	41	42	43	43 44	44	45

EXTRA GRAND	extra large (XL)
GRAND	large (L)
MOYEN	medium (M)
PETIT	small (S)

1 centimeter (cm.) = 0.39 in.   1 inch = 2.54 cm.
1 meter (m.) = 39.37 in.   1 foot = 30.5 cm.
10 meters = 32.81 ft.   1 yard = 0.91 m.

Health and beauty Santé et beauté

I'd like a ...
Je voudrais ...
zher voodray

facial
des soins du visage
day swang dew veezazh

manicure
une manucure *ewn manewkewr*

massage
un massage *ang massazh*

waxing
une épilation à la cire
ewn aypeelasyawng a la seer

Hairdresser's/Hairstylist Coiffeur

Tipping: France: 10% (generally included in price); Belgium: 15% (generally included); Switzerland: included.

I'd like to make an appointment for ...
Je voudrais prendre un rendez-vous pour ...
zher voodray prahngdr ang rahngday voo poor

Can you make it a bit earlier/later?
Est-ce que je peux venir un peu plus tôt/tard? *ess ker zher pur verneer ang pur plew toa/tar*

I'd like a ...
Je voudrais ... *zher voodray*

cut and blow-dry
une coupe et un brushing
ewn koop ay ang brursheeng

shampoo and set
un shampooing et une mise en plis
ang shahngpwang ayt ewn meez ahng plee

I'd like a trim.
Je voudrais me faire égaliser les pointes.
zher voodray mer fehr aygaleezay lay pwangt

I'd like my hair ...
Je voudrais ... *zher voodray*

highlighted
des mèches *day mesh*

permed
une permanente *ewn pehrmanahngt*

Don't cut it too short.
Ne les coupez pas trop court.
ner lay koopay pa tro koor

A little more off the ...
Pouvez-vous en couper un peu plus ...
poovay voo zahng koopay ang pur plews

back/front
derrière/devant *dehrryehr/devahng*

neck/sides
dans le cou/sur les côtés
dahng ler koo/sewr lay koatay

top
sur le dessus *sewr ler derssew*

That's fine, thanks.
Très bien, merci. *treh byang mehrsee*

Household articles Articles ménagers

	I'd like …	**Je voudrais …** *zher voodray*
	adapter	**un adaptateur** *ang nadaptaturr*
	aluminum foil	**du papier aluminium** *dew papyay alewmeenyom*
bottle opener		**un ouvre-bouteilles** *ang noovr bootayy*
candles		**des bougies** *day boozhee*
clothespins [pegs]		**des pinces à linge** *day pangss a langzh*
corkscrew		**un tire-bouchon** *ang teer booshawng*
light bulb		**une ampoule** *ewn ahngpool*
matches		**des allumettes** *day zalewmett*
paper napkins		**des serviettes en papier** *day sehrvyett ahng papyay*
plastic wrap [cling film]		**du film alimentaire** *dew feelm aleementair*
plug		**une prise** *ewn preez*
scissors		**des ciseaux** *day seezoa*
screwdriver		**un tournevis** *ang toornerveess*
can [tin] opener		**un ouvre-boîte** *ang noovr bwat*

Cleaning products Produits de nettoyage

bleach	**de l'eau de Javel** *der loa der zhavel*
dish cloth [tea towel]	**une lavette** *ewn lavet*
dishwashing [washing-up] detergent	**de la poudre pour lave-vaisselle** *der la poodr poor lav vessel*
garbage [refuse] bags	**des sacs poubelles** *day sak poobel*
sponge	**une éponge** *ewn aypawngzh*
detergent [washing powder]	**de la lessive** *der la lesseev*
dishwashing [washing-up] liquid	**du liquide vaisselle** *dew leekeed vessell*

Dishes/Utensils [Crockery/Cutlery] Vaisselle/Couverts

cups	**des tasses** *day tass*
forks	**des fourchettes** *day foorshet*
glasses	**des verres** *day vehr*
knives	**des couteaux** *day kootoa*
mugs	**des chopes** *day shop*
plates	**des assiettes** *day zassyet*
spoons	**des cuillères** *day kweeyehr*
teaspoons	**des cuillères à café** *day kweeyehr a kafay*

Jeweler's Chez le bijoutier

Could I see …?	**Est-ce que je pourrais voir …?** *ess ker zher pooray vwar*
this/that	**ceci/cela** *sersee/serla*
It's in the window/ display case.	**C'est en vitrine.** *set ahng veetreen*
I'd like …	**Je voudrais …** *zher voodray*
alarm clock	**un réveil** *ang rayvayy*
battery	**une pile** *ewn peel*
bracelet	**un bracelet** *ang brasleh*
brooch	**une broche** *ewn brosh*
chain	**une chaîne(tte)** *ewn shen(ett)*
clock	**une pendule** *ewn pahngdewl*
earrings	**des boucles d'oreilles** *day bookl dorayy*
necklace	**un collier** *ang kolyay*
ring	**une bague** *ewn bag*
watch	**une montre** *ewn mawngtr*

Materials Matériaux

Is this real silver/gold?	**Est-ce de l'argent/de l'or véritable?** *ess der larzhahng/der lor vayreetabl*
Is there a certificate for it?	**Y a-t-il un certificat?** *ee ateel ang sehrteefeeka*
Do you have anything in …?	**Avez-vous quelque chose en …?** *avay voo kelker shoaz ahng*
copper	**cuivre** *kweever*
crystal	**cristal** *kreestal*
cut glass	**verre taillé** *vehr tieyay*
diamond	**diamant** *deeamahng*
enamel	**émail** *aymie*
gold	**or** *or*
goldplate	**plaqué or** *plakay or*
pearl	**perle de culture** *pehrl der kewltewr*
pewter	**étain** *aytang*
platinum	**platine** *plateen*
silver	**argent** *arzhahng*
silverplate	**plaqué argent** *plakay arzhahng*
stainless steel	**acier inoxydable** *asyay eenoxeedabl*

Newsstand/Newsagent/Tobacconist
Marchand de journaux–Tabac

Newsstands (**maison de la presse** or **bureau de presse**), identifiable by their yellow sign with a red feather, sell magazines, newspapers, some paperbacks and stationery and sometimes cigarettes. Foreign newspapers can usually be found at railroad stations or airports or on newsstands in Paris and other major cities.

Do you sell English-language books/newspapers?	**Vendez-vous des livres/journaux en anglais?** *vahngday voo day leevr/zhoornoa ahng ahnggleh*
I'd like …	**Je voudrais …** *zher voodray*
book	**un livre** *ang leevr*
candy [sweets]	**des bonbons** *day bawngbawng*
chewing gum	**un chewing-gum** *ang shooweeng gom*
chocolate bar	**une tablette de chocolat** *ewn tablet der shokola*
pack of cigarettes	**un paquet de cigarettes** *ang pakeh der seegarett*
cigars	**des cigares** *day seegar*
dictionary	**un dictionnaire** *ang deeksyonehr*
French-English	**français-anglais** *frahngseh ahnggleh*
envelopes	**des enveloppes** *day zahngvlop*
guidebook of …	**un guide de/sur …** *ang geed der/sewr*
lighter	**un briquet** *ang breekeh*
magazine	**un magazine** *ang magazeen*
map of the town	**un plan de la ville** *ang plahng der la veel*
road map of …	**une carte routière de …** *ewn kart rootyehr der*
matches	**des allumettes** *day zalewmet*
newspaper	**un journal** *ang zhoornal*
American/English	**américan/anglais** *amayreekamg/ahnggleh*
paper	**du papier** *dew papyay*
pen	**un stylo** *ang steelo*
postcard	**une carte postale** *ewn kart postal*
stamps	**des timbres** *day tangbr*
candy	**des bonbons** *day bawngbawng*
tobacco	**du tabac** *dew taba*

Photography Photographie

I'm looking for a ... camera.	**Je cherche un appareil photo ...** *zher shehrsh ang naparayy foto*
automatic	**automatique** *oatomateek*
compact	**compact** *kawngpakt*
disposable	**jetable** *zhertabl*
SLR (single lens reflex)	**reflex** *rerflex*
I'd like ...	**Je voudrais** *zher voodray*
battery	**une pile** *ewn peel*
camera case	**un sac photo** *ang sak foto*
(electronic) flash	**un flash (électronique)** *ang flash (aylektroneek)*
filter	**un filtre** *ang feeltr*
lens	**un objectif** *ang nobzhekteef*
lens cap	**un couvercle** *ang koovehrkl*

Film/Processing Développement

I'd like a ... film for this camera.	**Je voudrais une pellicule ... pour cet appareil photo.** *zher voodray ewn peleekewl ... poor set aparayy foto*
black and white	**noir et blanc** *nwar ay blahng*
color	**couleur** *koolurr*
24/36 exposures	**24/36 poses** *vangtkatr/trahngtsee poz*
I'd like this film developed.	**Je voudrais faire développer cette pellicule.** *zher voodray fehr dayvlopay set peleekewl*
Would you enlarge this, please?	**Pourriez-vous agrandir ceci?** *pooryay voo zagrahngdeer sersee*
How much do ... exposures cost?	**Combien coûtent ... poses?** *kawnbyang koot ... poz*
When will the photos be ready?	**Quand est-ce que les photos seront prêtes?** *kahng tess ker lay foto serawng prayt*
I'd like to pick up my photos. Here's the receipt.	**Je viens chercher mes photos. Voilà le reçu.** *zher vyang shehrshay may foto. vwala ler rersew*

Police Police

Crime, theft, accidents or injuries should be reported to the **commissariat de police** in major cities or to the **gendarmerie nationale** in smaller towns.

To get the police in an emergency, ☎ 17 in France, ☎ 101 in Belgium, ☎ 117 in Switzerland.

Where's the nearest police station?	**Où est le commissariat le plus proche?** *oo eh ler komeessarya ler plew prosh*
Does anyone here speak English?	**Est-ce qu'il y a quelqu'un ici qui parle anglais?** *ess keel ee a kelkang eessee kee parl ahnggleh*
I want to report a(n) ... accident/attack	**Je veux signaler ...** *zher vur seeñalay* **un accident/une attaque** *ang nakseedahng/ewn atak*
mugging/rape	**une agression/un viol** *ewn agresyawng/ang vyol*
My child is missing.	**Mon enfant a disparu.** *Mawng nahngfahng a deesparew*
Here's a photo of him/her.	**Voilà sa photo.** *vwala sa foto*
Someone's following me.	**Quelqu'un me suit.** *kelkang mer swee*
I need an English-speaking lawyer.	**Il me faut un avocat qui parle anglais.** *eel mer foa ang navoka kee parl ahnggleh*
I need to make a phone call.	**Je dois téléphoner à quelqu'un.** *zher dwa taylayfonay a kelkang*
I need to contact the ... Consulate. American/British	**Je dois contacter le consulat ...** *zher dwa kawngtaktay ler kawngsewla* **américain/britannique** *amayreekang/breetaneek*

Pouvez-vous le/la décrire?	Can you describe him/her?
homme/femme	male/female
blond(e)/brun(e)/roux(-sse)/ aux cheveux gris	blonde/brunette/red-headed/ gray
aux cheveux longs/courts/ un peu chauve	long/short hair/balding
qui mesure environ ...	approximate height ...
qui a environ ... ans	aged (approximately) ...
Il/Elle portait ...	He/She was wearing ...

CLOTHES ➤ 144; COLORS ➤ 143

Lost property/Theft Pertes/Vol

I want to report a theft/break-in.	**Je veux signaler un cambriolage.** *zher vur seeñalay ang kahngbreeolazh*
I've been robbed/mugged.	**J'ai été volé/agressé.** *zhay aytay volay/agressay*
I've lost my …	**J'ai perdu …** *zhay pehrdew*
My … has been stolen.	**On m'a volé …** *awng ma volay*
bicycle	**mon vélo** *mawng vaylo*
camera	**mon appareil photo** *mawng naparayy foto*
(rental) car	**ma voiture (de location)** *ma vwatewr (der lokasyawng)*
credit cards	**mes cartes de crédit** *may kart der kraydee*
handbag	**mon sac à main** *mawng sak a mang*
money	**mon argent** *mawng arzhahng*
passport	**mon passeport** *mawng passpor*
purse	**mon porte-monnaie** *mawng port monayy*
ticket	**mon billet** *mawng beeyeh*
wallet	**mon portefeuille** *mawng portfuhy*
watch	**ma montre** *ma mawngtr*
What shall I do?	**Que dois-je faire?** *ker dwa zher fehr*
I need a police report/form for my insurance claim.	**Il me faut un certificat de police pour ma compagnie d'assurances.** *eel mer foa ang sehrteefeeka der poleess poor ma kawngpañee dassewrahngss*

Qu'est-ce qui (vous) manque?	What's missing?
Quand cela s'est-il passé?	When did it happen?
Où logez-vous?	Where are you staying?
Où a-t-il/elle été volé(e)?	Where was it taken from?
Où étiez-vous à ce moment-là?	Where were you at the time?
Nous allons vous procurer un interprète.	We're getting an interpreter for you.
Nous allons faire une enquête.	We'll look into the matter.
Pouvez-vous remplir ce formulaire, s'il vous plaît?	Please fill out this form.

153

Post Office Poste

In addition to the normal range of services at French post offices – **La Poste** – you can buy **Télécartes** (phonecards) and use a **Minitel terminal** (➤ 155) for free services such as finding addresses and telephone numbers.

Swiss and French post offices are recognized by the **PTT** sign and Belgian by **Postes** or **Posterijen**. Mailboxes (yellow in France and Switzerland, red in Belgium) may have separate slots for postcards (**cartes postales**), letters (**lettres**) and abroad (**l'étranger**).

General inquiries Questions d'ordre général

Where is the post office?	**Où est le bureau de poste?** *oo eh ler bewroa der post*
What time does the post office open/close?	**À quelle heure ouvre/ferme la poste?** *a kel urr oovr/fehrm la post*
Does it close for lunch?	**Est-elle fermée pour le déjeuner?** *eh el fehrmay poor ler dayzhurnay*
Where's the mailbox [postbox]?	**Où est la boîte aux lettres?** *oo eh la bwat oa letr*
Is there any mail for me?	**Est-ce qu'il y a du courrier pour moi?** *ess keel ee a dew kooryay poor mwa*

Buying stamps Pour acheter des timbres

A stamp for this postcard, please.	**Un timbre pour cette carte postale, s'il vous plaît.** *ang tangbr poor set kart postal seel voo pleh*
A …-franc stamp, please.	**Un timbre à … francs, s'il vous plaît.** *ang tangbr a … frahng seel voo pleh*
What's the postage for a letter to …?	**Quel est le tarif pour une lettre pour …?** *kel eh ler tareef poor ewn letr poor*
Is there a stamp machine here?	**Y a-t-il une machine à affranchir ici?** *ee ateel ewn masheen a afrahngsheer eessee*

– Bonjour, je voudrais envoyer ces cartes
postales aux États-Unis.
(Hello. I'd like to send these postcards to the U.S.)
– *Combien? (How many?)*
– Neuf, s'il vous plaît. (Nine, please.)
– *Ça fait deux francs cinquante, multiplié par neuf:*
vingt-deux francs cinquante, s'il vous plaît.
(That's 2.50 francs times nine: 22.50 francs please.)

Sending packages Pour envoyer des colis

I want to send this package [parcel] by …	**Je voudrais envoyer ce paquet …** *zher voodray ahngvwahyay ser pakeh*
airmail	**par avion** *par avyawng*
special delivery [express]	**en exprès** *ahng express*
It contains …	**Il contient …** *eel kawngtyang*

Veuillez remplir la déclaration de douane, s'il vous plaît.	Please fill out the customs declaration.
Quelle est la valeur?	What is the value?
Qu'y a-t-il à l'intérieur?	What's inside?

Telecommunications Télécommunications

I'd like a phonecard.	**Je voudrais une Télécarte/carte de téléphone.** *zher voodray ewn taylaykart/kart der taylayfon*
50/120 units.	**50/120 unités.** *sangkant/shangvangt ewneetay*
Do you have a photocopier?	**Est-ce qu'il y a un photocopieur?** *ess keel ee a ang fotokopyurr*
I'd like to send a message …	**Je voudrais envoyer un message …** *zher voodray engvoiyay ang mesarj …*
by E-mail/fax	**par e-mail/fax** *par eemail/fax*
What's your E-mail address?	**Quelle est votre adresse e-mail?** *kel eh votrer adres eemail*
Can I access the Internet here?	**Est-ce que je peux accéder à l'internet ici ?** *esker je pur aksedeh eesee a l'internet*
What are the charges per hour?	**C'est combien par heure?** *say combyang par hur*
How do I log on?	**Comment j'entre en communication?** *comong zhentr eng comunicasyon*

Minitel *meeneetel*

French telecommunications system with over 7,000 services (some in English). Terminals can be found in most public buildings, including the post office, for free services (including telephone directory). Access to a private terminal (charges go on the phone bill) allows booking tickets, home shopping, etc.

Souvenirs   Souvenirs locaux

Here are some suggestions for souvenirs from Belgium.

chocolate	**le chocolat**	*ler shokola*
crystal	**le cristal**	*ler kreestal*
glassware	**la verrerie**	*la vehrehree*
leather	**le cuir**	*ler kweer*
tapestry	**une tapisserie**	*ewn tapeessehree*

Popular souvenirs for visitors to Switzerland include chocolate, as well as:

cheese	**le fromage**	*ler fromazh*
cuckoo clocks	**les coucoux**	*lay kookoo*
Swiss Army knives	**les canifs**	*lay kaneef*
watches	**les montres**	*lay mawngtr*
wooden products	**les articles en bois**	*lay arteekl ahng bwa*
lace	**les dentelles**	*lay dahngtell*

Visitors to France may be attracted by cheeses, wines, liqueurs, as well as:

mustard	**la moutarde**	*la mootard*
perfume	**le parfum**	*ler parfahng*
porcelain	**la porcelaine**	*la poorserlehn*
pottery	**la poterie**	*la pottree*
(cast-iron) saucepans	**des casseroles (en fonte)**	*day cassrol (ahng font)*

Gifts   Cadeaux

bottle of wine	**une bouteille de vin**	*ewn bootayy der vang*
box of chocolates	**une boîte de chocolats**	*ewn bwat der shokola*
calendar	**un calendrier**	*ang kalahngdreeay*
cloth (for drying dishes)	**un torchon**	*ang torshawng*
key ring	**un porte-clefs**	*ang port klay*
postcard	**une carte postale**	*ewn kart postal*
souvenir guide	**un guide-souvenir**	*ang geed soovneer*
T-shirt	**un T-shirt**	*ang T-shirt*

Music Musique

I'd like a ...

Je voudrais ...
zher voodray

cassette

une cassette *ewn kassett*

compact disc

un compact disc
ang kawngpakt deesk

record

un disque *ewn deesk*

videocassette

une cassette vidéo *ewn kassett veedayo*

Who are the popular
French singers/bands?

**Quels sont les chanteurs/groupes
français populaires?** *kel sawng lay
shahngturr/groop frahngseh popewlehr*

Toys and games Jouets et jeux

I'd like a toy/game ...

Je voudrais un jouet/un jeu ...
zher voodray ang zhooeh/ang zhur

for a boy

pour un garçon *poor ang garsawng*

for a 5-year-old girl

pour une fille de cinq ans
poor ewn fee der sangk ahng

pail and shovel
[bucket and spade]

un seau et une pelle
ang soa ay ewn pel

chess set

un jeu d'échecs *ang zhur dayshek*

doll

une poupée *ewn poopay*

electronic game

un jeu électronique
ang zhur aylektroneek

teddy bear

un ours en peluche
ang oorss ahng perlewsh

Antiques   Antiquités

How old is this?

Cela a quel âge? *serla a kel azh*

Do you have anything
from the ... era?

**Avez-vous quelque chose de la
période ...?** *avay voo kelker shoaz
der la payryod*

Can you send it to me?

Pouvez-vous me l'envoyer?
poovay voo mer lahngvwahyay

Will I have problems
with customs?

**Est-ce que je risque d'avoir des
problèmes à la douane?** *ess ker zher
reesk davwar day problem a la doowan*

Is there a certificate
of authenticity?

Y a-t-il un certificat d'authenticité?
*ee ateel ang sehrteefeeka
doatahngteesseetay*

ARTISTIC PERIODS ➤ 104

Supermarket/Convenience store
Supermarché/Minimarché

Supermarkets such as **Monoprix**, **Prisunic** and **Casino** can be found in town centers; huge out-of-town hypermarkets such as **Carrefour**, **Leclerc**, **Mammouth** and **Auchan** encompass every shop you might find in the center. Convenience stores (**libres-services**) tend to be open until late, while **épiceries** – very small supermarkets – (including the **Félix Potin**, **Casino** and **Franprix** chains) offer good products and service.

At the supermarket Au supermarché

Excuse me. Where can I find …?	**Excusez-moi. Où se trouve(nt) …?** *exkewzay mwa. oo ser troov*
Do I pay for this here or at the checkout?	**Je paye ça ici ou à la caisse?** *zher payy sa eessee oo a la kess*
Where are the baskets/carts [trolleys]?	**Où sont les paniers/les chariots?** *oo sawng lay panyay/lay sharyoa*
Is there a … here?	**Y a-t-il … ici?** *ee ateel … eessee*
delicatessen	**un traiteur** *ang treturr*
pharmacy	**une pharmacie** *ewn farmassee*

EN ESPECE SEULEMENT	cash only
ARTICLES MÉNAGERS	household goods
BOUCHERIE	fresh meat
BOULANGERIE–PÂTISSERIE	bread and cakes
CONSERVES	canned fruit/vegetables
FRUITS ET LÉGUMES	fresh produce
POISSONNERIE	fresh fish
PRODUITS D'ENTRETIEN	cleaning products
PRODUITS LAITIERS/CRÉMERIE	dairy products
SURGELÉS	frozen foods
VINS ET SPIRITUEUX	wines and spirits
VOLAILLE	poultry

Weights and measures

- 1 kilogram or kilo (**kg.**) = 1000 grams (**g.**); 100 g. = 3.5 oz.; **1 kg.** = 2.2 lb [1 oz. = **28.35 g.**; 1 lb. = **453.60 g.**]
- 1 liter (**l.**) = 0.88 imp. quart or 1.06 U.S. quart [1 imp. quart = **1.14l.** 1 U.S. quart = **0.95l l.** 1 imp. gallon = **4.55 l.** 1 U.S. gallon = **3.8l.**]

Food hygiene Hygiène alimentaire

À CONSERVER AU FROID/ AU RÉFRIGÉRATEUR	keep refrigerated
À CONSOMMER DANS LES … JOURS APRÈS OUVERTURE	eat within … days of opening
CONVIENT AUX VÉGÉTARIENS	suitable for vegetarians
DATE LIMITE DE VENTE …	sell by …
POUR FOUR À MICRO-ONDES	microwaveable
RÉCHAUFFER AVANT DE CONSOMMER	reheat before eating

At the convenience store Au magasin d'alimentation

I'd like some of that/these.	**Je voudrais de ça/ceci.** _zher voodray der sa/sersee_
This one/Those	**Celui-ci/Ceux-là** _serlweesee/sur la_
To the left/right	**À gauche/droite** _a goash/drwaht_
Over there/Here	**Là-bas/Ici** _la ba/eessee_
Which one/ones?	**Lequel/lesquelles?** _lerkel_
That's all thanks.	**C'est tout, merci**. _seh too mehrsee_
I'd like …	**Je voudrais …** _zher voodray_
kilo of apples	**un kilo de pommes** _ang keelo der pom_
half-kilo of tomatoes	**une livre de tomates** _ewn leevr der tomat_
100 grams of cheese	**cent grammes de fromage** _sahng gram der fromazh_
liter of milk	**un litre de lait** _ang leetr der leh_
half-dozen eggs	**une demi-douzaine d'œufs** _ewn dermee doozayn dur_
… slices of ham	**… tranches de jambon** _trahngsh der zhahngbawng_
piece of cake	**un morceau de gâteau** _ang morsoa der gatoa_
bottle of wine	**une bouteille de vin** _ewn bootayy der vang_
carton of milk	**une brique de lait** _ewn breek der leh_
jar of jam	**un pot de confiture** _ang po der kawngfeetewr_
bag of chips [crisps]	**un paquet de chips** _ang pakeh der sheeps_
can of coke	**une boîte de coca** _ewn bwat der kola_

> – Je voudrais une livre de ce fromage, s'il vous plaît.
> (I'd like a pound of that cheese, please.)
> – *Celui-ci?* (This one?)
> – Oui, le Camembert, s'il vous plaît.
> (Yes, the "Camembert", please.)
> – *Très bien. Et avec ça?*
> (Certainly. Anything else?)
> – Quatre tranches de jambon, s'il vous plaît.
> (Four slices of ham, please.)
> – *Voilà.* (Here you are.)

Provisions/Picnic   Provisions/Pique-nique

beer	**de la bière**	*der la byehr*
butter	**du beurre**	*dew bur*
cheese	**du fromage**	*dew fromazh*
cookies [biscuits]	**des biscuits**	*day beeskwee*
eggs	**des œufs**	*day zur*
grapes	**du raisin**	*dew rezang*
instant coffee	**du café soluble**	*dew kafay solewbl*
loaf of bread	**du pain**	*dew pang*
margarine	**de la margarine**	*der la margareen*
milk	**du lait**	*dew leh*
rolls (bread)	**des petits pains**	*day pertee pang*
sausages	**des saucisses**	*day soasseess*
soft drinks/sodas	**des boissons gazeuses**	
	day bwassawng gazurz	
tea bags	**des sachets de thé**	*day sasheh der tay*
wine	**du vin**	*dew vang*

une baguette   *ewn baget*
traditional French bread loaf: variations include **une demi-baguette** (half-size), **une ficelle** (a thinner, crusty version), **une couronne** (ring-shaped) and **un bâtard** (baton).

un gâteau   *ang gatoa*
cake; for example **une tartelette aux fruits** (small fruit tart), **un mille-feuille** (napoleon/cream or vanilla slice), **un éclair** and **une religieuse** (frosted cream puff, shaped like a nun's habit).

un pain   *ang pang*
loaf of bread, which may be **complet** (wholemeal/wheat), **de campagne** (white bread dusted with flour), **de mie** (sliced, sandwich loaf), **de seigle** (like rye bread), **au son** (with added bran) or **brioché** (sweet and rich).

MEAT ➤ 45; VEGTABLES ➤ 47

Health

Before you leave, make sure your health insurance policy covers any illness or accident while on vacation.

You'll be expected to pay doctors and dentists on the spot. EU citizens with a Form E111 should be able to obtain reimbursement (but not in Switzerland). But make sure the doctor you see is a **médecin conventionné**. These doctors charge the minimum and their fees are accepted by the social security system. In an emergency, the doctor will come out to you: call **SOS Médecins**. Ambulance: France ☎ 18, Belgium ☎ 100, Switzerland ☎ 114; **SAMU** (French emergency ambulance) ☎ 567 50 50.

Doctor/General Médecin/Généralités

Where can I find a doctor/dentist [surgery]?	**Où est-ce que je peux trouver un médecin/dentiste?** *oo ess ker zher pur troovay ang maydsang/dahngteest*
Where's there a doctor who speaks English?	**Où y a-t-il un médecin qui parle anglais?** *oo ee a teel ang maydsang kee parl ahngleh*
What are the office hours?	**Quelles sont les heures de consultation au cabinet?** *kel sawng lay zurr der kawngsewltasyawng oa kabeeneh*
Could the doctor come to see me here?	**Est-ce que le médecin pourrait venir me voir?** *ess ker ler maydsang pooreh verneer mer vwar*
Can I make an appointment for ...?	**Est-ce que je peux prendre rendez-vous pour ...?** *ess ker zher pur prahngdr rahngdayvoo poor*
today/tomorrow	**aujourd'hui/demain** *oazhoordwee/dermang*
as soon as possible	**le plus tôt possible** *ler plew toa posseebl*
It's urgent.	**C'est urgent.** *seht ewrzhang*
I've got an appointment with Doctor ...	**J'ai rendez-vous avec docteur ...** *zhay rahngdayvoo avek dokturr*

TIME ➤ 220; DATE ➤ 218

Accident and injury Accidents et blessures

My … is hurt/injured.	**… s'est fait mal/est blessé(e).** *seh feh mal/eh blessay*
husband/wife	**Mon mari/Ma femme** *mawng maree/ma fam*
son/daughter	**Mon fils/Ma fille** *mawng feess/ma fee*
friend	**Mon ami(e)** *mawng amee*
He/She is …	**Il/Elle est …** *eel/el eh*
unconscious	**sans connaissance** *sahng konessahngss*
(seriously) injured	**(gravement) blessé(e)** *(gravmahng) blessay*
He/She is bleeding (heavily).	**Il/Elle saigne (beaucoup).** *eel/el señ (boakoo)*
I've got a/an …	**J'ai …** *zhay*
blister	**une ampoule** *ewn angpool*
boil	**un furoncle** *ang fewrawngkl*
burn	**une brûlure** *ewn brewlewr*
cut	**une coupure** *ewn koopewr*
insect bite	**une piqûre d'insecte** *ewn peekewr dangsekt*
lump	**une boule/bosse** *ewn bool/boss*
rash	**une éruption cutanée** *ewn ayrewpsyawng kewtanay*
scratch [graze]	**une égratignure** *ewn aygrateeñewr*
sprained muscle	**un muscle froissé** *ang mewskl frwassay*
swelling	**une enflure** *ewn ahngflewr*
It hurts here.	**J'ai mal ici.** *zhay mal eessee*

Short-term symptoms
Symptômes immédiats

I've been feeling sick [ill] for … days.
Je suis malade depuis … jours. *zher swee malad derpwee … zhoor*

I feel faint.
Je vais m'évanouir. *zher vay mayvanooweer*

I feel feverish.
J'ai de la fièvre. *zhay der la fyehvr*

I've been vomiting.
J'ai vomi. *zhay vomee*

I've got diarrhea.
J'ai la diarrhée. *zhay la deearay*

It hurts here.
J'ai mal ici. *zhay mal eessee*

I have (a/an) …
J'ai … *zhay*

backache
mal au dos *mal oa doa*

cold
un rhume *ang rewm*

cramps
des crampes *day krangp*

earache
mal à l'oreille *mal a lorayy*

headache
mal à la tête *mal a la tet*

sore throat
mal à la gorge *mal a la gorzh*

stiff neck
un torticolis *ang torteekolee*

stomachache
mal à l'estomac *mal a lestoma*

sunstroke
une insolation *ewn angsolasyawng*

Health conditions Problèmes médicaux

I have arthritis.
J'ai de l'arthrite *zhay der lartreet*

I have asthma.
J'ai de l'asthme. *zhay der lastm*

I am …
Je suis … *zher swee*

deaf
sourd *soor*

diabetic
diabétique *deeabayteek*

epileptic
épileptique *aypeelepteek*

handicapped
handicapé(e) *ahngdeekapay*

(… months) pregnant
enceinte (de … mois) *ahngsangt (der … mwa)*

I have a heart condition.
Je souffre du cœur. *zher soofr dew kurr*

I have high blood pressure.
J'ai de l'hypertension. *zhay der leepehrtahngsyawng*

I had a heart attack … years ago.
J'ai eu une crise cardiaque il y a … ans. *zhay ew ewn kreez kardyak eel ee a … ahng*

Doctor's inquiries Questions du docteur

Depuis combien de temps vous sentez-vous comme ça?	How long have you been feeling like this?
Est-ce que c'est la première fois que vous avez ça?	Is this the first time you've had this?
Est-ce que vous prenez d'autres médicaments?	Are you taking any other medicines?
Est-ce que vous êtes allergique à quelque chose?	Are you allergic to anything?
Est-ce que vous avez été vacciné(e) contre le tétanos?	Have you been vaccinated against tetanus?
Est-ce que vous avez perdu l'appétit?	Have you lost your appetite?

Examination Examen (médical)

Je vais prendre votre température/tension.	I'll take your temperature/ blood pressure.
Remontez votre manche, s'il vous plaît.	Roll up your sleeve, please.
Déshabillez-vous jusqu'à la ceinture, s'il vous plaît.	Please undress to the waist.
Allongez-vous, s'il vous plaît.	Please lie down.
Ouvrez la bouche.	Open your mouth.
Respirez profondément.	Breathe deeply.
Toussez, s'il vous plaît.	Cough please.
Où est-ce que vous avez mal?	Where does it hurt?
Est-ce que ça vous fait mal ici?	Does it hurt here?

Diagnosis Diagnostic

Il faut vous faire une radio.	I want you to have an x-ray.
J'ai besoin d'une prise de sang/ d'un examen des selles/ d'une analyse d'urine.	I want a specimen of your blood/stool/urine.
Je veux que vous alliez voir un spécialiste.	I want you to see a specialist.
Je veux vous hospitaliser.	I want you to go to the hospital.
C'est cassé/foulé.	It's broken/sprained.
C'est disloqué/déchiré.	It's dislocated/torn.

Vous avez ...	You have (a/an) ...
les amygdales	tonsillitis
l'appendicite	appendicitis
le cancer	cancer
une cystite	cystitis
une fracture	fracture
une gastrite	gastritis
la grippe	flu
des hémorroïdes	hemorrhoids
une hernie	hernia
une inflammation de ...	inflammation of ...
une intoxication alimentaire	food poisoning
la jaunisse	jaundice
une maladie vénérienne	venereal disease
une pneumonie	pneumonia
la rougeole	measles
une sciatique	sciatica
une tumeur	tumor
C'est infecté.	It's infected.
C'est contagieux.	It's contagious.

Treatment Traitement

Je vais vous donner	I'll give you ...
un antiseptique	an antiseptic
un calmant/analgésique	a pain killer
Je vais vous prescrire ...	I'm going to prescribe ...
des antibiotiques	a course of antibiotics
des suppositoires	some suppositories
Est-ce que vous êtes allergique à certains médicaments?	Are you allergic to any medicines?
Prendre une pilule/un comprimé	Take one pill
toutes les ... heures	every ... hours
... fois par jour	... times a day
avant/après les repas	before/after each meal
en cas de douleurs	in case of pain
pendant ... jours	for ... days
Consultez un médecin à votre retour.	Consult a doctor when you get home.

Parts of the body Parties du corps

appendix	**l'appendice** *lapangdeess*
arm	**le bras** *ler bra*
back	**le dos** *ler doh*
bladder	**la vessie** *la vessee*
bone	**l'os** *loss*
breast	**le sein** *ler sang*
chest	**la poitrine** *la pwatreen*
ear	**l'oreille** *lorayy*
eye	**l'œil** *loy*
face	**le visage** *ler veezazh*
finger	**le doigt** *ler dwa*
foot	**le pied** *ler pyay*
gland	**la glande** *la glahngd*
hand	**la main** *la mang*
head	**la tête** *la tet*
heart	**le cœur** *le kurr*
jaw	**la mâchoire** *la mashwar*
joint	**l'articulation** *larteekewlasyawng*
kidney	**le rein** *ler rang*
knee	**le genou** *ler zhernoo*
leg	**la jambe** *la zhangb*
lip	**la lèvre** *la levr*
liver	**le foie** *ler fwa*
mouth	**la bouche** *la boosh*
muscle	**le muscle** *ler mewskl*
neck	**le cou** *ler koo*
nose	**le nez** *ler nay*
rib	**la côte** *la koat*
shoulder	**l'épaule** *laypoal*
skin	**la peau** *la poa*
stomach	**l'estomac** *lestoma*
thigh	**la cuisse** *la kweess*
throat	**la gorge** *la gorzh*
thumb	**le pouce** *le pooss*
toe	**l'orteil** *lortayy*
tongue	**la langue** *la lahngg*
tonsils	**les amygdales** *lay zameegdal*
vein	**la veine** *la ven*

Gynecologist Le gynécologue

I have …
**J'ai … ** *zhay*

abdominal pains
des douleurs abdominales
day doolurr abdomeenal

period pains
des règles douloureuses
day regl dooloorurz

a vaginal infection
une infection vaginale
ewn angfeksyawng vazheenal

I haven't had my period for … months.
Je n'ai pas eu mes règles depuis … mois.
zher nay pa ew meh regl derpwee … mwa

I'm on the Pill.
Je prends la pilule.
zher prahng la peelewl

Hospital À l'hôpital

Please notify my family.
Est-ce que vous pouvez prévenir ma famille? *ess ker voo poovay prayvneer ma famee*

I'm in pain.
J'ai mal./Je souffre.
zhay mal/zher soofr

I can't eat/sleep.
Je ne peux pas manger/dormir.
zher ner pur pa mahngzhay/dormeer

When will the doctor come?
Quand est-ce que le docteur passera? *kahng ess ker ler dokturr passra*

Which section [ward] is … in?
Dans quelle chambre est …?
dahng kel shangbr eh

I'm visiting …
Je viens voir … *zher vyang vwar*

Optician Chez l'opticien

I'm nearsighted/farsighted [shortsighted/longsighted]
Je suis myope/hypermétrope.
zher swee meeop/eepehrmaytrop

I've lost …
J'ai perdu … *zhay pehrdew*

one of my contact lenses
une de mes lentilles de contact
ewn der meh lahngtee der kawngtakt

my glasses
mes lunettes *meh lewnett*

a lens
un verre *ang vehr*

Could you give me a replacement?
Est-ce que vous pourriez m'en donner un(e) de remplacement? *ess ker voo pooryay mahng donnay ang (ewn) der rahngplassmahng*

Dentist Chez le dentiste

I have a toothache.	**J'ai mal aux dents.** *zhay mal oa dahng*
This tooth hurts.	**Cette dent me fait mal.** *set dahng mer feh mal*
I've lost a filling/tooth.	**J'ai perdu un plombage/une dent.** *zhay pehrdew ang plawngbazh/ ewn dahng*
Can you repair this denture?	**Est-ce que vous pouvez réparer ce dentier?** *ess ker voo poovay rayparay ser dahngtyay*
I don't want it extracted.	**Je ne veux pas que vous me l'arrachiez.** *zher ner vur pa ker voo mer larashyay*

Je vais vous faire une piqûre/ une anesthésie locale.	I'm going to give you an injection/ a local anesthetic.
Il faut vous faire un plombage/ vous mettre une couronne.	You need a filling/cap [crown].
Je dois l'arracher.	I'll have to take it out.
Je ne peux vous donner qu'un traitement provisoire.	I can only fix it temporarily.
Ne mangez rien pendant … heures.	Don't eat anything for … hours.

Payment and Insurance Paiement et assurance

How much do I owe you?	**Combien vous dois-je?** *kawnbyang voo dwazh*
I have insurance.	**J'ai une assurance.** *zhay ewn assewrahngss*
Can I have a receipt for my health insurance?	**Puis-je avoir un reçu pour mon assurance maladie?** *pweezh avwar ang rersew poor mawng nassewrahngss maladee*
Would you fill out this health insurance form, please?	**Pouvez-vous remplir cette feuille d'assurance maladie?** *poovay voo rahngpleer set fuhy dassewrahngss maladee*
Do you have …?	**Est-ce que vous avez …?** *ess ker voo zavay*
Form E111/health insurance	**un imprimé E111/une assurance maladie** *ang angpreemay er sang awngz/ewn assewrahngss maladee*

Dictionary
English – French

A-Z

Many terms in this dictionary are cross-referenced to pages
where the word appears in a full phrase. In addition, the notes
below provide some basic grammar guidelines.

Nouns

Nouns in French are classed as either masculine (m) or feminine (f).
Their plurals (pl) are usually formed by adding -s. The articles they
take (a, an, the, some) depend on their gender:

masculine			feminine		
le train	the train		**la voiture**	the car	
un train	a train		**une voiture**	a car	
les trains	the trains		**les voitures**	the cars	
des trains	some trains		**des voitures**	some cars	

Note that **le** and **la** become **l'** before a vowel or a silent **h** (eg. **l'hôtel**)

Adjectives

Adjectives agree in gender and number with the noun they are describ-
ing. In this dictionary the feminine form (where it differs from the
masculine) is shown in brackets, e.g.

	feminine form:	
grand(e) - large		**grande**
heureux(-euse) - happy		**heureuse**
dernier(-ière) - last		**dernière**

Note: most adjectives follow the noun.

Verbs

Here are two useful verbs in the present tense.

être	to be	**avoir**	to have
je suis	I am	**j'ai**	I have
tu es	you are	**tu as**	you have
il/elle est	he/she (it) is	**il/elle a**	he/she (it) has
nous sommes	we are	**nous avons**	we have
vous êtes	you are	**vous avez**	you have
ils/elles sont	they are	**ils/elles ont**	they have

Verbs are generally shown in the infinitive (to say, to eat, etc.) Although
there isn't space here to show how every verb declines, the infinitive
form can be used after the following phrases:

je vais + inf.	I'm going to	**j'aime** +inf.	I love to
nous allons +inf.	we're going to	**je voudrais** +inf.	I'd like to
je dois +inf.	I ought to	**nous voudrions** +inf.	we'd like to
nous devons +inf.	we ought to	**je ne veux pas** +inf.	I don't want to

Negatives are generally formed by putting **ne** before the verb and **pas**
after it.

a few quelques un(e)s 15
a little un peu 15
a lot beaucoup 15
a.m. du matin
able, to be (also ►can, could) pouvoir
about (approximately) environ 15
above (place) au-dessus de
abroad à l'étranger m
abscess abcès m
abseiling descente f en rappel
accept, to accepter 136;
do you accept...? acceptez-vous?
access (n) accès m 100
accessories accessoires mpl 144
accident accident m 152; (road) accident (de la route) m 92
accommodations logement m
accompany, to accompagner 65
accountant comptable m
ace (cards) as m
across de l'autre côté de, en face de 12
acrylic acrylique
action film film m d'aventure/d'action
activities activités fpl
actor/actress acteur m/actrice f
adapter adaptateur m 148
address adresse f 84, 93, 126
adjoining room chambre f à côté 22
admission charge prix m d'entrée
adult adulte m 81, 100
advance, in à l'avance
aerial (car/tv) "antenne" f
after après 13, 95; **aftershave lotion** lotion f après-rasage 142; **after-sun lotion** lotion f après-soleil 142
afternoon, in the l'après-midi 221
age: what age? quel âge?
aged, to be avoir... ans 152
... ago il y a... 13
agree: I agree je suis d'accord
air air m; **~ conditioning** climatisation f 22, 25; **~ mattress** matelas m pneumatique 31; **~ pump** compresseur m (pour l'air) 87; **~ freshener** désodorisant m
airline compagnie f aérienne
airmail par avion m 155
airport aéroport m 96

airplane avion m
air steward/hostess hôtesse f de l'air
aisle seat siège m côté couloir 69, 74
alarm clock réveil m 149
alcoholic (drink) alcoolique
all tous/toutes
all-night pharmacy pharmacie f de garde 140
allergic, to be être allergique 164
allergy allergie f
allowance quantité f autorisée 67
allowed: is it allowed? est-ce que c'est permis?
almost presque
alone seul(e)
already déjà 28
also aussi
alter, to faire des retouches 137
always toujours 13
am: I am je suis
ambassador ambassadeur m
ambulance ambulance f 92
American (adj) américain(e) 150, 152; (n) américain; **~ football** football m américain
amount somme f, montant m 42
amusement arcade salle f de jeux 113
anchor, to mouiller l'ancre
and et
anesthetic anesthésie f
angling pêche f (à la ligne)
animal animal m 106
anorak anorak m
another un(e) autre 21; **~ day** un autre jour 125
antibiotics antibiotiques mpl
antifreeze antigel m
antiques antiquité f 157; **~ shop** antiquaire m 130
antiseptic antiseptique 165; **~ cream** crème f antiseptique 141
any du, de l', de la
anyone quelqu'un; **~ else** quelqu'un d'autre m 93
anything cheaper quelque chose de moins cher 21
anything else? autre chose?
apartment appartement m 28
apologize: I apologize excusez-moi
apples pommes f/p 159

A-Z

appointment rendez-vous m 161; **to make an ~** prendre rendez-vous 147
approximately environ 152
April avril m 218
archery tir m à l'arc
architect architecte 104
architecture architecture f
are you...? est-ce que vous êtes...?
area région f
area code code m 127
arm bras m 166
armbands *(swimming)* brassards mpl gonflables, flotteurs mpl
around *(place)* autour de; *(time)* vers 13
arrange, to: can you arrange it? pouvez-vous vous en occuper?
arrest, to be under être en état d'arrestation
arrive, to arriver 68, 70, 71; **to ~ in** arriver à 76
art art; **~ gallery** galerie f d'art/ de peinture 99
artery artère f
arthritis, to have avoir de l'arthrose/arthrite 163
artificial sweetener édulcorant m 38
artist artiste 104
as soon as possible dès que possible
ashore, to go débarquer
ashtray cendrier m 39
ask, to demander; **I asked for...** j'ai demandé... 41
asleep, to be être endormi, dormir
aspirin aspirine f 141
asthma, to have avoir de l'asthme 163
at *(place)* à la, à l', au, aux 12; *(time)* à 13
at least au moins 23
attack attaque f 152; *(medical)* crise f, attaque f
attendant gardien(ne) m/f
attractive joli(e)
August août m 218
aunt tante 120
Australia Australie f 119
Australian *(adj)* australien(ne); *(n)* Australien(ne) m/f
authenticity authenticité f 157
automated teller/ATM distributeur m automatique 139

automatic *(car, camera)* automatique 86, 151
autumn automne m 219
avalanche avalanche f
away loin de 12
awful affreux(-se)

B **baby** bébé m 39, 113; **~ bottle** biberon m; **~ food** aliments mpl pour bébé 142; **~ seat** siège m pour bébé m; **~ sitter** baby-sitter f, garde f d'enfants; **~ wipes** lingettes fpl 142
back dos m 166
backache mal m au dos 163
backpacking faire du tourisme à pied
bad mauvais(e) 14
baggage bagages mpl 32, 71; **~ allowance** poids m de bagages; **~ check** (**office**) consigne f 71, 73; **~ reclaim** consigne f
bakery boulangerie f 130, 158
balance of account bilan m des comptes
balcony balcon m 29
ball ballon m, balle f
ballet ballet m 108, 111
band *(musical)* groupe m 111, 157
bandage bandage m 141
bank banque f 130, 138; **~ account** compte m bancaire; **~ card** carte f bancaire 139; **~ loan** prêt m bancaire
bar bar m 112; *(hotel)* bar m 26
barbecue barbecue m
barber coiffeur m (pour hommes)
barge péniche m
basement sous-sol m
basin lavabo m
basket panier m 158
bath: to take a bath prendre un bain; **~ towel** serviette f de bain 27; **~ room** salle f de bains 29
bathrooms toilettes fpl 26, 98; WC mpl
battery pile f 137, 149, 151; *(car)* batterie f 88
battleground champ m de bataille 99
be, to *(also ➤ am, are)* être 17; **I am** je suis; **we are** nous sommes

beach plage f 116
beard barbe f
beautiful beau (belle) 14, 101
because parce que 15; ~ **of** à cause de 15
bed lit m 21; ~ **room** chambre f 29; **I'm going to** ~ je vais au lit; ~ **and breakfast** chambre f et petit déjeuner m 24
bedding literie f 29
bee abeille f
beer bière f 40, 160
before *(time)* avant 13, 221
begin, to *(also* ➤*start)* commencer
beginner débutant(e) m/f 117
beginning commencement m, début m
beige beige 143
Belgian *(adj)* belge; *(n)* Belge m/f
Belgium Belgique f 119
below 15°C en-dessous de 15 degrés
belt ceinture f 144
beneath sous
berth couchette f 74, 77
best meilleur(e)
better mieux 14
between entre
bib bavoir m
bicycle vélo m 75, 83, 153; ~ **hire/rental** location f de vélo 83; ~ **parts** 82
bidet bidet m
big grand(e) 14, 24, 117, 134
bikini bikini m 144
bill note f 32; billet m; addition f 42; **put it on the bill** mettez-le sur l'addition
bin liner sac m poubelle
binoculars jumelles fpl
bird oiseau m 106
birthday anniversaire m 219
biscuits *(cookies)* biscuits mpl
bishop *(chess)* fou m
bite *(insect)* piqûre f (d'insecte)
bitten: I've been bitten by a dog j'ai été mordu par un chien
bitter amer(-ère) 41
black noir(e) 143; ~ **and white film** *(camera)* pellicule f noir et blanc 151
blanket couverture f 27
bleeding, to be saigner 162

bless you! à vos souhaits!
blind *(window)* store m 25
blister ampoule f 162
blocked, to be être bouché(e) 25; **the road is** ~ la route est barrée
blood sang m 164; ~ **group** groupe m sanguin; ~ **pressure** tension f (artérielle 163, 164
blouse chemisier m 144
blow-dry brushing
blue bleu(e) 143
blusher fard m à joues
boarding pass carte f d'embarquement
boat bateau m 81; ~ **trip** voyage m en bateau 81
body: parts of the body 166; corps, m, parties du corps fpl
boil furoncle m 162
boiler chaudière f 29
bone os m 166
book livre m 150; ~ **store** librairie f 130
booked up, to be être complet 115
book of tickets carnet de tickets m 79
boots bottes fpl 145; *(for sport)* chaussures fpl 115
border *(country)* frontière f
boring ennuyeux(se) 101
born: I was born in... je suis né(e) à *(place)*/en *(year)*
borrow: may I borrow...? est-ce que je peux emprunter...?
botanical garden jardin botanique m 99
bottle bouteille f 37, 159; ~ **bank** container à verre m; ~ **opener** ouvre-bouteilles m 148
bow *(ship)* proue f
bowel intestins mpl
box boîte f; ~ **of chocolates** boîte f de chocolats 156; ~ **office** bureau de location m
boxing boxe f
boy garçon m 120, 157
boyfriend copain 120
bra soutien-gorge m 144
bracelet bracelet m 149
brand marque f

brass laiton m
bread pain m 38
break, to casser 28
breakage casse f, bris m
breakdown panne f 88; **to have a ~** tomber en panne 88
break-in cambriolage m 153
breakfast petit déjeuner m 26, 27
breast sein m 166
breathe, to respirer 92, 164
breathtaking époustouflant(e) 101
bridge pont m 107; *(cards)* bridge m
briefcase attaché-case, porte-document m
briefs culotte f 144
brilliant fantastique, superbe 101
bring, to apporter
Britain Grande-Bretagne f 119
British *(adj)* britannique 152
Briton *(n)* Britannique m/f
brochure dépliant m
broken, to be être cassé(e), 25, 137, 164
bronchitis bronchite f
bronze *(adj)* de bronze
brooch broche f 149
brother frère m 120
brown marron 143
browse, to regarder 133
bruise bleu m 162
brush brosse f
buffet car wagon-restaurant m
build, to construire 104
building bâtiment m
built construit(e) 104
bum-bag sac banane m
burger hamburger m 40; **~ stand** kiosque à hamburger m 35
burglary *(also ►theft)* cambriolage m
burn brûlure f 162
burnt, to be *(food)* être brûlé(e)
bus bus m 70, 78, 79; *(bus)* car m 78; **~ pass** passe-bus m; **~ route** itinéraire m des bus 96; **~ station** gare f routière 78; **~ stop** arrêt m d'autobus 65, 96; arrêt m de car 78
business affaires fpl; **~ class** passe f affaires 68; **~man** homme m d'affaires; **~ trip** voyage m d'affaires 123;

~ woman femme f d'affaires; **on ~** pour affaires 66
busy, to be être occupé(e), avoir à faire 125
but mais
butane gas gaz butane m 30, 31
butcher shop la boucherie f 130
butter beurre m 38, 160
button bouton m
buy, to acheter 67, 80
buying tickets *(travel)* acheter des billets 79
by *(time)* avant *(at the latest)* pour 13; **~ car** en voiture f 17, 94; **~ credit card** avec une carte de crédit f 17
bye! au revoir!, salut!
bypass route f de contournement

C **cabaret** cabaret m
cabin cabine f
cable car téléphérique m
café café m 35, 40
cake gâteau m 40; **~ shop** pâtisserie f
calendar calendrier m 156
call, to *(phone)* téléphoner 92; appeler 127, 128; **to ~ collect** appeler en P.C.V. 127; **call the police!** appelez la police!; **I'll call back** je rappellerai; **I'll call round** je passerai
camcorder caméscope m
camera appareil-photo m 151, 153; **~ case** sac-photo m 151; **~ shop** magasin m de photos 130
campbed un lit de camp 31
camping camping m 30; **~ equipment** matériel m de camping 31
campsite terrain m de camping 30
can boîte f 159
can I (have)…? est-ce que je peux (avoir)…? 18
can you help me? pouvez-vous m'aider? 18
can you recommend…? pouvez-vous recommander…? 112

can opener ouvre-boîte m
Canada Canada m 119
Canadian (adj)
canadien(ne);
(n) Canadien(ne) m/f
canal canal m
cancel, to annuler 68
cancer cancer m
candle bougie f 148
candy bonbons mpl 150
canoe canoë m
canoeing faire du canoë(-kayak)
cap casquette f; (dental) couronne f 168
capital city capitale f
captain (boat) capitaine m
car voiture f 81, 85–89; **~ alarm** alarme
de voiture m; **~ ferry** car-ferry m 81;
~ rental location de voiture f 70, 86;
~ parts 90, 91; **~ pound** fourrière f;
~ repairs 89; **~ wash** laverie f
automatique (de voiture); **by ~** en
voiture 95; **rental ~** voiture f de
location 153; (train) wagon m 75
carafe carafe f 37
caravan caravane f 30, 81;
~ site/park terrain de camping/
caravaning m
card (➤ cash, credit, business, greeting,
playing, telephone)
careful: be careful! soyez prudent;
(urgent) faites attention!
carpet (fitted) moquette f; (rug) tapis m
carrier bag sac (plastique) m 136
carry-cot lit-auto m (pour bébé)
cart chariot m 158
carton (of milk) brique f (de lait) 159
cash liquide m 136; **~ card** carte f
bancaire 139; **~ desk** caisse f 132;
~ machine distributeur
automatique m 139
cash, to encaisser 138
cassette cassette f 157
castle château m 99
casualty dept. urgences fpl
cat chat(te) (m/f)
catch, to (bus) attraper
cathedral cathédrale f 99
cause, to causer
cave grotte f 107

CD CD m, disque compact m;
~ player lecteur m de CD
cemetery cimetière m 99
central heating chauffage m central
center of town centre-ville m 21
ceramics céramique f
certificate certificat m 149, 157
chair chaise f; **~ lift** télésiège m 117
change (coins) monnaie f 87, 136; **keep
the change** gardez la monnaie 84
change, to (buses) changer 78, 79;
(money) 27, 138; (reservation) 68;
(trains) 75, 80; (baby) 39; (lanes) 93;
(clothes) se changer
changing facilities salle f de change 113
changing rooms cabines fpl d'essayage
Channel (English) Manche f
chapel chapelle f
charge prix m; tarif m 30
charter flight vol m charter
cheap bon marché 14, 134
cheaper moins cher(-ère) 21, 24,
109, 134
check in, to (plane) faire enregistrer ses
bagages 68
check out, to (hotel) partir
check note f 32; ticket de caisse m;
addition f 42; **put it on the check**
mettez-le sur l'addition
check chèque; **~ book** carnet m de
chèque; **~ guarantee card** carte f
bancaire (de garantie)
check: please check pouvez-vous
vérifier
check-in desk bureau m
d'enregistrement 69
checked (patterned) à carreaux
checkers dames fpl
checkout caisse f 158
cheers! santé!
cheese fromage m 48, 160
chemical toilet WC m chimique
cheque ➤ check
chess échecs mpl 121; **~ set** jeu m
d'échecs 157
chest poitrine f 166
chickenpox varicelle f
child enfant m 98, 152; **~ seat** (car) siège
auto bébé/enfant; (high chair) chaise f
haute (pour bébé) 39

children enfants mpl 66, 81, 113, 120; (reduction) 24, 74, 100; (meals) 39

children's meals repas mpl pour enfants 39

chips frites

choc-ice glace f au chocolat 110

chocolate chocolat m; ~ bar tablette f de chocolat 150; box of ~s boîte f de chocolats; hot ~ chocolat m chaud

Christian (adj) chrétien(ne); (n) Chrétien(ne) m/f

Christmas Noël m 219

church église f 96, 99, 105

cigarette cigarette f 150; ~ machine distributeur m de cigarettes

cigars cigares mpl 150

cinema cinéma m 96, 110

circle (balcony) balcon m; (U.S.) (road) rond-point m

city wall rempart m

civil servant fonctionnaire m

claim ticket ticket de consigne m 71

clamp, to mettre un sabot 87

class: first class première classe f 68

clean (adj) propre 14, 39, 41; to ~ nettoyer 137; I'd like my shoes cleaned je voudrais faire nettoyer mes chaussures

cleaner femme f de ménage 28

cleansing lotion lotion f démaquillante

cliff falaise f 107

cloakroom vestiaire m

clock pendule f 149

close (near) près 95

close, to fermer 100, 132, (shop) 140

clothes vêtements mpl 144; ~ pins épingles/pinces fpl à linge 148; ~ store/shop magasin m de vêtements 130

cloudy: it's cloudy il y a des nuages 122

clubs (golf) clubs mpl 115

coast côte f

coat manteau m 144

coat hanger cintre m

coat room vestiaire m 109

cockroach cafard m

code (area/dialling) code m

coffee café m 40

coil (contraceptive) stérilet m

coin pièce f

cold (adj) froid(e) 14, 41, 122; (n) rhume m 141, 163

collapse: he's collapsed il s'est effondré

collect, to venir chercher

college université f

color couleur f 134, 143; ~ film pellicule f couleur 151

comb peigne m 142

come back , to (return) revenir 36, 165; ~ for (collection) revenir chercher 140

commission commission f 138

communion communion f

compact disc/disk compact disc m 157

company (business) compagnie f; (companionship) 126

compartment (train) compartiment m

compass boussole f

complaint, to make a se plaindre

complaints (restaurant) 41; (hotel) 25

computer ordinateur m

concert concert m 108, 111; ~ hall salle de concert f 111

concussion, to have a avoir une commotion cérébrale/un traumatisme crânien

condoms préservatifs mpl 141

conference conférence f

confirm, to (reservation) confirmer 22, 68

confirmation confirmation f

congratulations! félicitations! fpl

connection (transport) correspondance f

conscious, to be être conscient(e)

constipated, to be être constipé(e)

constipation constipation f

Consulate consulat m 152

consult, to consulter 165

consultant (medical) médecin m spécialiste

contact, to contacter 28

contact lens lentille f de contact 167; ~ fluid liquide m pour lentilles de contact

contagious, to be être contagieux(-se) 165

contain, to contenir 39, 69, 155

contemporary dance danse f contemporaine 111

contraceptive contraceptif m

convenience store mini marché m 158

convenient pratique

conversion charts 85, 158

convertible *(n) (car)* voiture f décapotable

cook cuisinier(-ière) m/f

cook, to faire la cuisine

cookbook livre m de cuisine

cookies biscuits mpl 160

cooking *(cuisine)* cuisine f

coolbox glacière f

copper cuivre m 149

copy copie f

corduroy velours m côtelé

corkscrew tire-bouchon m 148

corner coin m 95

correct (➤ right) correct(e)

cosmetics produits mpl de beauté, cosmétiques mpl

cotton coton m 145

cotton wool coton m (hydrophile) 141

cough toux f 141; ~ **syrup** sirop m contre la toux; **to ~** tousser 164

could I have…? est-ce que je peux avoir…? 18

counter caisse f, comptoir m

country *(nation)* pays m

countryside paysage m

course *(meal)* plat m

courthouse palais m de justice m

cousin cousin(e) m/f

cover *(lid)* couvercle m

cover charge prix d'admission m

craft shop magasin m d'artisanat

cramps crampes fpl 163

crash: I've had a crash j'ai eu un accident

creak: the bed creaks le lit grince

creche crèche f

credit card carte f de crédit 42, 136, 153; ~ **number** numéro m de carte de crédit 109

credit status état m du crédit

credit, to be in avoir un compte provisionné

crisps chips fpl 160

crib lit m d'enfant 22

crockery vaisselle f 148

cross *(crucifix)* croix f, crucifix m

cross, to *(road)* traverser 95

cross-country skiing track piste f de ski de fond

crossing *(boat)* traversée f

crossroads carrefour m 95

crowded encombré(e)

crown *(dental)* couronne f 168

cruise croisière f

crutches béquilles fpl

cup tasse f 39, 148

cupboard placard m

curlers bigoudis mpl

currency devises fpl 138; monnaie f 67; ~ **exchange office** bureau m de change 70, 138

curtains rideaux mpl

cushion coussin m

customs douane f 67, 157; ~ **declaration** déclaration f de douane 155

cut coupure f 162

cutlery couverts mpl 29, 148

cycle vélo m; ~ **helmet** casque m à vélo; ~ **path** piste f cyclable; ~ **route** circuit m cycliste 106; route f cycliste

cycling cyclisme m 114

cyclist cycliste m

cystitis cystite f 165

D

daily tous les jours, quotidiennement

damaged, to be être abîmé(e) 28, 71

damp *(n)* humidité f; *(adj)* humide

dance spectacle m de danse 111

dancing, to go aller danser 124

dangerous dangereux(-se)

dark sombre 24, 134; *(color)* foncé 14, 134, 143

darts, to play jouer aux fléchettes

daughter fille f 120, 162

day jour m 97; ~ **ticket** ticket/billet m pour la journée; ~ **trip** excursion f d'une journée

dead mort(e); *(battery)* à plat 88
deaf, to be être sourd(e) 163
dear *(greeting)* cher (chère)
December décembre m 218
decide: we haven't decided yet nous n'avons pas encore décidé
deck *(ship)* pont m
deck chair chaise f longue 116
declare, to déclarer 67
deep profond
defrost, to décongeler
degrees *(temperature)* degrés mpl
delay retard m 70
delicate fragile
delicatessen charcutier m, traiteur m 130
delicious délicieux(-se) 14
deliver, to livrer
denim jean 145
dental floss fil m dentaire
dentist dentiste m 131, 168
dentures dentier m 168
deodorant déodorant m 142
depart, to *(train, bus)* (➤ leave) partir
department *(in store)* rayon m; **~ store** grand magasin m 130
departure *(train)* départ m 76; **~ lounge** salle f de départ
depend: it depends on celà dépend de f
deposit *(hotel)* arrhes fpl 24, *(bicycle rental)* 83; *(car rental)* caution f
describe, to décrire 152
design *(dress)* création f
designer dessinateur m, créateur m
destination destination f
details détails mpl
detergent détergent m
develop, to *(photos)* développer 151
diabetes diabète m
diabetic, to be être diabétique 39, 163
diagnosis diagnostic m 164
diamonds *(cards)* carreau m
diapers couches fpl 142
diarrhea diarrhée f 141
dice dés mpl
dictionary dictionnaire m 150
diesel diesel m 87
diet: I'm on a diet je suis au régime
difficult difficile 14

digital (watch) (montre) f à affichage numérique
dinghy canot m pneumatique
dining car wagon-restaurant m 75, 77
dining room salle f à manger 26, 29
dinner jacket smoking m
dinner, to have dîner 124
direct direct(e) 75
direct, to indiquer 18
direct-dial telephone téléphone m à ligne directe
direction direction f; **in the ~ of** en direction de 95
director *(film)* réalisateur m; *(of company)* directeur m, PDG m
directory *(telephone)* annuaire m
directory Enquiries Renseignements mpl 127
dirty sale 14, 28
disabled *(n)* handicapés mpl 22, 100
disco discothèque f 112
discount réduction f 24, 68, 100
discount: can you offer me a discount? pouvez-vous me faire une remise?
disgusting dégoûtant(e)
dish *(meal)* plat m
dish cloth lavette f 148
dish washing detergent poudre pour lave-vaisselle f 148
disk film pellicule f disque
dislocated, to be être disloqué(e) 164
display cabinet vitrine f 149
display case vitrine f 134
disposable camera appareil-photo m jetable 151
distilled water eau f distillée
district région f, quartier m
disturb: don't disturb ne pas déranger
dive, to plonger 116
diversion déviation f
divorced, to be être divorcé(e) 120
DIY (Do It Yourself) store magasin m de bricolage
dizzy, to feel avoir le vertige
do: things to do choses à faire 123
doctor médecin m 131, 161; docteur m 167
doctor's office cabinet m médical

does anyone here speak English? y a-t-il quelqu'un ici qui parle anglais? 67
dog chien m
doll poupée f 157
dollar dollar m 67, 138
door porte f 25, 29
dosage posologie f 140
double *(room)* (chambre f) pour deux personnes 21; **~ bed** grand lit m
downstairs en bas 12
downtown area centre-ville m 99
dozen douzaine f 159, 217
drain tuyau m (d'écoulement)
drama drame m
draught *(wind)* courant m d'air
dress robe f 144
drink boisson f; quelque chose à boire 70, 125, 126; verre m 124
drinking water eau f potable 30
drinks 49
drive, to conduire 93
driver *(bus, etc.)* conducteur m
driver's license [licence] permis m de conduire
drop off, to déposer 83; amener 113
drowning: someone is drowning quelqu'un se noie
drugstore droguerie f 130; pharmacie f
drunk ivre
dry cleaner's pressing m, nettoyage m à sec 131
dry cut coupe f sur cheveux secs
dry-clean, to nettoyer à sec
dual carriageway route f à quatre voies
dubbed, to be être doublé(e) 110
due, to be *(payment)* être dû (due)
during pendant 13
dusty poussiéreux(-se)
duty-free hors-taxe; **~ goods** marchandises fpl hors-taxe; **~ shop** magasin m hors-taxe; **~ shopping** 67
duty: to pay duty payer une taxe 67
duvet couette f

E
each: how much each? combien chacun?
ear oreille f 166

earache mal m à l'oreille 163
earlier plus tôt 125, 147
early tôt 13, 221
earrings boucles fpl d'oreilles 149
east est m 95
Easter Pâques fpl 219
easy facile 14
eat, to manger 41, 167; **places to eat** endroits pour manger 123
eaten: have you eaten? avez-vous mangé?;
we've already eaten nous avons déjà mangé
economical économique
economy class classe f économique 68
eight huit 216
either... or soit... soit; ou... ou
elastic *(adj)* élastique
electric blanket couverture f chauffante
electric meter compteur m électrique 28
electric shaver rasoir m électrique
electrical appliance store magasin m d'électroménager
electrician électricien m
electricity électricité f
elevator ascenseur m 26, 132
eleven onze 216
else: something else quelque chose d'autre
E-mail courrier m électronique, e-mail 155
embark, to *(boat)* embarquer
embassy ambassade f
emergency urgence f 127, 152; **~ exit** sortie f de secours; **~ room** urgences fpl; **it's an emergency** c'est urgent
empty vide 14
end, to finir 108
end: at the end au bout m
engaged, to be être fiancé(e) 120
engine moteur m
engineer ingénieur m
England Angleterre f 119
English *(language)* anglais m 11, 67, 110, 152, 161; **in ~** en anglais 150; **~-speaking** qui parle anglais 98
English person Anglais(e) m/f
enjoy, to aimer 124
enlarge, to *(photos)* agrandir 151
enough assez 15, 42, 136

entertainment guide
  guide m des spectacles
entrance fee prix m d'entrée 100
entry visa visa m d'entrée
envelope enveloppe f 150
epileptic, to be être épileptique 163
equipment *(sports)* équipement m 115
error erreur f
escalator escalier m roulant 132
essential essentiel(le) 89
estate agent agent m immobilier
EU UE f
Eurocheque eurochèque m
evening dress tenue f de soirée 112
evening, in the le soir 221, 132; dans la
  soirée 221
events spectacles mpl 108
every day tous les jours
every week chaque semaine 13
examination *(medical)* examen m
example, for par exemple
except sauf
excuse me *(getting attention)*
  excusez-moi 10, 94
excess luggage
  bagages (mpl) trop lourds 69
exchange, to changer 138
exchange rate taux m de change 138
excursion excursion f 97
excuse me *(getting attention)*
  excusez-moi 10, 94
exhausted, to be être épuisé(e) 106
exhibition exposition f
exit sortie f 70; **at the ~** à la sortie
expected: it's expected il faut 111
expensive cher (chère) 14, 134
expire: when does it expire?
  quand expire-t-elle?
expiration date date d'expiration f 109
expressway autoroute f
extension *(telephone)* poste f 128
extension cord rallonge (électrique) f
extra *(additional)* supplémentaire 23, 27
extracted, to be *(tooth)* arracher 168
extremely
  extrêmement 17
eye œil m *(pl* yeux) 166
eyeliner crayon pour les yeux m
eyeshadow
  ombre f/fard m à paupières

F **fabric** *(material)*
    tissu
face visage m 166
facilities équipement m
  30; aménagements mpl 22
factor *(sun cream)* facteur 142
faint, to feel être prêt(e) à
  s'évanouir 163
fairground fête f foraine 113
fall *(autumn)* automne m 219
fall: he's had a fall il a fait une chute
family famille f 66, 74, 120, 167
famous célèbre
fan *(air)* ventilateur m 25
fan: I'm a fan of
  je suis un fan/passionné(e) de
far loin 95; **is it far?** c'est loin? 73
farce farce f
fare prix m
farm ferme f 107
farsighted hypermétrope 167
fashionable, to be être à la mode
fast vite 93; **~ food** fast food m 40
fast, to be *(clock)* avancer 221
fat gras m
father père m 120
faucet *(tap)* robinet m 25
fault, it's my/your ~ c'est ma/votre
  faute
faulty, to be avoir un défaut m
favorite préféré(e), favori(te)
fax fax m 155; télécopieur m; **~ office**
  bureau m de fax/de télécopie;
  ~ machine fax m
February février m 218
feed, to allaiter 39
feeding bottle biberon m
feel ill, to se sentir malade 163
feel sick, to se sentir malade 163
feel nauseous, to avoir envie de vomir
female femme f 152; *(adj)* femelle
ferry ferry m 81
festival festival m
fetch help! allez chercher de l'aide!
feverish, to feel se sentir fiévreux(-se)
few quelques 15
fiancé(e) fiancé(e) m/f
field champ m 107

fifth cinquième 217
fight *(brawl)* bagarre f
fill out, to remplir
filling *(dental)* plombage
m 168;
(in sandwich) garniture f
filling station station-service f
film *(movie)* film m 108, 110; *(camera)*
pellicule f151; ~ speed vitesse f
de pellicule
filter filtre m 151;
~ paper *(for coffee)* filtre m en papier
fine *(penalty)* amende f 93; *(well)* très
bien 118
finger doigt m 166
fire: there's a fire! il y a le feu!;
~ alarm alarme f d'incendie;
~ escape escalier m de secours; ~
extinguisher extincteur m; ~
department pompiers mpl 92;
~lighters allume-feu mpl; ~place
cheminée f; ~wood bois m de
chauffage
first premier(-ière) 68, 75, 81, 217; ~
class première classe f 68, 74; ~ floor
(U.K.) premier étage m; *(U.S.)* rez-de-
chaussée m
first-aid kit trousse f de secours
fish store poissonnerie f 130
fishing rod canne f à pêche
fishing, to go aller à la pêche
fit: it fits *(clothes)* ça va 146
fitting room cabine f d'essayage 146
five cinq 216
fix: can you fix it? pouvez-vous le
réparer?
flag drapeau m
flannel *(fabric)* flanelle f; *(face-cloth)*
gant m de toilette
flash *(photo)* flash m 151
flashlight lampe de poche f 31
flat, have a être crevé f 83,
être à plat 88
flea puce f;
~ market marché m aux puces
flight vol m 70; ~ number numéro m de
vol 68; ~ attendant hôtesse f de l'air
flip-flops tongs fpl 145
flood inondation f

floor *(storey)* étage m 132; ~ mop balai
m laveur; ~ show spectacle m de
cabaret
florist fleuriste m 130
flower fleur f 106
flu grippe f 165
fluent: to speak fluent French
parler français couramment
fly *(insect)* mouche f
foggy: it's foggy il y a
du brouillard 122
folding chair/table chaise/table f
pliante
follow, to *(signs)* suivre 95;
(pursue) suivre 152
food plats 39; nourriture f 41;
cuisine 119;
~ poisoning intoxication f
alimentaire 165
foot pied m 166
footpath sentier m, chemin m 107
for a day pour une journée 86
for a week pour une semaine 86
forecast prévisions fpl météo 122
foreign étranger(-ère); ~ currency
devises fpl étrangères 138
forest forêt f 107
forget, to oublier 42
for hire libre
fork fourchette f 39, 41, 148;
(in the road) embranchement m
form fiche f 23; formulaire m 153;
feuille 168
formal dress tenue f de soirée 111
fortnight quinzaine f
fortunately heureusement 19
forwarding address
adresse f pour faire suivre le courrier
foundation *(make-up)* fond m de teint
fountain fontaine f 99
four quatre 216
four-door car voiture f quatre portes 86
four-wheel drive à quatre roues f
motrices
fourteen quatorze 216
fourth quatrième 217
foyer *(hotel/theater)* hall m d'entrée
frame *(glasses)* monture f
France France f 119
Francs francs mpl 67

free *(of charge)* sans payer; *(available/vacant)* libre 36, 124
freezer congélateur m 29
French *(language)* français m 110, 126
French person Français(e) m/f
frequently souvent
fresh frais (fraîche)
Friday vendredi m 218
fridge réfrigérateur m, frigo m 29
friend ami(e) m/f 162
friendly aimable
fries frites fpl 38, 40
fringe frange f
from *(place)* de 12; *(time)* 13
front door porte f d'entrée 26; **~ key** clé f de la porte d'entrée
frozen surgelé(e)
fruit juice jus m de fruit
frying pan poêle f 29
fuel *(gasoline)* carburant m 86
full plein(e) 14
full board pension f complète 24
full insurance assurance f tous risques 86
fun, to have s'amuser
funny *(amusing)* amusant(e); *(odd)* drôle
furniture mobilier m, meubles mpl
fuse fusible m 28; **~ box** boîte f à fusibles 28; **~ wire** plomb m (à fusible)

G **gallon** gallon m (4,5 litres)
gamble, to jouer pour de l'argent
game *(toy)* jeu m 157
garage garage m
garbage bag sac m poubelle 148
garden jardin m
gardener jardinier m
gardening jardinage m
gas: I smell gas! ça sent le gaz!; **~ bottle** bouteille f de gaz 28
gasoline essence f 87, 88; **~ can** bidon m d'essence
gastritis gastrite f 165
gate *(airport)* porte f 70
gauze bandage 141
gay club club m gay 112

general delivery poste f restante
generous généreux (-euse)
genuine authentique; original(e) 134
Germany Allemagne f
get by: may I get by? est-ce que je peux passer?
get off, to *(transport)* descendre 79
get to, to arriver à 77; *(find)* se rendre à, aller à 84; **how do I get to…?** pour aller à…? 73, 94
gift cadeau m 67, 156; **~ shop** magasin m de cadeaux 130
girl fille f 120, 157
girlfriend copine 120
give, to donner
glass verre m 37, 39, 148
glasses *(spectacles)* lunettes fpl 167
gliding vol m plané
glossy finish *(photos)* brillant(e)
glove gant m
go, to aller; **to ~ back** *(turn around)* retourner 95; **to ~ for a walk** aller se promener 124; **to ~ out** *(in evening)* sortir; **to ~ shopping** aller faire des courses fpl 124; **where does this bus go?** où va ce bus?; **go away!** allez-vous en!
goggles lunettes fpl de protection
gold or m 149
gold plate plaqué-or m 149
golf golf m 114; **~ course** terrain m de golf 115
good *(adj)* bon(ne) 14, 35, 42; **~ afternoon** bonjour 10; **~ evening** bonsoir 10; **~ morning** bonjour 10; **~ night** bonne nuit 10
good-bye au revoir 10
got: have you got…? avez-vous…?
grade *(fuel)* qualité f
gram [gramme] gramme m 159
grandparents grands-parents mpl
grass herbe f; *(lawn)* pelouse f
gratuity pourboire m
gray [grey] gris(e) 143
graze égratignure f 162
greasy *(hair)* gras
great fun très amusant

green vert(e) 143
greengrocer marchand m
de fruits et légumes 130
grocery store/grocer
épicerie f 130
ground *(camping)*
terrain m (de camping) 30
ground floor rez-de-chaussée m
group groupe m 66, 100
guarantee garantie f 135; **is it guaranteed?** est-ce sous garantie?
guide *(tour)* guide m 98;
~book guide m 150
guided tour visite f guidée 100
guitar guitare f
gynecologist gynécologue m 167

H **hair** cheveux mpl 147; **~ brush**
brosse f à cheveux; **~ dryer**
sèche-cheveux m; **~ gel** gel m
pour cheveux; **~ mousse** mousse f
pour cheveux 142; **~ spray** laque f 142
haircare 142
haircut coupe f de cheveux 147
hairdresser's coiffeur m 131, 147
hairstylist coiffeur m styliste 147
half board demi-pension f 24
half fare demi-tarif m
half past … et demie 220
half, a moitié f, demi m 217
hammer marteau m 31
hand main f 166; **~ cream** crème f pour
les mains; **~ luggage** bagages mpl à
main 69; **~ towel** torchon m/serviette f
pour les mains; **~ washable** lavable à
la main 145
handbag sac m à main 144, 153
handicapped, to be être
handicapé(e) 163
handicrafts artisanat m
handkerchief mouchoir m
handle poignée f
hang-gliding vol m libre
hanger cintre m 27
hangover *(n)* gueule f de bois 141
happen: what happened?
qu'est-ce qui s'est passé?
happy: I'm not happy with the service
je ne suis pas content(e) du service

harbor/harbour port m
hard shoulder *(road)*
bande f d'arrêt d'urgence
hardware store quincaillerie f
hat chapeau m 144
hatchback coupé m avec hayon arrière
have to, to *(must)* devoir 79
have, to (➤ 18, 133; **I have** j'ai;
we have nous avons
hay fever rhume m des foins 141
head tête f 166
head waiter maître m d'hôtel 41
headache mal m à la tête 163
health food store/shop magasin m
de diététique 130
health insurance assurance f
maladie 168
hear, to entendre
hearing aid appareil m de surdité
heart cœur m 166; **~ attack** crise f
cardiaque 163; **~ condition** problèmes
mpl de cœur 163
hearts *(cards)* cœur m
heater radiateur m
heating chauffage m 25
heavy lourd(e) 14
height taille f; hauteur f
helicopter hélicoptère m
hello bonjour 10, 118
help aide f 94
help, to aider 18; **could you help me?**
pourriez-vous m'aider? 92
hemorrhoids hémorroïdes fpl
her la; *(to her)* à elle 16; *(possessive)*
son/sa/ses 16
here ici 12, 17
hers: it's hers c'est le sien/la sienne
hi! salut! 10
high haut(e); **~ tide** marée f haute
highlight, to *(hair)* faire des mèches 147
highway autoroute f
hike *(walk)* randonnée f 106
hill colline f 107
him le; *(to him)* à lui 16
his à lui 16; *(possessive)* son/sa/ses 16;
it's his c'est le sien/la sienne
history histoire f
hitchhike, to faire de l'auto-stop
hitchhiking auto-stop m 83
HIV-positive séropositif(-ive)

hobby hobby m, passe-temps m 121

hockey *(field)* hockey m

hold, to *(contain)* contenir;
~ on *(phone)* patienter; **~ on** ne
raccrochez pas 128

hole *(in clothes)* trou m

holiday resort station f de vacances

home, to go rentrer chez soi

homosexual *(adj)* homosexuel(le)

honeymoon, to be on
être en lune de miel

horse cheval m

horseracing courses fpl
de chevaux

horseback trip promenade f à cheval

hospital hôpital m 131, 164, 167

hot *(warm)* chaud(e) 14; *(weather)* très
chaud 122; **~ dog** hot dog m 110; **~
water** eau f chaude 25; **~ water bottle**
bouillotte f

hotel hôtel m 21; **~ reservation** 21

hour heure f 97;
in an ~ dans une heure 84

house maison f, villa f

housewife femme f au foyer 121

hovercraft hovercraft m 81

how? comment? 17; **~ are you?**
comment allez-vous? 118

how far? à combien de km? 94, 106; à
quelle distance? 106

how long?
combien de temps? 23, 75, 76, 88;

how many? combien? 15, 80

how much? combien? 15, 84, 109

how often? combien de fois? 140

how old? quel âge? 120

however toutefois

hundred cent 216

hungry, to be avoir faim

hurry, to be in a être pressé(e)

hurt: it hurts j'ai mal 162;
to be ~ être blessé(e) 162

husband mari m 120, 162

hypermarket hypermarché m

I **I'd like...** je voudrais... 18, 36,
37, 40, 74

ice glaçons mpl 38; **~ dispenser**
distributeur m de glace; **~ hockey**

hockey m sur glace; **~
pack** pack m de glace; **~
rink** patinoire f

ice cream glace f 40; **~
cone** cornet m de glace

identification pièce f
d'identité 136

ill, to be être malade

illegal, to be être illégal(e)

illness maladie f

immediately tout de suite 13

impressive impressionnant(e)

in *(place)* à, en 12; *(time)* dans 13

in-law: mother~ belle-mère f; **father~**
beau-père m

included: is... included? est-ce que...
est compris? 86, 98

indicate, to *(car)* mettre son
clignotant

indigestion indigestion f

indoor pool piscine f couverte 116

indoors à l'intérieur

inexpensive bon marché 35

infected, to be être infecté(e) 165

infection infection f 167

inflammation inflammation f 165

informal *(dress)* tenue f de ville

information renseignements mpl 97;
~ desk bureau m des renseignements
73; **~ office** office m du tourisme 96

injection piqûre f 168

injured, to be être blessé(e) 92, 162

innocent innocent(e)

insect insecte m 25; **~ bite** piqûre f
d'insecte 141; **~ repellent**
crème/lotion f contre les insectes 141

inside à l'intérieur 12

insist: I insist j'insiste

insomnia insomnie f

instead of au lieu de

instructions instructions fpl 135

instructor moniteur m

insulin insuline f

insurance assurance f 86, 89, 93, 168; **~
certificate** certificat m d'assurance 93;
~ claim demande f d'indemnité; **~
company** compagnie f d'assurance 93

interest *(hobby)* intérêt m, hobby m 121

interest rate taux m d'intérêt

interesting intéressant(e) 101

international international(e)
International Student Card carte f d'étudiant internationale 29
Internet Internet m 155
interpreter interprète m 93, 153
intersection croisement m 95
interval intervalle m
into dans
introduce oneself, to se présenter
invitation invitation f 124
invite, to inviter 124
involved, to be être impliqué(e) 93
Ireland Irlande f 119
Irish irlandais(e)
Irish person Irlandais(e) m/f
iron *(for clothing)* fer m à repasser
iron, to repasser
is there…? y a-t-il…? 17
island île f
it is… c'est… 17
Italian *(adj)* italien(ne) 35
Italy Italie f
itemized bill note f détaillée 32

jack/knave *(cards)* valet m
jacket veste f 144
jammed, to be être coincé(e) 25
January janvier m 218
jar pot m 159
jaw mâchoire f 166
jeans jean m/*sing* 144
jet lag décalage m horaire
jet ski scooter m des mers 116
Jew *(n)* Juif(-ve) m/f
jeweler bijoutier m 149
jewelry store bijouterie f 131
Jewish *(adj)* juif(-ve)
job: what's your job? quelle est votre profession?
joint passport passeport m joint 66
joke plaisanterie f
joker *(cards)* joker m
journalist journaliste m/f
jug (of water) pichet m/pot m (d'eau)
July juillet m 218
jumper cables [jump leads] câbles mpl de secours (pour batterie)

junction *(exit)* sortie f (d'autoroute);
  (intersection) bretelle f, intersection f
June juin m 218

keep the change gardez la monnaie
ketchup ketchup m
kettle bouilloire f 29
key clé f 27, 28, 88;
  ~ ring porte-clé m 156
kidney rein m 166
kilo(gram) kilo(gramme) m 159
kilometer kilomètre m
kind *(pleasant)* gentil(le)
kind: what kind of…? quelle sorte de…?, quel genre de…?
king *(cards/chess)* roi m
kiosk kiosque m
kiss, to embrasser 126
kitchen cuisine f 29;
  ~ paper papier m absorbant
knapsack sac m à dos 31, 145
knave *(cards)* valet m
knee genou m 166
knife couteau m 39, 41, 148
knight *(chess)* cavalier m
knocked down, to be être renversé(e)
know: I don't know je ne sais pas
kosher kascher

label étiquette f
lace dentelle f 145
ladder échelle f
ladies *(toilet)* femmes/dames fpl
lake lac m 107
lamp lampe f 29; *(oil)* lampe à pétrole
land, to atterrir 70
landing *(house)* palier m
landlord/landlady propriétaire m/f
lane voie f
language course cours m de langue
large *(adj)* gros(se) 40; *(drink)* grand(e) 110; *(clothing)* grand 134
last *(final/previous)* dernier(-ière) 68, 75, 80, 81; **to last** *(time)* durer
late tard 221; *(delayed)* en retard 70
later plus tard 125, 147
laugh, to rire 126
laundromat laverie f automatique 131

laundry service service m de nettoyage

lavatory toilettes fpl, WC mpl

lawn pelouse f

lawyer avocat(e) m/f 152

laxative laxatif m

lead-free (gas) sans plomb m

leader (of group) chef m

leaflet dépliant m

leak: it leaks (car, roof, pipe) il fuit

learn, to (language/sport) apprendre

learner étudiant(e) m/f

leather cuir m 145

leave, to (depart) partir 68, 126; (leave behind: car) laisser 73; (luggage) laisser; **to ~ from** (transport) partir de 78; **leave me alone!** laissez-moi tranquille! 126

left, on the à gauche 76, 95

left-hand side gauche

left-handed gaucher(-ère)

left: are there any left? est-ce qu'il en reste?

leg jambe f 166

legal, to be être légal(e)

leggings legging m/sing 144

lemon citron m 38

lemonade limonade f

lend: could you lend me...? pourriez-vous me prêter...?

length longueur m

lens (camera) objectif m 151; (optical) verre m 167

lesbian club club m pour lesbiennes

less moins 15

lesson leçon f

let: please let me know pourriez-vous me faire savoir

letter lettre f 154; **~ box** boîte f aux lettres

library bibliothèque f 131

license plate number numéro m d'immatriculation 88, 93

lie down, to s'allonger, se coucher

lifebelt bouée f de sauvetage

lifeboat canot m de sauvetage

lifeguard maître-nageur m 116

lifejacket gilet m de sauvetage

lift (hitchhiking) trajet m; **~ pass** forfait m 117

light (adj) (color) clair(e) 14, 134, 143; (weight) léger(-ère) 14, 134; (n) (bicycle) phare m, feu m 83; (cigarette) feu m;

(electric) lumière f 25; **~ bulb** ampoule f 148

lighter (cigarette) briquet m 150

lightning foudre f

like: I'd like... je voudrais... 133; j'aimerais; **like this** (in this way) comme ça

line (subway) ligne f 80; (profession) branche f 121; queue f, file f (d'attente); **to stand in line** faire la queue 112; (phone) **an outside line, please** je voudrais appeler à l'extérieur

linen lin m 145

lip lèvre f 166

lipbalm stick-lèvres m

lipstick rouge m à lèvres

liqueur liqueur f

liter litre m 87, 159

little petit(e)

live, to vivre; **~ together** vivre ensemble 120

liver foie m 166

living room salon m, salle f de séjour 29

lobby (theatre/hotel) hall m d'entrée

local local(e) 35, 37; **~ anesthetic** anesthésie f locale 168; **~ road** route f locale/départementale

lock serrure f 25; (canal) écluse f

locked, to be fermé (à clé) 26; **it's locked** c'est fermé(e) à clé

locker casier m

lock-up coffre-fort m

London Londres

long long(ue); (clothing) 146; (time) longtemps; **how ~?** combien de temps? 164

long-distance bus (auto)car m 78

long-distance call appel m à longue distance

longer: how much longer? encore pour combien de temps? 41

look for, to chercher 18

look like, to ressembler à

look, to have a (check) vérifier

look: I'm just looking je jette (juste) un coup d'œil

loose ample 146; (clothing) large

lorry camion m

A-Z

lose, to perdre 28, 100, 153;
I've lost... j'ai perdu...71
loss perte f 71
lost, to be être perdu(e)
lost-and-found bureau m
des objets trouvés 73
lots beaucoup de
loud: it's too loud c'est trop fort
love, to aimer, adorer; **I love you** je
t'aime
low-fat allégé(e), à teneur peu élevée
en matière grasse
lower (berth) inférieur(e) 74
luck: good luck! bonne chance! 219
luggage bagages mpl 67, 69, 71; ~
allowance poids m de bagages
autorisé; ~ **carts** chariots mpl à
bagages 71~ **locker** consigne f
automatique 71, 73; ~ **tag** étiquette f
pour bagages; ~ **ticket** ticket m de
consigne
lump boule f, bosse f 162
lumpy (mattress) défoncé(e)
lunch déjeuner m 98
lung poumon m
Luxembourg Luxembourg m

M **machine washable**
lavable en machine 145
(dear) madam (chère) madame
made of, what is it en quoi est-ce (fait)?
magazine magazine m 150
magnificent magnifique 101
maid femme f de chambre 27
maiden name nom m de jeune fille
mail (post) courrier m 27, 154; ~ **box**
boîte f aux lettres 154; **by ~** par lettre
22; ~ **office** (bureau de) poste f
mail, to poster
main principal(e) 130; ~ **course** plat m
principal; ~ **railway station** gare f
principale 95, ~ **street** rue f
principale 95, 96
make (brand) marque f
make, to faire; ~ **tea/coffee** faire du
thé/café; ~ **an appointment** prendre
rendez-vous 161
make-up maquillage m

male (n) homme m 152; (adj) mâle
man homme m
manager directeur m 25, 137;
patron m 41
manicure manucure f 147
many beaucoup
map carte f 106, 150; (road) carte f
routière
March mars m 218
margarine margarine f 160
market marché m 99; ~ **day** jour m
de marché
married, to be être marié(e) 120
mascara mascara m
mass messe f 105
massage massage 147
match (game) match m 114
matches allumettes fpl 31, 148, 150
material tissu m
matinée matinée f 109
matte finish (photos) mat m
matter: it doesn't matter ça ne fait rien;
what's the matter? que se passe-t-il?
mattress matelas m
May mai m 218
may I? puis-je? 37
maybe peut-être
me me; (to me) à moi 16
meal repas m 38, 125; (dish) plat m 38
mean, to signifier 11
measure, to mesurer 146
measurement mesures fpl
meat viande f 41
medical certificate
certificat m médical 168
medicine (medication)
médicament m 164, 165
medium (adj) moyen(ne) 40;
(steak) à point
meet, to se retrouver 125; **pleased to
meet you** enchanté(e) 118
meeting place point m de rendez-vous
member (of club) membre m 112, 115
memorial monument m (aux morts) 99
men (toilets) messieurs/hommes mpl
mend, to réparer
mention: don't mention it je vous en
prie, il n'y a pas de quoi 10; de rien
menu menu m
message message m 27

metal métal m
meter (taxi) compteur m
methylated spirits alcool à brûler
microwave oven four m à micro-ondes
midday midi m
midnight minuit m 220
migraine migraine f
mileage kilométrage m 86
milk lait m 160; with ~ au lait 40; ~ of
magnesia magnésie f (hydratée)
million million m 216
mind: do you mind? est-ce que ça vous
dérange? 77, 126; I've changed my
mind j'ai changé d'avis
mine à moi 16;
it's mine c'est le mien/la mienne
mineral water eau f minérale
minibar mini-bar m 32
minibus minibus m
minimum (n) minimum m
minister pasteur m
minute minute f 76
mirror miroir m, glace f; (car)
rétroviseur m 90
miss, to manquer
missing, to be (lacking) manquer 137;
(person) avoir disparu 152;
there is... missing il manque...
mistake erreur f 32, 42
misunderstanding, there's been a il y a
eu un malentendu m
mittens moufles fpl
mobile home camping car m
modern moderne 14; ~ art art m
moderne
Monday lundi m 218
money argent m 42, 139, 153;
~ belt ceinture f pour transporter de
l'argent; ~ order mandat m
month mois m 218
monument monument m
moor, to amarrer
mooring amarrage m
moped mobylette f 83
more plus 15, 67; d'autre 67; I'd like
some more j'en voudrais un peu
plus 39
morning, in the le matin 218, 221
morning-after pill pilule du lendemain f

Moslem (adj)
musulman(e);(n)
Musulman(e) m/f
mosque mosquée f 105
mosquito moustique m; ~
bite piqûre f de moustique
mother mère f 120
motorboat canot m automobile 116
motorcycle moto f 83; ~ parts 82
mountain montagne f 107; ~ bike VTT
(vélo m tout terrain); ~ pass col m (de
montagne) 107; ~ range chaîne f de
montagnes 107
mountaineering alpinisme m
moustache moustache f
mouth bouche f 166; ~ ulcer aphte m
move, to (house) déménager; (rooms)
changer de 25; don't move him! ne le
déplacez pas! 92
movie film m 108, 110; ~ theater
cinéma m 96, 110
Mr. M (monsieur)
Mrs. Mme (madame)
much beaucoup 15
mugged, to be être agressé 153
mugging agression f 152
multiplex cinema cinéma m multiplex
mumps oreillons mpl
muscle muscle m 166
museum musée m 99
music musique f 111;
~ box boîte f à musique
musician musicien(ne) m/f
my mon, ma, mes 16

N nail polish vernis m à ongles
nail scissors ciseaux mpl à
ongles
name nom m 22, 36, 93, 118, 120
name: my name is je m'appelle 118;
what's your name? comment vous
appelez-vous 118
nappies/diapers couches fpl 142
narrow étroit(e) 14
national national(e)
nationality nationalité f
nature reserve parc naturel m 107
nature trail circuit forestier éducatif m
nausea nausée f

navy blue bleu marine m
near près 12
nearby près d'ici 21, 87
nearest le/la plus proche 80, 88, 92, 130
nearsighted myope 167
necessary nécessaire 89
neck cou m 166; *(clothes)* encolure f 144
necklace collier m 149
need: I need to je dois +inf. 18
needle aiguille f
negative *(photo)* négatif m
neighbor voisin(e) m/f
nephew neveu m
Netherlands Pays-Bas mpl
never jamais 13
new neuf (neuve) 14
new year Nouvel An m 219
New Zealand Nouvelle Zélande f 119
newsdealer/newsagent's marchand m de journaux 150
newspaper journal m 150
newsstand kiosque m à journaux
next prochain(e) 75, 81, 87; suivant(e) 68; **next stop!** prochain arrêt! 79
next to à côté de 12, 95
niece nièce f
night porter gardien de nuit m
night/at night la nuit 218, 221; **per night** par nuit f
nightclub nightclub m 112
nightdress chemise de nuit f
nine neuf 216
nipple *(for baby)* tétine f
no non 10
no one personne 16, 92
noisy bruyant(e) 14, 24
non-alcoholic non alcoolisé(e)
non-smoking *(adj)* non-fumeur 36; **~ area** zone f non-fumeur 69
none aucun(e) 15, 16
noon midi m 220
normal normal(e) 67
north nord m 95
North Africa Afrique f du Nord
Northern Ireland Irlande f du Nord
nose nez m 166
nosebleed saignement m de nez
not that one pas celui-ci (celle-ci) 16
not yet pas encore 13

notebook cahier m, carnet m
nothing else rien d'autre 15
nothing for me rien pour moi
nothing to declare rien à déclarer
notice board tableau m d'affichage
notify, to informer, prévenir 167
November novembre m 218
now maintenant 13, 84
nudist beach plage f pour nudistes
number *(telephone)* numéro m 84; **sorry, wrong number** désolé, faux numéro
number plate plaque f d'immatriculation
nurse infirmière f
nursery slope *(skiing)* piste f pour débutants
nylon nylon m

O

o'clock, it's... il est... heures 220
observatory observatoire m
occupied occupé(e) 14
October octobre m 218
odds *(betting)* cote f 114
of de
of course bien sûr 19
off-peak hors saison
off-road (multipurpose) vehicle véhicule m tout-terrain, quatre-quatre m
office bureau m
often souvent 13
oil huile f
oily *(hair)* gras
okay d'accord 10
old vieux (vieille) 14
old-fashioned démodé(e) 14
on *(day, date)* le... 13; *(position)* sur 12
on, to be *(showing)* passer
on/off switch interrupteur m
on board *(ship)* à bord; *(train)* dans le train
on foot à pied 17, 95
on the left à gauche 12
on the other side of... de l'autre côté de... 12, 95
on the right à droite 12
once une fois f 217; **once a week** une fois par semaine
one un(e) 216; **one like that** un(e) comme ceci 16

one-way ticket aller-simple m 68; 74; ticket/billet aller m 79

open ouvert(e) 14; ~ to the public ouvert(e) au public 100

open, to ouvrir 132; *(shop)* 140

opening hours heures fpl d'ouverture 100, 132

opera opéra m 108, 111; ~ house opéra m 99, 111

operation opération f

operator *(tel.)* conducteur m

opposite en face de 12

optician opticien m 131, 167

or ou

orange *(color)* orange 143; *(fruit)* orange f

orchestra orchestre m 111

order, to commander 37, 41, 89, 135; *(taxi)* appeler 32

organized organisé(e) 106

others autres 134

our notre, nos 16; ours à nous 16

out: he's out il est sorti

outdoor(s) à l'extérieur

outdoor pool piscine f en plein air 116

outside dehors 12, 36

oven four m

over there là-bas 12, 36, 76

overcharged: I've been overcharged on m'a fait payer trop cher

overdone *(food)* trop cuit(e) 41

overdraft découvert m

overdrawn à découvert

overheat, to surchauffer

overnight service *(photo)* développement en 24h

owe: how much do I owe you? combien vous dois-je?

own: on my own tout(e) seul(e) 65

owner propriétaire m

P

p.m. de l'après-midi m

pacifier sucette f, tétine f

pack paquet m 159; ~ of cigarettes paquet m de cigarettes 150

pack of cards jeu m de cartes

pack, to faire les valises 69

package colis m

packed lunch panier m repas m, repas m froid

paddling pool petit bassin m 113

padlock cadenas m

pail seau m 157

pain, to be in avoir mal, souffrir 167

pain killer analgésique m 141, 165; calmant m 165

paint, to peindre

painter peintre m

painting tableau m

pair of, a une paire, deux 217

pajamas pyjama m/sing.

palace palais m 99

panorama panorama m 107

panties culotte f

pantomime pantomime f

pants pantalon m 144

paper papier m; ~ napkin serviette f en papier 148

paraffin pétrole m 31

paralysis paralysie f

parcel *(package)* paquet m 155

pardon? pardon? 11

parents parents mpl 120

park parc m 96, 99, 107

park, to se garer

parking stationnement m 87; ~ disc disque m de stationnement 87; ~ lot parking m 26, 87, 96; ~ meter parcmètre m 87; ~ space emplacement m de parking

parliament building parlement m 99

partner partenaire m/f

parts *(components)* pièces fpl 89

party *(social)* soirée f, réception f 124; *(celebration)* fête f

pass col m 107

pass, to passer 77

pass through, to être en transit 66

passenger passager(-ère) m/f

passport passeport m 66, 69, 153; ~ control 66

pastry shop pâtisserie f

patch, to raccommoder 137

path sentier m, chemin m 107

patient patient m 161

pavement trottoir m

pay, to payer 42, 136; **~ a fine** payer une amende 93; **~ by credit card** payer avec une carte de crédit
pay phone téléphone payant m
paying (hotel) 32; (restaurant) 42; (shopping) 136
peak pic m, sommet m 107
pebbly beach plage f de galets 116
pedalo pédalo m
pedestrian crossing passage m piétons 96
pedestrian zone zone f piétonnière 96
pen stylo m 150
pencil crayon m de papier
penicillin pénicilline f
penknife canif m
penpal correspondant(e) m/f
pensioner retraité(e) m 100
people gens mpl 119;
~ carrier (minivan) monospace m
pepper poivre m 38
per: per day par jour m 30, 83, 86, 87, 115; **per hour** par heure f 87, 115; **per night** par nuit f 21; **per week** par semaine f 83, 86
performance représentation f
perhaps peut-être 19
period période f 105; (menstrual) règles fpl 167; **~ pains** règles fpl douloureuses 167
perm permanente f 147
permit permis m
personal stereo balladeur m, walkman® m
pet (n) animal m de compagnie
petrol essence f 87, 88;
~ can bidon m d'essence
pharmacy pharmacie f 130, 140; droguerie f 130
phone téléphone m; **~ call** appel m téléphonique; **~ card** télécarte f 127, 155; carte f de téléphone 155 (➤ telephone)
photo, to take a prendre une photo
photo (passport-size) photo f d'identité 115
photocopier photocopieur m 155
photographer photographe m
photography photographie f 151

phrase expression f 11;
~ book guide m de conversation
piano piano m
pick up, to (ticket) aller chercher 109; (children) venir chercher 113
picnic pique-nique m
picnic area aire f de pique-nique 107
piece morceau m 15;
a ~ of un morceau de 40
Pill (contraceptive) pilule f 167
pillow oreiller m 27;
~ case taie m d'oreiller
pilot light veilleuse f
pink rose 143
pint (= 0.56 liter) pinte f
pipe pipe f; **~ cleaners** cure-pipe m;
~ tobacco tabac m à pipe
piste map plan m des pistes
pitch (for camping) emplacement m;
~ charge prix m de l'emplacement
pity: it's a pity c'est dommage
place (area) endroit m; (space) place f
place a bet, to faire un pari 114
plain (not patterned) uni(e)
plane avion m 68
plans projets mpl 124
plant plante f
plastic bag sac m plastique
plate assiette f 39, 148
platform quai m 73, 76, 77
play, to jouer 121; (drama) jouer 110;
~ an instrument jouer (d'un instrument); **~ music** jouer (de la musique) 111
playground cour f de récréation 113
playgroup garderie f 113
playing cards cartes fpl à jouer
playwright auteur m 110
pleasant (nice) agréable 14
please s'il vous plaît 10
pliers pinces fpl, tenailles fpl
plug (socket) prise f 148; (on flex) fiche f
plumber plombier m
point to, to montrer 11
poison poison m
poisonous toxique
police police f 92, 152; **~ report** [certificate] certificat de police 153; **~ station**

commissariat m (de police) 96, 131, 152

pollen count taux m de pollen 122

pond étang m 107

pony ride promenade f sur un poney

pop music musique f pop

popular populaire 157

port (harbor) port m

porter (hotel) porteur m; (station) porteur m 71

portion portion f 40

possible, as soon as dès que possible

possibly peut-être

post (mail) courrier m

post office (bureau m de) poste f 96, 154

post, to poster

postbox boîte f aux lettres 154

postcard carte f postale 150, 154, 156

poste restante poste f restante

poster affiche f, poster m

postman facteur m

pottery poterie f

pound (sterling) livre f (sterling) 138

power failure [cut] coupure f de courant

power point prise f électrique

practice: to practice speaking French s'entraîner à parler français

pregnant, to be être enceinte 163

prescribe, to prescrire 165

prescription ordonnance f 140, 141

present (gift) cadeau m

press, to (iron) repasser 137

pretty joli(e)

priest prêtre m

primus stove réchaud m (de camping)

prison prison f

private bathroom salle f de bains particulière

probably probablement

program programme m; ~ of events programme m des spectacles 108

prohibited interdit(e)

promenade deck pont m promenade

pronounce, to prononcer

properly correctement

Protestant protestant(e)

public building bâtiment m public 96

public holiday jour m férié 219

pullover pullover m, pull m 144

pump pompe f; (gas) pompe f à essence

puppet show spectacle m de marionettes

pure (fabric) pur(e) 145

purple violet(tte) 143

purse porte-monnaie m 153

push-chair poussette f

put aside [by], to (in shop) mettre de côté

put up: can you put me up for the night? pouvez-vous m'héberger pour la nuit?

put: where can I put…? où puis-je mettre…?

pyjamas pyjama m/sing.

Q-Z

Q quality qualité f 134

quantity quantité f 134

quarantine quarantaine f

quarter past/after et quart 220

quarter to/before moins le quart 220

quarter, a un quart 217

quarter-deck (ship) gaillard m d'arrière

quartz à quartz

quay quai m

Quebec Québec m

Quebecois Québécois m/f

queen (cards) reine f; (chess) reine f

question question f

quick rapide 14

quickest: what's the quickest way to…? quel est le chemin le plus court à…?

quickly vite 17

quiet silencieux(-ieuse) 14

quieter plus calme 24, 126

quoits jeu m de palet

R rabbi rabbin m

race (cars/horses) course f; ~ track [course] (track) hippodrome m 114

racing bike vélo m de course

racket (tennis, squash) raquette f 115

radiator radiateur m électrique

radio radio f

railroad/railway voie ferrée f

rain, to pleuvoir 122

raincoat imperméable m 144

rape viol m 152

A-Z

rappeling descente f en rappel
rare *(steak)* saignant; *(unusual)* rare
rarely rarement
rash éruption f cutanée 162
razor rasoir m; ~ **blades** lames fpl de rasoir 142
re-enter, to entrer à nouveau
reading *(interest)* lecture f; ~ **glasses** lunettes fpl de vue
ready, to be être prêt(e) 89, 137, 151
real *(genuine)* véritable 149
real estate agent agent m immobilier
receipt reçu m 32, 89, 151; ticket de caisse m 136, 137
reception (desk) accueil m 133; réception f
receptionist réceptioniste m/f
reclaim, to réclamer
reclining seat siège inclinable m
recommend, to recommander 21, 35, 141; **can you ~...?** pouvez-vous recommander...?35, 37, 97
record *(lp)* disque m 157
red rouge 143; ~ **wine** vin m rouge 40
refreshments boissons fpl
refrigerator réfrigérateur m, frigo m 29
refund remboursement m 137
regards to amitiés à 219
region région f 106
register receipt ticket m de caisse
registered mail courrier m en recommandé
registration form fiche f d'inscription 23
registration number numéro m d'immatriculation
regular *(gas)* ordinaire 87; *(size of drink)* moyen(ne) 110
religion religion f
remember: I don't remember je ne me souviens pas
rent, to louer 83, 86, 115, 116, 117; **to rent out** louer 29; **for ~** à louer
repair, to réparer 89, 137, 168
repairs réparations fpl 137; *(car)* 89
repeat, to répéter 94, 128; **please repeat that** pouvez-vous répéter ça? 11

replacement remplacement m 167; ~ **part** pièce de rechange f 137
report, to signaler 152
representative représentant m 27
required, to be il faut +inf. 112
reservation *(table)* réservation f; *(hotel)* 22; *(train)* 36; *(restaurant)* 68; ~ **desk** bureau m des réservations
reserve, to *(tickets)* réserver 109; *(table)* 36
rest, to se reposer
restaurant restaurant m 33, 35
restrooms toilettes fpl; WC mpl
retired, to be être retraité(e) 121
return ticket (ticket/billet) m aller-retour 68, 74, 79
return, to *(give back)* rapporter; *(come back)* revenir 81
reverse the charges, to appeler en P.C.V. 127
revolting dégoûtant(e) 14
rheumatism rhumatisme m
rib côte f 166
right juste 14; *(correct)* bon(ne) 77, 79, 80, 94; **that's ~** c'est vrai; **on the ~** à droite 76, 95
right of way priorité f 106; droit de passage m 106
right-hand drive volant m à droite
right-handed droitier(-ière)
ring bague f 149
rip-off: it's a rip-off c'est du vol 101
river rivière f 107; ~ **cruise** croisière f sur la rivière 81
road route f 94, 95; ~ **accident** accident m de la route; ~ **assistance** assistance f routière 88; ~ **map** carte f routière 150; ~ **signs** pancartes fpl (routières) 96
robbed, to be être volé 153
robbery cambriolage m
rock climbing escalade f
rocks rochers mpl
roller blades patins mpl à roulettes
romantic romantique 101
roof *(house/car)* toit m
roof-rack fixe-au-toit m
rook *(chess)* tour f
room chambre f 21; ~ **with a bath** suite f avec bain; **service ~ service** service m de chambre 26

rope corde f

rouge fard m à joues

round *(adj)* rond(e) 134; *(of golf)* partie f 115; **it's my round** c'est ma tournée

roundabout rond-point m

round-trip ticket (ticket/billet) m aller et retour 68, 74, 79

route chemin m 106; route f 106; itinéraire m

row boat canot m (à rames)

rubbish *(trash)* ordures fpl 28

rude, to be être impoli(e)/ grossier(-ière)

rugby rugby m

ruins ruines fpl 99

run into, to *(crash)* rentrer dans 93

run out: I've run out of gas je suis en panne d'essence 88

rush hour heure f de pointe

S **safe** coffre-fort m 27; *(not dangerous)* sans danger 116 en sécurité 65

safe, to feel se sentir en sécurité 65

safety sécurité f 65

safety pins épingles fpl de sûreté

sag: the bed sags le lit fait le ventre

sailboat bateau m à voiles, voilier m

sailboard planche f à voile

sailboarding faire de la planche à voile

salad salade f

sales tax TVA f 24, 136; **~ receipt** reçu m pour la TVA

salt sel m 39

same le/la même; **the same again please** la même chose, s'il vous plaît

sand sable m

sandals sandales fpl 145

sandwich sandwich m 40

sandy beach plage f de sable 116

sanitary napkins serviettes fpl hygiéniques 142

satellite TV télévision f par câble 22

satisfied: I'm not satisfied with it je n'en suis pas satisfait(e)

Saturday samedi m 218

sauna sauna m

saw *(tool)* scie f

say: how do you say...? comment dites-vous...?; **what did he say?** qu'a-t-il dit?

scarf écharpe f 144

scenic route route f touristique 106

scheduled flight vol m normal

school école

scientist scientifique m/f

scissors ciseaux mpl 148

scooter scooter m

Scotland Écosse f 119

Scottish écossais(e)

scouring pad tampon à récurer

screw vis f

screwdriver tournevis m 148

scrubbing brush brosse f dure

sculptor sculpteur

sea mer f 107

seasick, I feel j'ai le mal de mer

season ticket carte f d'abonnement

seasoning assaisonnement m 38

seat siège m 77; *(place)* place f 74, 109

second second(e), deuxième 217; **~ class** deuxième classe f 74; **~ floor** *(UK)* deuxième étage m; *(US)* premier étage

second-hand d'occasion

secretary secrétaire f/m

security guard garde m chargé de la sécurité

sedative sédatif m

see, to voir 37; *(inspect)* 24; *(witness)* 93

see s.o. again, to revoir quelqu'un 126

self-employed, to be être à son compte 121

self-service self-service m 87

sell, to vendre

send, to envoyer 155; *(help)* 88

senior citizen personne f âgée 74

separated, to be être séparé(e) 120

separately séparément 42

September septembre m 218

serious grave

served, to be *(meal)* être servi 26

service (charge) service m 105; **is service included?** le service est-il compris? 42

service station *(gas)* station f service

services 131

set menu menu m à prix fixe 37
seven sept 216
sex *(gender)* sexe m; *(act)* rapports mpl sexuels
shady ombragé(e)
shallow peu profond(e)
shampoo shampooing m 142; **~ for dry/oily hair** shampooing m pour cheveux secs/gras
shape forme f 134
share, to partager
sharp pointu(e)
shatter, to *(windshield/windscreen)* casser
shaver rasoir m (électrique); **~ socket** prise f pour rasoir
shaving brush blaireau m (à raser)
shaving cream crème f à raser
she elle
sheet *(bed)* drap m 28
shelf rayon m, étagère f
sherbet sorbet 63
ship bateau m 81; navire m
shirt chemise f 144
shivery, to feel avoir des frissons
(electric) shock choc (électrique) m
shoelaces lacets mpl
shoepolish cirage m
shoe repair ressemelage m
shoemaker cordonnier m
shoes chaussures fpl 145
shop magasin m 130
shop assistant vendeur(-euse) m/f
shopkeeper commerçant(e) m/f
shopping: ~ area rues fpl commerçantes 99; **~ basket** panier m; **~ cart** chariot m **~ mall** centre m commercial 131; **~ list** liste f de commissions **shopping, to go** aller faire les courses
shore *(sea/lake)* rivage m
short court(e) 146
shorts short m 144
shoulder épaule f 166
shovel pelle f 157
show, to montrer 97, 133; **can you show me?** pouvez-vous me montrer? 94, 106
shower douche f 26, 30; **~ gel** gel m pour la douche

shrunk: they've shrunk ils ont rétréci
shut fermé(e) 14
shutter volet m
shy timide
sick: to feel ~ être malade **I'm going to be ~** je vais vomir
sickbay *(ship)* infirmerie f
side *(of road)* côté m 95
side street rue f transversale 95
sidewalk, on the sur le trottoir
sights panorama m
sightseeing tour visite f touristique 97
sightseeing, to go faire du tourisme; *(in town)* visiter la ville
sign *(road)* panneau f 93, 95
signpost pancarte f
silk soie f
silver argent m 149
silverplate plaqué-argent m 149
similar, to be ressembler à
since *(time)* depuis
singer chanteur m 157
single room chambre f à un lit 21
single, to be être célibataire 120
sink évier m
sister sœur f 120
sit, to s'asseoir 36, 77, 126
sit down, please asseyez-vous, s'il vous plaît
six six 216
size taille f 146; *(shoes)* pointure f 115
skates patins mpl 117
skating rink patinoire f
ski: ~ bindings fixations fpl; **~ boots** chaussures fpl de ski 117; **~ instructor** moniteur m de ski; **~ poles** bâtons mpl 117; **~ suit** combinaison f de ski; **~ trousers** pantalon m de ski
ski lift remonte-pente m 117
ski school école f de ski 117
skid: we skidded nous avons glissé
skiing ski m 117
skin peau f 166
skirt jupe f 144
skis skis mpl 117
slalom slalom m
sledge luge m
sledge run piste f de luge
sleep, to dormir 167

sleeping bag sac m de couchage 31
sleeping car wagon-lit m 77
sleeping pill somnifère m
sleeve manche f 144
slice tranche f 159
slide film pellicule f pour diapositives
slip *(undergarment)* combinaison f
slippers pantoufles fpl 145
slope *(ski)* piste f, pente f
slot machine machine f à sous
slow lent(e) 14
slow down! ralentissez!
slow, to be *(clock)* être de retard 221
slowly lentement 17; *(speak)* 11, 128
SLR camera appareil-photo m
  reflex 151
small petit(e) 14, 24, 40, 117, 134;
  (drink) 110
small change (petite) monnaie f 139
smoke, to fumer 126;
  I don't smoke je ne fume pas
smoking *(adj)* fumeur 36, 69
smoky: it's too smoky c'est trop enfumé
snack bar snack bar m, buffet m 73
snacks casse-croûte m
sneakers (chaussures fpl de) tennis
snorkel tuba m (plongée)
snow neige f 117
snow, to neiger 122
snowed in, to be être bloqué par
  la neige
snowplow chasse-neige m
soap savon m 142
soap powder lessive f
soccer football m 114
socket prise f électrique
socks chaussettes fpl 144
sofa canapé m
sofabed canapé-lit m
soft drink *(soda)* boisson f gazeuse 110
solarium solarium m
sold out *(concert)* complet
sole *(shoes)* semelle f
some du/de la/de l'/des
someone quelqu'un 16
something quelque chose 16
sometimes quelquefois 13
son fils m 120, 162
soon bientôt 13

soon: as soon as possible
  dès que possible 161
sore throat mal m de
  gorge 141;
  mal m à la gorge 163
sore: it's sore ça fait mal
sorry! désolé(e)! 10
sort sorte f 134; **a ~ of** une sorte de
sour acide 41
south sud m 95
South Africa Afrique f du Sud
South African *(n)* Sud-africain(e) m/f
souvenir souvenir m 98, 156
spa ville f thermale
space place f 30
Spain Espagne f
spare *(extra)* supplémentaire
speak, to parler 11, 41, 67, 128; **do you
  speak English?** parlez-vous anglais? 11
special requirements régimes mpl
  spéciaux 39
specialist spécialiste m 164
specimen prise f, analyse f 164
spectacles lunettes fpl
speed limit limite f de vitesse
speed, to aller trop vite 93
spell, to épeler 11
spend, to *(money)* dépenser;
  (time) passer
spin-dryer essoreuse f
spine colonne f vertébrale
spoon cuillère f 39, 41, 148
sport sport m 114
sports club club m sportif 115
sprained, to be être foulé(e) 164
spring *(season)* printemps m 219;
  (water) source f
square *(adj)* carré(e) 134
squash *(sport)* squash m
stadium stade m 96
stain tache f
stainless steel acier m inoxydable 149
stairs escalier m/sing.
stale rassis(e)
stall: the engine stalls le moteur cale
stalls *(orchestra)* parterre m
stamp timbre m 150, 154
stamp machine distributeur m
  (automatique) de timbres
stand in line, to faire la queue 112

standby ticket billet m sans garantie
start (n) début m
start, to (begin) commencer 98, 108, 112; (car) démarrer 88
starter entrée f
statement déclaration f; (police) déposition f 93
station gare f 73, 96
station wagon (voiture f) break m
statue statue f 99
stay (n) séjour m 32
stay, to (lodge) rester 23; loger 123; (remain) rester 65
steak house (restaurant)-gril m 35
stereo stéréo f
stern (ship) poupe f
stiff neck torticolis m 163
still: I'm still waiting j'attends encore
sting piqûre f
stocking bas mpl 144
stolen, to be être volé(e) 71
stomach estomac m 166; **~ ache** mal m à l'estomac 163
stool (feces) selles fpl 164
stop (bus/tram) arrêt m 79; (metro) station f 80
stop, to s'arrêter 77, 78, 98; **~ here** arrêtez-vous ici; **I'll stop by** je passerai
stopover halte f
store magasin m 130
store detective agent m de surveillance
store guide plan du magasin m 132
storekeeper commerçant(e) m/f
stove cuisinière f 28, 29
straight ahead tout droit 95
strained muscle muscle m froissé 162
strange étrange
straw (drinking) paille f
stream ruisseau m 107
string ficelle f
striped (patterned) à rayures
stoller poussette f
strong fort
student étudiant(e) m/f 74, 100
study, to étudier 121
stunning stupéfiant(e) 101
stupid: that was stupid! c'était bête!

sturdy solide
style style m 104
styling mousse mousse f coiffante
subtitled, to be être sous-titré 110
subway métro m 80; **~ station** station de métro m 80, 96
suede daim m
suggest, to suggérer 123
suit costume m 144
suitable for, to be convenir à 140
summer été m 219
sun block écran m total 142
sun lounger chaise f longue
sunbathe, to prendre un bain de soleil
sunburn coup m de soleil 141
Sunday dimanche m 218
sunglasses lunettes fpl de soleil
sunstroke insolation f 163
suntan lotion crème f solaire 142
super (gas) super 87
superb superbe 101
supermarket supermarché m 158
supplement supplément m 68, 69
suppositories suppositoires mpl 165
sure: are you sure? êtes-vous sûr(e)?
surfboard planche f de surf 116
surname nom m de famille
suspicious suspect(e)
swallow, to avaler
sweater pullover m, pull m
sweatshirt sweatshirt m 144
sweet (taste) sucré(e)
sweets bonbons mpl 150
swelling enflure f 162
swim, to nager, se baigner 116
swimming natation f 114; **~ pool** piscine f 22, 26, 116; **~ trunks** slip de bain m 144
swimsuit maillot de bain m 144
Swiss (person) Suisse m/f
switch (electric) interrupteur m
switch on, to allumer
switch off, to éteindre
Switzerland Suisse f 119
swollen, to be être enflé(e)
symptoms symptômes mpl 163
synagogue synagogue f 105
synthetic synthétique 145

T

T-shirt T-shirt m 144, 156
table (restaurant) table f 36, 112
table cloth nappe f
table tennis tennis m de table
tablet (medicine) comprimé m 140
take away, to à emporter 40
take photographs, to prendre des photos 98, 100
take someone home, to raccompagner
take, to (bus) prendre; (carry) emporter 71; (medicine) prendre 140, 165; (last) durer 78; (to a place) emmener 84; **I'll take it** (purchase) je le/la prends 135; (room) 24
takeaway (takeout) plats mpl à emporter
taken (occupied) occupé(e), pris(e) 77
talcum powder talc m
talk, to parler
tall grand(e) 14
tampons tampons mpl 142
tan bronzage m
tarpaulin tapis de sol 31
taste goût m
taxi taxi m 70, 71, 84
taxi driver chauffeur m de taxi
taxi stand station f de taxi 96
tea thé m 40
tea bags sachets mpl de thé 160
teacher instituteur m, professeur m
team équipe f 114
teaspoon cuillère f à café 140, 148
teenager adolescent(e) m/f
telephone téléphone m 22, 92, 127; **~ bill** note f de téléphone; **~ booth** cabine f téléphonique 127; **~ calls** coups mpl de téléphone 32; **~ directory** annuaire m; **~ kiosk** cabine f téléphonique; **~ number** numéro m de téléphone 127 (➤ phone)
telephone, to téléphoner 128
television télévision f
tell, to dire 18, 79; **tell me** dites-moi 79
temperature (water) température f; (body) 164
temporary temporaire
ten dix 216
tendon tendon m

tennis tennis m 114; **~ ball** balle m de tennis; **~ court** court m de tennis 115
tent tente f 30, 31; **~ pegs** piquets mpl de tente 31; **~ pole** montant m de tente; grand piquet de tente 31
terrible terrible 101
tetanus tétanos m 164
thank you merci 10, 94
that cela; **~ one** celui-là (celle-là) 16, 134; **that's all** c'est tout 133
thawing snow neige f fondue
theater théâtre m 96, 99, 110
theft vol m 71, 153; cambriolage m 153
their leur 16
theirs à eux (à elles) 16; **it's ~** c'est le/la/les leur(s)
them les; (to them) à eux (à elles) 16; **for ~** pour eux/elles
theme park parc m d'attraction
then (time) alors, ensuite 13
there là 17
there is... il y a... 17
thermometer thermomètre m
thermos flask bouteille f thermos
these ceux-ci, celles-ci 134
they eux (elles)
thick épais(se)
thief voleur m
thigh cuisse f 166
thin mince
think: I think je pense 42, 77
third troisième 217; **a ~** un tiers 217
third party insurance assurance f au tiers
thirsty assoiffé(e)
this one celui-ci (celle-ci) 16, 134
those ceux-là (celles-là) 134
thousand mille 216
thread fil m
three trois 216
throat gorge f 166; **~ lozenges** pastilles fpl pour la gorge
thrombosis thrombose f
through à travers
thumb pouce m 166
Thursday jeudi m 218

A-Z

ticket billet m 69, 75, 77, 100, 114, 153; ticket m 79, 80, 100, 114, 153; ~ **agency** agence f de spectacles; ~ **office** guichet m 73

tie cravate f 144

tie pin épingle f à cravate

tight (clothing) serré(e) 146

tights collant m 144

time heure f 76, 78, 220; free ~ temps m libre 98; on ~ à l'heure 76

timetable horaire m 75

tin (can) boîte f; ~ **opener** ouvre-boîte m 148

tin foil papier m d'aluminium

tinted (glass/lens) teinté(e)

tip pourboire m 32

tipping 32, 42, 71

tire (auto) pneu m 83

tired, to be être fatigué(e)

tissues mouchoirs mpl en papier 142

to (place) jusqu'à 12

toaster grille-pain m

tobacco tabac m 150

tobogganing, to go faire de la luge

today aujourd'hui 124, 218

toe orteil m 166

together ensemble 42

toilet paper papier m toilette 25, 29, 142

toiletries 142

tomorrow demain 84, 124, 218

tongs pinces fpl

tonight ce soir 110, 124; for tonight pour ce soir 108

tonsillitis angine f

tonsils amygdales fpl 166

too (also) aussi; (extreme) trop 17, 93; ~ **much** trop 15

tooth dent f 168

toothache mal m de dent

toothbrush brosse f à dents

toothpaste dentifrice m 142

top sommet m, bouchon m

top floor étage m supérieur

torch lampe f de poche/électrique 31

torn, to be (muscle) être déchiré(e) 164

tote totalisateur m

tough (food) dur(e) 41

tour tour m; visite f 97

tour guide guide m touristique

tour operator organisateur m de voyages 26

tour representative représentant m de vacances 27

tourist touriste m

tourist information office office m de tourisme 97

tow rope corde f de remorquage

tow, to remorquer

towards vers, en direction de 12

towel serviette f

tower tour f 99

town ville f 70, 94

toy jouet m 157

track piste f, sentier m

tracksuit jogging m, survêtement m

traditional traditionnel(le) 35

traffic circulation f

traffic jam embouteillage m, bouchon m

traffic violation/offence infraction f au code de la route

trail chemin m, sentier m 106

trailer caravane f 30, 81

trailer park terrain m de camping caravaning

train train m 75, 76, 77; (subway) rame f 80

train station gare f 73

train times horaires mpl des trains 75

trainers chaussures fpl de sport 145

tram tram m 78, 79

translate, to traduire 11

translation traduction f

translator traducteur(-trice) m/f

trash ordures fpl 28

trash can poubelle f 30

travel agency agence f de voyages 131

travel sickness mal m des transports 141

travel, to voyager

traveler's check chèque m de voyage 136, 138

tray plateau m

tree arbre m 106

tremendous formidable 101

trip voyage m, 76, 78, 97, 123; promenade f 97

truck camion m

true north plein nord m
true: that's not true ce n'est pas vrai
try on, to essayer 146
Tuesday mardi m 218
tunnel tunnel m
turn, to tourner 95;
~ **down** (volume, heat) baisser;
~ **off** arrêter, éteindre 25; ~
~ **on** mettre en marche, allumer 25; ~
up (volume, heat) monter, augmenter
turning intersection f
TV télévision f 22; ~ **room** salle f de
télévision; ~-**listings magazine**
magazine m de télévision
tweezers pince f à épiler
twelve douze 216
twice deux fois 217
twin beds lits mpl jumeaux
two deux 216
two-door car voiture f deux portes 86
type type m; **what** ~? quel nom? 109;
quel genre? 112
typical typique 37

U **ugly** laid(e) 14, 101
U.K. Royaume-Uni
ulcer ulcère m
umbrella parapluie m; **beach** ~ parasol
116
uncle oncle m 120
unconscious, to be avoir perdu
connaissance 92; être sans
connaissance 162
under (place) sous
underdone (food) pas assez cuit(e) 41
underpants slip m/sing. 144
underpass passage m sous-terrain 96
understand, to comprendre 11;
do you understand? vous comprenez?
11; **I don't understand** je ne comprends
pas 11, 67
undress, to se déshabiller 164
unfortunately malheureusement 19
uniform uniforme m
unit unité f 155
university université f
unleaded gas essence f sans plomb 87
unlock, to ouvrir

unpleasant désagréable
14
unscrew, to dévisser
until jusqu'à 221
upper (berth) supérieur(e)
74
upset stomach mal m de ventre 141
upstairs en haut 12
up to jusqu'à 12
urgent urgent 161
us: for/with us pour/avec nous
U.S. États-Unis mpl 119
use, to utiliser 139
use: for my personal use pour mon
usage personnel 67
useful utile

V **vacancy** chambre f libre 21
vacant libre 14
vacate, to libérer 32
vacation, on en vacances fpl 66, 123
vaccinated against, to be
être vacciné(e) contre 164
vaccination vaccin m, vaccination f
valet service service m de
nettoyage complet
valid valable 75
validate, to (ticket) composter
valley vallée f 107
valuable de (grande) valeur
value valeur f 155
vegetables légumes mpl 38
vegetarian (adj/n) végétarien(ne) m/f
35; **to be vegetarian** être
végétarien(ne) 39
vehicle véhicule m; ~ **registration**
document carte f grise 93
vein veine f
velvet velours m
venereal disease maladie f
vénérienne 165
very très 17
vest maillot m de corps
vet(erinarian) vétérinaire m
video cassette vidéo f; ~ **game** jeu
vidéo m; ~ **recorder** magnétoscope m
view: with a view of the sea
avec vue sur la mer

viewpoint belvédère m 99 107;
point m de vue 107
village village m 107
vineyard vigne f 107
visa visa m
visit visite f
visit, to (sights) visiter 123; (person in hospital) venir voir 167
visiting hours heures fpl de visite
visitor center centre m pour visiteurs
vitamin pills vitamines fpl 141
voice voix f
voltage voltage m
vomit, to vomir 163

W **waist** taille f
wait, to attendre 41, 140; ~ **for** attendre 76, 89; **wait!**
attendez! 98
Waiter! garçon! m 37
waiting room salle f d'attente 73
Waitress! mademoiselle! f 37
wake, to (self) se réveiller; (s.o. else) réveiller 27
wake-up call appel m de réveil
Wales Pays de Galles m 119
walk promenade f 106; **to go for a ~** aller faire une promenade
walk home, to rentrer chez moi à pied 65
walking marche f; ~ **boots** chaussures fpl de marche 145; ~ **route** circuit m de randonnée 106; ~ **(hiking) gear** équipement m pour la marche 145
wall mur m
wallet portefeuille m 42, 153
want, to vouloir 18
ward (hospital) chambre f 167
warm (weather) chaud 24, 122
warm, to réchauffer 39
warmer plus chaud(e) 24
wash, to laver
washbasin lavabo m
washer (for faucet) joint m
washing: ~ **instructions** conseils mpl de lavage; ~ **machine** machine f à laver; ~ **powder** lessive f 148
washing, to do faire la vaisselle

washing-up liquid liquide m vaisselle m 148
wasp guêpe f
watch montre f 149, 153
watch band bracelet m de montre m
watch TV, to regarder la télé(vision)
watchmaker horloger m
water eau f 87, 116; ~ **bottle** bouillote m; ~ **heater** chauffe-eau m 28
water skis skis mpl nautiques 116
waterfall cascade f 107
waterproof imperméable, étanche; ~ **jacket** blouson m imperméable 145
waterskiing ski m nautique
wave vague f
waxing épilation f à la cire 147
way: I've lost my ~ je me suis perdu(e) 94; **on the ~** sur la route
we nous
weak (coffee) clair; **I feel ~** je me sens faible
wear, to porter 152
weather temps m 122
weather forecast météo f 122
wedding mariage m; ~ **ring** alliance f
Wednesday mercredi m 218
week semaine f 23, 97, 218
weekend weekend m; **on [at] the weekend** le weekend 218; **weekend rate** tarif m de week-end 86
weekly ticket ticket m/billet m pour la semaine
weight: my weight is... je pèse...
welcome to... bienvenue à...
Welsh (adj) gallois(e)
Welsh person Gallois(e) m/f
west ouest m 95
wetsuit combinaison f de plongée
what? qu'est-ce que? 18
what sort of? quel genre de? 14, 106
what time...? à quelle heure...? 68, 76, 78, 81
what's the time? quelle heure est-il? 220
when? quand?, à quelle heure? 13
where? où 12, 99; ~ **are you from?** d'où êtes-vous? 119; ~ **can we...?** où pouvons-nous...?
which quel(le) 80; ~ **one?** lequel (laquelle)? 16

while pendant que

white blanc(he) 143; **~ wine** vin m blanc 40

who? qui? 16

whole: the whole day toute la journée

whose? à qui? 16

why? pourquoi 15

wide large 14

wife femme f 120, 162

wildlife faune f et flore f

window fenêtre f 25, 77; *(shop)* vitrine f 134, 149; **~ seat** siège m côté hublot 69, 74

windshield [windscreen] pare-brise m

windsurfer planche f à voile

windy, it's il y a du vent m 122

wine vin m 40, 160; **~box** vin m en boîte; **~ list** carte f des vins 37

winery vigne f 107

winter hiver m 219

wishes: best wishes to… meilleurs vœux à… 219

with avec 17

withdraw, to *(money)* retirer 139

without sans 17

witness témoin m 93

wood *(forest, material)* bois m

wool laine 145

work, to *(job)* travailler 121; *(function)* marcher 25, 28, 83, 89; fonctionner 28

worry: I'm worried je me fais du souci

worse pire 14; **it's become worse** ça a empiré

worst le/la/les pire(s)

worth: is it worth seeing? est-ce que ça vaut la peine d'être vu?

wound blessure f

wrap up, to faire un paquet-cadeau

write down, to écrire 136

write soon! écrivez [écris] vite!

writing pad papier m à lettres

wrong faux (fausse) 14, 136; mauvais(e) 88, 136; **~ number** *(phone)* faux numéro m 128

 X Y Z

x-ray radio f 164

yacht yacht m

year année f 218

yellow jaune 143

yes oui 10

yesterday hier 218

yogurt yaourt m

you *(sing/pl)* vous, tu 16; **to ~** à vous; à toi 16

young jeune 14

your votre/vos; ton/ta/tes 16

yours à vous, à toi 16; **it's ~** c'est le/la vôtre/les vôtres; c'est le tien/la tienne/les tien(ne)s

youth hostel auberge f de jeunesse 29

zebra crossing passage m piéton

zero zéro m

zip(per) fermeture f éclair

zone zone f

zoo zoo m 113

zoology zoologie f

Dictionary
French – English

This French-English dictionary concentrates on all the areas where you may need to decode written French: hotels, public buildings, restaurants, shops, ticket offices and transportation. It will also help with understanding forms, maps, product labels, road signs and operating instuctions (for telephones, parking meters, etc.).
If you can't locate the exact sign, you may find key words or terms listed separately.

[Note: entries are not listed under the particles: **à**, **au**, **aux**, **d'**, **de**, **des**, **le**, **l'**, **la**, or **les**.]

A à la ... ... style
abonnement season ticket
abribus bus shelter
l'accès aux véhicules est interdit pendant la traversée
  no access to car decks during crossing
accès réservé aux voyageurs munis de billets ticket holders only
accôtements non stabilisés soft edges
ACF French automobile association
acier steel
ACS Swiss Automobile Association
administration public building
adresse domicile home address
adressez-vous à la réception
  ask at reception
aérogare airport, air terminal
affranchissements stamps
agence de spectacles ticket agency
agence de voyage travel agent
agence immobilière real estate agent
agent de la RATP subway ticket inspector
aire de croisement passing area
aire de pique-nique picnic area
aire de repos/de stationnement
  rest area
aller-retour round-trip
aller-simple one-way trip
allumez vos feux de route/croisement/phares
  switch on/use headlights
alpinisme mountaineering
altitude par rapport au niveau de la mer
  height above sea level

ambassade embassy
amélioré improved
ameublement furniture
ampoules auto-cassables
  easy-to-open capsules [ampules]
anglais English
annuaire téléphonique directory
annulé cancelled
août August
appareils photo interdits
  no photography
appuyer pour ouvrir press to open
après-demain the day after tomorrow
l'après-midi p.m.
argent money; silver
arrêt de bus bus stop
arrêt facultatif request stop
arrêt interdit no stopping
arrêtez votre moteur
  turn off your engine
arrivées arrivals
arrondissement administrative district
articles vendus avec défaut
  damaged goods
ascenseur elevator
atelier d'artiste studio
attachez vos ceintures (de sécurité)
  fasten your seat belt
attendez votre billet
  wait for your ticket
attendre la tonalité wait for tone
attente d'environ ... mn
  wait approx ... mins.
attention caution, warning
attention à la fermeture automatique des portières warning! automatic doors!

attention à la marche mind the step
attention bétail warning! cattle!
attention station en courbe
  mind the gap (subway)
auberge de jeunesse youth hostel
aujourd'hui today
autocar coach
automne fall/autumn
autoroute highway
autoroute à péage toll route
autres directions other directions
avant … before …
avant les repas before meals
avec douche with shower
avec nos remerciements
  paid (with thanks)
avec plomb leaded
avec salle de bains
  with bathroom
avec vue sur mer with sea view
avion plane
avis de coup de vent gale warning
avril April

B baie bay
baignade surveillée
  supervised swimming
bains publics baths
bande d'arrêt d'urgence
  hard-shoulder
banlieue suburbs, outskirts
banque bank
bassin pond
bassin d'alimentation reservoir
bateau ship
bateau à vapeur steamer
bateaux-mouches river boats
bazar general store
bd boulevard
berge river bank
bibliothèque library
bienvenue! welcome!
bière beer
bijoutier jeweler's
billet ticket
billet Section Urbaine ticket valid for
  métro, RER and suburban train
billets périmés used tickets
"le blanc" household linen
blanchisserie laundry
bois wood
boissons drinks
bonnes affaires bargains

bonnets de bain
obligatoires
  bathing caps must be
  worn
boucherie butcher
bouchons traffic jams:
  delays likely
boulangerie bakery/baker's
boules French game of bowls
bourse stock exchange
bouteille consignée returnable bottle
boutique hors-taxes duty-free shop
BP P.O. Box
braderie discount store, clearance sale
bricolage et jardinage
  hardware and garden store
brocante(ur) secondhand shop
brouillard fréquent risk of fog
bureau d'accueil reception center
bureau d'information information desk
bureau de change
  currency exchange office
bureau de vente (des billets) ticket office
bureau des objets trouvés lost and
  found

C cabine d'essayage fitting room
cabine de bain bathing
  cabana/hut
cabine de téléphérique cable car cabin
cabinet médical/dentaire
  doctor's/dentist's office [surgery]
cachets pills, tablets
cadeau gratuit free gift
cadeaux gifts
caisse checkout, please pay here
caisse 5 articles 5 items or less
caisse d'épargne savings bank
caisse livraison à domicile
  checkout for home delivery
caisse rapide/éclair express checkout
caissiers cashiers
camion truck
canne à pêche fishing rod
canton Swiss administrative district
caravane trailer
carnet book (of tickets)
carrosserie repair garage
carte d'abonnement season ticket
carte d'assuré social
  national insurance card
carte d'embarquement boarding card
carte d'identité ID card
carte orange pass for Paris metro/bus
carte routière road map

carte verte green (insurance) card
carte téléphonique phonecard
les cartes de crédit ne sont pas acceptées credit cards not accepted
caserne de pompiers fire station
casque crash helmet
casser la vitre en cas d'urgence break glass in case of emergency
ce bus dessert … this bus is going to …
ce matin this morning
ce soir this evening
ce train desservira les gares de … this train stops at …
cet appareil rend la monnaie this machine gives change
cédez le passage give way (yield)
ceinture circle (ramparts or mountains)
ceinture de sauvetage lifebelt
centre commercial shopping mall
centre médico-social health clinic
centre ville downtown area
cet après-midi this afternoon
cette machine ne rend pas la monnaie this machine does not give change
CH Switzerland
chaise longue deck chair
chambre d'hôte bed & breakfast
la chambre a besoin d'être faite this room needs making up
chambres à louer rooms to let
chambres libres vacancies
champ field
change currency exchange
changer à change at …
charcuterie delicatessen
charge maximum load limit
chariots carts
chasse hunting
château castle, stately home
chaud hot
chaussée déformée poor/uneven road surface
chaussée glissante/verglacée icy road
chaussures shoes
chemin walk(way), path
les chèques ne sont pas acceptés checks not accepted
chez at (the home/place of)
chien méchant beware of the dog

choisir la destination/la zone select destination/zone
au choix of your choice
Chronopost® express mail
chutes de pierres falling rocks
cimetière cemetery
cinéma permanent continuous performance
cinq ampères 5 amp
circulation interdite closed to traffic
circulation opposée traffic from the opposite direction
circulation ralentie slow traffic
citoyens (non-)européens (non-)EU citizens
classé monument historique listed building
clé minute keys while you wait
climatisé air conditioned
club de voile sailing club
coiffeur hairdresser
coiffeur pour hommes barber
coiffeur-visagiste stylist
col (mountain) pass
Colissimo express parcel post
collège secondary (U.S. high) school
colline hill
commence à … begins at …
commissariat (de police) police station
complet full, sold out
complexe industriel industrial estate
composez votre code confidentiel dial your PIN
composez votre numéro dial number
compostez votre billet validate/punch your ticket
compris included (in the price)
compteur électrique electric meter
comptoir d'enregistrement check-in counter
concierge caretaker
concours contest
conducteur/conductrice driver
confiseur confectioner's
confiture jam
congelé frozen
conseillé recommended
conseils de préparation cooking recommendations
conservateurs preservatives

à conserver au congélateur/réfrigérateur keep frozen/refrigerated
à conserver au frais keep in a cool place
conservez votre ticket de caisse/titre de transport keep your receipt/ticket
consigné returnable
consigne automatique luggage lockers
consigne manuelle baggage check
consommation au comptoir drink at the bar
à consommer de préférence avant fin … best before end …
consultations consulting room, outpatients
conteneur papier newspapers only
conteneur verre bottle bank
contre-allée service road
contrôle des douanes customs control
convient aux végétariens/végétaliens suitable for vegetarians/vegans
convoi exceptionnel long vehicle
cordonnier cobbler's
correspondances connection
côte coast
couloir d'autobus bus lane
cour yard
cours du change exchange rate
cousu main hand-sewn
crème peaux grasses/sèches moisturizer for oily/dry skin
crème solaire (indice 8) (factor 8) sun cream
crémerie dairy
croisement crossing, intersection
croisières cruises, river trips
à croquer chewable
CRS French riot police
c centime (1/100 of a franc)
cuir leather
cuisine kitchen
cuisson sans décongélation cook without defrosting
CV horsepower

D **dames** ladies (toilets)
danger de mort danger of death
date d'expiration expiration date
date de fraîcheur best before (date)
date de naissance date of birth
date de péremption use-by date
date limite de vente sell by date
de … à … from … to …

débranché disconnected
début d'autoroute expressway entrance
déchetterie waste point
déchirer ici tear here
décoration home furnishings
décrochez lift receiver
défense d'entrer keep out
dégustation de vins wine tasting
demain tomorrow
demander un vendeur please ask for assistance
demi-pension half board
déposer vos clés à la réception leave keys at reception
dépôt d'ordures interdit don't dump trash
dépôts et retraits deposits and withdrawals
dernière entrée à … latest entry at … p.m.
dernière station essence avant l'autoroute/la voie rapide last gas station before the expressway
descente en rappel abseiling
deuxième étage second (U.S. third) floor
déviation obligatoire pour véhicules lourds diversion for trucks, truck route
devises étrangères foreign currency
dimanche Sunday
Dimanche de Pâques Easter Sunday
directeur manager
disquaire record dealer
dissoudre dans un peu d'eau dissolve in water
distribanque/distributeur automatique ATM/cash-dispenser
dons donations
dos d'âne (en voie de formation) ramps
douanes customs
doublé dubbed
douches showers

E **eau courante** running water
eau (non) potable (non) drinking water
échange exchange
échangeur (d'autoroute) freeway interchange/junction
échelle: … scale: …
école school

écran total sun block cream
effets indésirables side effects
église church
électro-ménager electrical goods
embarquement en cours boarding now
embarquement immédiat last call
emplacement gravier/herbeux/sableux stone/grass/sand (camping site)
empruntez le passage souterrain use the underpass
en bas downstairs
en cas d'accident, prière de téléphoner à.../de contacter... in case of breakdown, phone/contact …
en cas d'incendie in the event of fire
en chantier under construction/proposed
en dehors des repas without food
en haut upstairs
en plein air open air
en (projet de) construction under construction/proposed
en retard delayed
... en vente ici ... on sale here
enceinte city wall
enfants children
entre ... et ... between ... and ... (time)
entrée entrance, way in
entrée gratuite admission free
entrée interdite no entry
entrée - ne pas stationner do not block entrance
entrer par la porte arrière/avant enter by the rear/front door
enregistrement check in
envois en nombre bulk mailing
épicerie grocer's
épicerie fine delicatessen
équitation horseback riding
escalade rock climbing
escalier de service back stairs/service stairs
espèces cash
essence (sans plomb) (unleaded) gas
essorage dry spin
(d')est east(ern)
étang pond
été summer
éteignez/éteindre switch off
étranger foreign
étudiant student

EU (États-Unis) United States
événement event
évêque bishop
excédent de bagages excess baggage
exigez votre reçu ask for a receipt
exp./expéditeur sender
extincteur fire extinguisher

F **F(F)** French franc
fabriqué en ... made in ...
faille fault (geol.)
faire la queue derrière la barrière please wait behind barrier
fait main handmade
fait maison homemade
fait sur mesure made to measure
falaise cliff
farine flour
fauteuil (près du) hublot window seat
FB Belgian franc
femmes women (toilets); ladies wear
fer iron
ferme farm
fermé closed
fermé pendant les travaux closed for renovations
fermer la porte close the door
fermeture annuelle closed for vacation [holiday]
fermeture automatique des portières automatic doors
fête nationale National holiday
feux d'artifice fireworks
feux interdits no fires/barbeques
février February
film en version française/originale film in French/original version
fin d'autoroute freeway exit
fin d'interdiction de stationner end of no parking zone
fin de BAU end of hard shoulder
fin de travaux end of construction (road)
fleuriste florist's
foire fair
... fois par jour ... times a day
forêt forest
frais fresh
frais d'opérations bank charges
français French
frapper knock
frère brother
froid cold
fromage cheese
fumeurs smoking

G galerie viewing gallery; arcade
garage en sous-sol underground garage
gardien caretaker
gare (ferroviaire/SNCF) railroad station
gare routière haulage depot
gazoil fuel; diesel
gélules capsules, gel caps
gendarmerie nationale highway police
généraliste general practitioner
gilets de sauvetage lifejackets
gîte d'étape self-catering cottage, B&B
gîte rural self-catering cottage
gouttes drops
gradin tier
grand large
grand bassin deep end
grand magasin department store
grand teint colorfast
grande surface department store
grandes lignes intercity trains
gratuit free
gravillons loose stones (road)
grotte cave
groupes acceptés parties welcome
groupe sanguin blood group
guichet box office, ticket office

H h. hour, o'clock
habit de rigueur formal wear
habitation à loyer modéré (H.L.M) low rent apartment
halle covered market; hall
hammam Turkish bath
haut-lieu historique important historical feature
haute tension high voltage
hauteur limitée à … m headroom/height restriction: …
hebdomadaire weekly
heures d'ouverture business hours/opening
heure hour
heures de levée times of collection
hippodrome racetrack
hiver winter
hommes menswear; men (toilets)
hôpital hospital
horaires (d'été/ d'hiver) (summer/winter) timetable
horaires d'ouverture visiting hours
horaires de vacances holiday timetable
horloger watchmaker

horodateur parking meter
hors service out of order
hôtel de ville town hall
hôtesse de l'air flight attendant
huile oil
hydroptère jetfoil

I ici here
ici on brade tout prices slashed
ici on vous sert service
immeuble apartment building
impasse dead end
indéformable will not lose its shape
infirmerie infirmary
infirmières nurses
information clientèle customer information
informations de vol flight information
insérez pièce insert coin
insérez votre billet insert ticket
insérez votre carte insert credit card
interactions médicamenteuses interference with other drugs
interdiction de déposer des ordures no littering, no dumping
... interdit (de) … forbidden
interdit à toute circulation traffic-free zone
interdit aux deux roues no access for cyclists and motorcyclists
interdit aux enfants de moins de .... no children under …
interdit aux mineurs non accompagnés no unaccompanied children
interdit sauf aux riverains access only
intérieur indoor
introduire carte/ les pièces insert card/coins
issue de secours fire exit
itinéraire bis alternative route
itinéraire de déviation diversion, detour
itinéraire obligatoire pour véhicules lourds truck route

J janvier January
jardin public public gardens/park
jardinerie garden center
jeudi Thursday
à jeun on an empty stomach
jeunesse young adult/youth
jeux de ballon interdits no ball games

A-Z

jouets toys
jour de fermeture: day off/closed
jour férié Bank/National Holiday
le jour de l'An New Year's Day
journal féminin women's magazine
jours de semaine weekdays
jours pairs/impairs (parking allowed on) even/odd days
juillet July
juin June
jus de fruits fruit juices
jusqu'à until

L

lac lake
laine wool
laisser descendre les passagers let passengers off first
laisser fondre dans l'eau/la bouche dissolve in water/suck
laisser vos sacs à l'entrée du magasin leave your bags here
langues étrangères foreign languages
lavable en machine machine washable
lavabos wash bowl
lavage à la main hand wash only
laver séparément wash separately
layette baby wear
légumes vegetables
lettre recommandée registered letter
lever de rideau curtain up
libérer votre chambre avant ... vacate your room by ...
librairie bookstore
libre vacant, for hire
libre-service bancaire ATM/cashpoint
lieu de bataille battle site
lieu de naissance place of birth
lieu touristique tourist spot
ligne de bus bus route
ligne directe direct service
ligne réservée reserved lane
limitation de vitesse speed limit
lin linen
linge de maison household linen
liquidation clearance
liquide cash
livraisons uniquement deliveries only
livre sterling pound sterling
livres de poche paperbacks

location de voitures car rental
locations accommodations available
logement accommodations
loisirs hobbies and interests
lot multi pack
lotion après-soleil after sun lotion
lotissement housing area [estate]
loto lottery
à louer for hire/for rent
lundi Monday
Lundi de Pâques Easter Monday
lunettes de soleil sunglasses
lycée secondary (U.S. high) school

M

M (Monsieur) Mr.
magasin d'antiquités antiques store
magasin de diététique health-food store
magasin de jouets toy store
magasin d'usine factory outlet
mai May
maigre fat-free
mairie town hall
la maison house and home
maison de la presse newsstand
maison de village terraced house
maison à louer house to rent
mandats postaux money orders, postal orders
manoir manor house
manette du signal d'alarme pull for alarm
marais swamp, marsh
marchand de légumes greengrocer's
marchandises hors-taxes duty-free goods
marche walking, hiking
marché market
marché aux puces flea market
mardi Tuesday
mare pond
mars March
match aller first leg
match retour second leg
matière grasse fat content
mazout fuel oil
le matin a.m.
Me (Maître) lawyer (title)
médecin doctor
meilleur au monde world leader
mensuel monthly
menu fixe/à ... F set menu/for ... francs
menu minceur dieter's menu

mer sea
merci pour vos dons
  thank you for your contribution
mercredi Wednesday
mère mother
messieurs gentlemen (toilets)
météo weather forecast
métro subway
mettez vos chaînes
  use chains or snow tires
mettre la pièce et prendre le ticket
  insert money in machine and
  remove ticket
meublé self-catering; furnished
  accommodations
meubles furniture
midi noon
(du) midi south(ern)
minuit midnight
mise en fourrière immédiate
  unauthorized vehicles will be towed
  away
Mlle (Mademoiselle) Miss
Mme (Madame) Mrs.
mode d'emploi instructions for use
au moins at least
à moitié prix half price
moniteur (de voile) (sailing) instructor
montagne mountain
montant exact exact change
monument aux morts war memorial
monument classé listed historic
  building
mosquée mosque
mouillage interdit no anchorage
moulin à vent windmill
mur wall
musée museum

N **natation** swimming
  navette shuttle service
  ne circule pas le dimanche
doesn't run on Sundays
ne contient pas de ... contains no ...
**ne laissez pas vos bagages sans
  surveillance** do not leave baggage
  unattended
ne pas affranchir free post
ne pas avaler not to be taken orally
ne pas brûler do not burn
ne pas consommer sans avis médical
  consult your doctor before use
ne pas courir no running
ne pas déranger do not disturb

ne pas doubler no
  passing
**ne pas exposer à la
  lumière**
  do not expose to
  sunlight
**ne pas fumer dans le pont des
  véhicules**
  no smoking on car decks
ne pas klaxonner use of horn
  prohibited
ne pas laisser à la portée des enfants
  keep out of reach of children
**ne pas laisser d'objets de valeur dans
  les voitures**
  do not leave valuables in your car
ne pas marcher sur les pelouses
  keep off the grass
ne pas parler au conducteur
  do not talk to the driver
ne pas repasser do not iron
ne pas se pencher hors des fenêtres
  do not lean out of windows
ne pas traverser les voies do not cross
neige glacée icy (snow)
neige lourde/mouillée/poudreuse
  heavy/wet/powdery (snow)
nettoyage à sec dry-cleaner's
ni repris, ni échange goods cannot be
  refunded or exchanged
nids de poules potholes
niveau intermédiaire intermediate level
niveau de la mer sea level
Noël Christmas
nom de famille surname, last name
nom de jeune fille maiden name
nom de l'époux/l'épouse name of
  spouse
non comris not included (in the price),
  exclusive
non consigné non-returnable
non-fumeurs non-smoking
(du) nord north(ern)
normal two-star/regular gas
normes de qualité quality standard
nos suggestions serving suggestions
notez le numéro de votre emplacement
  note your parking space number
n'oubliez pas de ... don't forget to ...
n'oubliez pas de composter votre billet
  don't forget to validate your ticket
n'oubliez pas le guide
  remember to tip your guide
nous acceptons les cartes de crédit
  we accept credit cards

A-Z

nous achetons et revendons ...
we buy and sell ...
nous déclinons toute responsabilité en cas de dommage ou vol
the owners can accept no responsibility for any damage or theft.
nouveau brand-new
nouveautés new titles, new releases
Nouvel an New Year
nouvel signalisation
new traffic system in operation
nouvelles news
nuit night
numéro d'immatriculation
car license plate number
numéro de secours
emergency number
numéro de siège seat number
numéro de vol flight number
numéro vert toll-free number
numérotez dial

O **objets perdus/trouvés**
lost property, lost and found
oblitérez votre billet punch your ticket
occasions opportunity, second-hand
(d')occident west(ern)
office du matin morning mass
office du soir evening service
l'office est commencé
service in progress
on achète à ... currency bought at ...
on demande des ... ... required
on n'accepte pas les cartes de crédit
no credit cards
on parle anglais English spoken
on vend à ... currency sold at ...
opticien/optique optician's
or gold
ordinaire regular (gas)
ordinateurs computers
ordonnance prescription
(de l')orient east(ern)
orientations directions; plan
(de l')ouest west(ern)
ouvert open
ouvert 24 heures sur 24
24-hour service
ouvert le/les ... open until/on ...
ouvert(ure) open

ouvrir ici open here

P **pages jaunes** yellow pages
pain bread
palais de justice courthouse
palais des congrès convention hall
panier shopping basket
papiers trash
papeterie stationer's
Pâques Easter
paquets packages
par jour/semaine per day/week
parapente parasailing
parc d'attractions amusement park
parcmètre parking meter
parcotrain parking for train users
parfum flavoring, perfume
parking à étages
multi-story parking lot
parking clients/clientèle
customer parking lot
parking longue/courte durée
long-/short-term parking
parking payant pay parking lot
paroisse parish
parterre orchestra [stalls]
à partir de... commencing ...
passage à niveau automatique/manuel
railroad crossing
passage clouté pedestrian crossing
passage interdit no access
passage piétons pedestrian crossing
passage sous-terrain underground passage
passe au lave-vaisselle dishwasher-proof
passe au micro-ondes microwaveable
pâtes pasta
patientez please wait
patinage ice skating
patins à glaces skates
pâtisserie pastry shop
pavillon pavilion; ward (separate building)
pavillon de banlieue bungalow
payez à l'horodateur pay at the meter
payez à l'ordre de ... payable to ...
payer au guichet pay at counter
payer avant de vous servir
pay for gas before filling car
payer comptant pay cash
payez en entrant pay on entry
PCV collect call/reverse-charge
péage toll

pêche à la ligne angling
pêche interdite no fishing
peinture fraîche wet paint
pendant ... jours for ... days
pendant le service during services
pendant les repas with food/meals
péniches pleasure steamers, river boats
péninsule peninsula
pension complète full board
pension de famille guest house
pente incline
Père/père fr. (Father) (rel.)/father
périphérique (extérieur/intérieur)
 (outer/inner) ring-road
permis de conduire driver's license
permis obligatoire permit-holders only
pétanque bowls/boules
petit small
petit bassin shallow end
petit déjeuner breakfast
p.ex. e.g.
phare lighthouse; headlight
pharmacie (de garde)
 (all-night/duty) drugstore
pièce coin; play
piétons pedestrians
piscine (dé)couverte
 indoor (outdoor) swimming pool
piste (skiing) trail
piste bleue ski trail for intermediates
piste cyclable cycle lane/path
piste de cours racing track
piste rouge/noire for advanced skiers
piste verte beginner slope
PJ criminal investigation dept.
place square
placer le ticket derrière le pare-brise
 place ticket on windshield
places assises seulement no standing
plage (nudiste) (nudist) beach
plan du magasin store guide
planche à voile
 windsurf, sailboard; windsurfing
planche de surf surfboard
plaque minéralogique
 license plate
plongée interdite no diving
plat du jour dish of the day
plats à emporter take-away
plongeoir diving board
poids de bagages autorisé
 luggage allowance
poids lourd heavy goods vehicle
poids maximum autorisé en charge
 load limit

poids net net weight
point d'eau water tap
point de rassemblement
 meeting place
point de rendez-
 vous/rencontre
 meeting point
point de vue view point
point noir blackspot
point téléphone pay phone
poisson fish
poissonnerie fish stall
police (de la route) (traffic) police
pompe à essence pump
pompiers firefighters
pont bridge; deck
pont basculant drawbridge
pont cabines cabin decks
pont des véhicules car deck
pont promenade sun deck
port port, harbor
port du casque obligatoire crash
 helmets obligatory
porte (d'embarquement)
 (boarding) gate , door
porte anti-incendie fire door
porte de secours fire (protection) door
les portes seront fermées ... minutes
 après le début de la représentation
 doors close ... minutes after
 performance begins
portier de nuit night porter
posologie dosage
poste post office
poulailler gallery
pour cheveux gras/normaux/secs
 for oily/normal/dry hair
pour débutants for beginners
pour deux personnes for two
pour obtenir la réception,
 composez le ... dial ... for reception
pour obtenir un numéro à l'extérieur,
 composez le ... dial ... for an outside
 line
pour tout échange, conservez votre
 ticket de caisse keep your receipt for
 exchange or refund
pour tous renseignements, s'adresser à
 for inquiries, see ...
pour usage externe
 not to be taken internally
2 pour le prix d'1 buy 2 get 1 free
pourboire tip
pousser push

A-Z

A-Z

précautions d'emploi instructions for use
premier balcon dress circle
premier étage first (U.S. second) floor
première classe first class
premiers secours first aid
prendre/prenez le ticket take ticket
à prendre après les repas/à la fin des repas take after meals
prenez un jeton à la caisse buy a token at cash desk
préparation rapide easy-cook
présentez vos papiers show your registration documents
présenter vos sacs ouverts à la sortie du magasin show your bags before leaving the store
pressing dry-cleaner's
prière de … please …
prière de présenter la somme exacte exact fare, no change given
prière de s'essuyer les pieds avant d'entrer please wipe your feet
prières prayers
primeur greengrocer's
printemps spring
priorité à droite right of way
prise en charge minimum (standard) charge
prise pour rasoirs seulement shavers only
privé private
prix au litre price per liter
prix cassés reduced prices, sale prices
prix des chambres room rate
prix nets no discounts
prochain arrêt bus stopping
prochaine levée à … h next collection at …
prochaine séance/visite à … next performance/tour at …
proche des commerces/plages within easy reach of shops/the sea
produits congelés frozen foods
produits diététiques health foods
produits laitiers dairy products
propriété privée private property
P&T Post & telecommunications

PTT Post, Telegraph, Telephone (Bel., Sw.)
puits well
PV parking ticket

Q

quai platform; docks
quartier d'affaires business district
quincaillerie hardware store

R

rabais discount
radeaux de sauvetage lifeboats
rafraîchissements refreshments available
ralentir slow down
ralentissement slowdown [tailback]
ralentisseurs speed bumps
Rameaux Palm Sunday
rangée row, tier
RATP Parisian transport authority
rayon department
réactualisé updated
réduction money off
refermer la barrière keep gate shut
régime diet
remboursement refund
remis à jour updated
renseignements information desk
réparations repairs
représentation performance
RER Paris suburban subway
réseau network
réservations faites à l'avance advance bookings
réservations pour la représentation de ce soir tickets for tonight
réservé reserved
réservé au fret freight only
réservé aux riverains access (to residents) only
réservés aux abonnés season ticket holders only
résidence apartment building
résiste aux chocs shockproof
restez en première leave your car in first gear
retard de … mn/h … minutes/hours delay
retardé delayed
retirez votre argent/carte take your money/card
retrait des bagages baggage claim

retraits withdrawals
revue magazine, periodical
revue de bandes dessinées comics
rez-de-chaussée ground floor
rez-de-jardin garden apartment
RF French Republic
rien à déclarer nothing to declare
risque d'orages storm warning
riverains autorisés residents only
rivière river
RN national highway
rocade bypass
romans fiction/novels
rond-point circle/roundabout
roulez à droite drive on the right
roulez au pas dead slow
route road
route à péage toll road
route à quatre voies two-lane highway
route départementale secondary road
route en travaux road under
 construction
route étroite narrow road
route fermée road closed
route nationale main road
route verglacée icy road
RU (Royaume-Uni) UK
rue street
rue à double sens two-way street
rue à sens unique one-way street
ruelle lane, alley
ruisseau stream

S s/ on, at
SA Ltd., Inc.
 sables mouvants quicksand
la Saint-Sylvestre New Year's Eve
salle hall; ward
salle à manger dining room
salle d'attente waiting room
salle de bains bathroom
salle de jeux game room
salle de petit déjeuner breakfast room
salle de réunion conference room
salle de soins treatment room
salle en étage seats upstairs
salon lounge
samedi Saturday
SAMU emergency medical service
sanisette automated public toilet
sans arrêt jusqu'à ... non-stop to ...
sans entracte no intermission
sans issue dead-end
sans plomb unleaded

sans sucre sugar-free
sauf le ... except on ...
saut à l'élastique
 bungee-jumping
sèche-cheveux hairdryer
secours emergency
sel salt
self self-service restaurant
selon arrivage/disponibilité
 subject to availability
selon saison according to season
(à la) semaine (per) week
la semaine seulement weekdays only
sens interdit no entry
sens unique one-way street
sentier (balisé) (marked) path, footpath
serrez à droite keep to the right
serrez à gauche keep to the left
service service charge; department
service clientèle customer service
service compris service included
service des chambres room service
service non-compris service not
 included
service omnibus local [stopping] service
le service n'est pas compris
 service charge not included
services de secours emergency services
SI tourist office
servir froid best served chilled
seulement only
siège (près de l')allée aisle seat
siège réservé aux personnes ayant des
 difficultés à se tenir debout please give
 up this seat to the old or infirm
signal d'alarme emergency brake
site classé conservation area
ski de descente downhill skiing
ski de fond/de randonnée
 cross-country skiing
ski hors-piste interdit
 no skiing off the trail [off-piste]
ski nautique waterskiing
skooter des mers jet ski
société de dépannage
 emergency road [breakdown] service
soie silk
soins de beauté beauty care
soins intensifs intensive care
soldes (clearance) sale
soldes avant changement d'activités
 closing down sale
les soldes ne seront pas échangés sale
 goods cannot be exchanged

A-Z

sommet peak
sonner, SVP please ring the bell
sonnette de nuit night bell
sortie exit, way out
sortie de poids lourds/de camions truck exit
sortie de secours emergency exit, fire exit
sortie interdite no exit
sortir par la porte arrière/avant exit by the rear/front door
SOS amitié helpline
... sous peine d'amende/de poursuites ... under penalty of a fine/prosecution
sous-titré subtitled
sous-vêtements lingerie, underwear
soyez prudent drive carefully
spectacle show
stade stadium
standardiste operator
station de gonflage air pump
station de péage toll booth
station de taxis taxi stand
stationnement autorisé parking permitted
stationnement gênant keep clear
stationnement interdit no parking
station essence/service service/filling station
sucre sugar
(du) sud south(ern)
suivre le mode d'emploi follow usage instructions
super four-star/super gasoline
sur on, at
sur commande made to order
surf des neiges snowboard
surveillée supervised
SVP (s'il vous plaît) please
syndicat d'initiative tourist office

T

taille économique economy size
taille unique one size fits all
tarif de jour/nuit day/night rate
tarif des consommations price list
tarif normal/réduit first-/second-class mail
tarif postaux intérieurs/pour l'étranger inland/overseas postage
tarif réduit/spécial reduced/special fare
tarifs rates

taux d'achat buying rate
taux de change exchange rate
taux de vente selling rate
télécarte phonecard
télécopie faxes sent
téléphérique cable car, gondola
téléphone à cartes card telephone
téléphone bureau work phone number
téléphone de secours emergency telephone
téléphone domicile home phone number
télévision dans toutes les chambres TV in every room
tenez votre droite keep to the right
tenir au frais et au sec keep cool and dry
tenue de ville informal wear
tergal® terylene®
terminer le traitement finish the treatment
terrain d'aviation airfield
terrain vague vacant lot
tête de station taxi stand
TGV (train à grande vitesse) extra-high-speed train
théâtre de boulevard farce
timbres stamps
tir à l'arc archery
tire-fesses ski tow
tirer pull
tissus fabrics
tissus d'ameublement soft furnishings
titre de transport ticket
tour de hanches/poitrine/taille hip/chest/waist measurement
tour tower
tous les jours sauf ... every day except ...
tous les plats ci-dessus sont servis accompagnés de ... all the above served with ...
tout article cassé doit être payé all breakages must be paid for
tout compris all inclusive
tout contrevenant sera puni penalty for traveling without ticket
tout public universal (movie)
toutes directions all directions
toutes les ... heures every ... hours
toutes opérations all transactions
train à supplément supplement to pay on this train
train auto-couchettes motorail train
train corail local train
train de nuit sleeper (train)

train grandes lignes intercity train
train omnibus local train
tranchée cutting
travaux construction [roadworks] ahead
tribunal courthouse
tribune stand, grandstand
trousse de secours first-aid kit
TTC inclusive of tax
TVA comprise VAT/sales tax included

U **UE** European Union
un train peut en cacher un autre
one train may hide another
une collation vous sera servie
a snack will be served
une pièce d'identité sera exigée
proof of identity required
uniquement only
... unités disponibles
... units remaining
utiliser avant ... use before ...
urgences emergency
usage externe for external use only
usine factory

V **vacances** vacation [holiday]
valable jusqu'au valid until ...
valeur nutritionnelle nutritional
information
valide jusqu'au ... valid until ...
validez validate
variétés popular music
véhicules lents slow vehicles
véhicules lourds heavy vehicles
veilleuses sidelights, parking lights
vélo bicycle
vélomoteur moped
à vendre for sale
vendredi Friday
verglas black ice
vérifier votre monnaie
check your change
vernissage preview, opening
verre glass
vestiaires changing rooms
vêtements pour femmes/hommes
ladies wear/menswear
veuillez ... please ...
veuillez attendre votre tour please wait
your turn
**veuillez composter votre titre
de transport** please cancel your ticket
veuillez laisser descendre les passagers
let passengers off first

**veuillez payer avant
de vous servir**
please pay for gas before
filling car
**veuillez respecter ce lieu
de culte**
please respect this place of
worship
viande meat
vidange graissage oil change
vignes vineyard
vignoble winery
villa individuelle detached house
village de vacances holiday village
ville city/town
vin wine
virage dangereux dangerous bend
viseur viewfinder
vitesse limitée à ... speed limit ...
vitesse maximum maximum speed
VO in original language (movie)
voie lane; platform
voie à double sens two-way traffic
voie ferrée railroad/railway
voie rapide expressway
voie sans issue no through road
voile sailing
voir date fond de la boîte
see date on bottom of can/box
voiture car, automobile
vols intérieurs domestic flights
vous êtes ici you are here
voyages travel
vu à ... as seen on ...

 wagon-lit sleeping car
zone à stationnement limité
limited parking zone
zone bleue restricted parking zone
zone commerciale shopping area
zone de déchargement loading bay
zone piétonne pedestrian zone

Reference

Numbers	216	Public holidays	219
Days/Months/		Time	220
Dates	218	Maps	222
Greetings	219	Quick reference	223

Numbers

GRAMMAR

Larger numbers are built up using the components below: e.g.
  2,567,498 = **deux million, cinq cents soixante-dix-sept mille, quatre cents quatre-vingt-dix-huit**

Note that the French use a comma for a decimal point and a period or space to indicate '000s; e.g. 4.575.000; 265.932; 4,95 FF

In certain areas of Belgium and Switzerland, 70 = **septante**, 80 = **huitante**, 90 = **nonante**.

0	**zéro** *zayroa*		18	**dix-huit** *deezweet*
1	**un** *ang*		19	**dix-neuf** *deesnurf*
2	**deux** *dur*		20	**vingt** *vang*
3	**trois** *trwa*		21	**vingt et un** *vangt ay ang*
4	**quatre** *katr*		22	**vingt-deux** *vangt dur*
5	**cinq** *sangk*		23	**vingt-trois** *vangt trwa*
6	**six** *seess*		24	**vingt-quatre** *vangt katr*
7	**sept** *set*		25	**vingt-cinq** *vangt sangk*
8	**huit** *weet*		26	**vingt-six** *vangt seess*
9	**neuf** *nurf*		27	**vingt-sept** *vangt set*
10	**dix** *deess*		28	**vingt-huit** *vangt weet*
11	**onze** *awngz*		29	**vingt-neuf** *vangt nurf*
12	**douze** *dooz*		30	**trente** *trahngt*
13	**treize** *trez*		31	**trente et un** *trahngt ay ang*
14	**quatorze** *katorz*		32	**trente-deux** *trahngt dur*
15	**quinze** *kangz*		40	**quarante** *karahngt*
16	**seize** *sez*			
17	**dix-sept** *deesset*			

50	**cinquante** *sangkahngt*
60	**soixante** *swassahngt*
70	**soixante-dix** *swassahngt deess*
71	**soixante et onze** *swassahngt ay awngz*
80	**quatre-vingts** *katr vang*
81	**quatre-vingt-un** *katr vang ang*
90	**quatre-vingt-dix** *katr vang deess*
100	**cent** *sahng*
101	**cent un** *sahng ang*
102	**cent deux** *sahng dur*
200	**deux cents** *dur sahng*
500	**cinq cents** *sangk sahng*
1 000	**mille** *meel*
10 000	**dix mille** *dee meel*
35 750	**trente cinq mille sept cent cinquante** *trahngt sangk meel set sahng sangkahngt*
1 000 000	**un million** *ang meelyawng*
first	**premier(-ière)** *prermyay(-yehr)*
second	**second/deuxième** *sergawng/durzyem*
third	**troisième** *trwazyem*
fourth	**quatrième** *katryem*
fifth	**cinquième** *sangkyem*

once	**une fois** *ewn fwa*
twice	**deux fois** *dur fwa*
three times	**trois fois** *trwa fwa*
a half	**une moitié** *ewn mwatyay*
half an hour	**une demi-heure** *ewn dermee urr*
half a tank	**un demi réservoir** *ang dermee rayzehrvwar*
half eaten	**à moitié mangé** *a mwatyay mahngzhay*
a quarter	**un quart** *ang kar*
a third	**un tiers** *ang tyehr*
a pair of ...	**deux .../une paire de ...** *dur/ewn pehr der*
a dozen ...	**une douzaine de/d' ...** *ewn doozayn der/d*
1997	**mille neuf cent quatre-vingt-dix-sept** *meel nurf sahng katr vang deesset*
2001	**deux mille un** *dur meel ang*
the 1990s	**les années mille neuf cent quatre-vingt-dix** *lay zanay meel nurf sahng katr vang dees*

Days Jours

Monday	**lundi** *langdee*
Tuesday	**mardi** *mardee*
Wednesday	**mercredi** *mehrkrerdee*
Thursday	**jeudi** *zhurdee*
Friday	**vendredi** *vahngdrerdee*
Saturday	**samedi** *samdee*
Sunday	**dimanche** *deemahngsh*

Months Mois

January	**janvier** *zhahngvyay*
February	**février** *fayvryay*
March	**mars** *marss*
April	**avril** *avreel*
May	**mai** *may*
June	**juin** *zhwang*
July	**juillet** *zhweeyeh*
August	**août** *oot*
September	**septembre** *setahngbr*
October	**octobre** *oktobr*
November	**novembre** *novahngbr*
December	**décembre** *daysahngbr*

Dates Dates

It's …	**Nous sommes …** *noo som*
July 10	**le dix juillet** *ler dees zhweeyeh*
Tuesday, March 1	**mardi premier mars** *mardee prermyay marss*
yesterday	**hier** *yehr*
today	**aujourd'hui** *oazhoordwee*
tomorrow	**demain** *dermang*
this …/last …	**ce …/… dernier** *ser/dehrnyay*
next week	**la semaine prochaine** *la sermayn proshayn*
every month/year	**tous les mois/ans** *too lay mwa/zahng*
on [at] the weekend	**(pendant) le weekend** *(pahngdahng) ler weekend*

Seasons Saisons

spring	**printemps**	*prangtahng*
summer	**été**	*aytay*
fall [autumn]	**automne**	*oatonn*
winter	**hiver**	*eevehr*
in spring	**au printemps**	*oa prangtahng*
during the summer	**pendant l'été**	*pahngdahng laytay*

Greetings Souhaits et vœux

Happy birthday!	**Bon anniversaire!**	*bon aneevehrsehr*
Merry Christmas!	**Joyeux Noël!**	*zhwahyur nowell*
Happy New Year!	**Bonne année!**	*bon annay*
Happy Easter!	**Joyeuses Pâques!**	*zhwahyurz pak*
Best wishes!	**Meilleurs vœux!**	*mayurr vur*
Congratulations!	**Félicitations!**	*fayleesseetasyawng*
Good luck!	**Bonne chance!**	*bon shahngss*
Have a good trip!	**Bon voyage!**	*bawng vwahyazh*
Give my regards to …	**Donnez le bonjour à …**	
	donnay ler bawngzhoor a	

Public holidays Jours fériés

National holidays in France (F), Belgium (B) and Switzerland (CH):

			F	CH	B
January 1	**Nouvel An**	New Year's Day	F	CH	B
January 2				CH	
May 1	**Fête du Travail**	Labor Day	F		
May 8	**Fête de la Libération**	Victory Day (1945)	F		
July 14	**Fête Nationale**	Bastille Day	F		
July 21	**Fête Nationale**	National Holiday			B
August 1	**Fête Nationale**	National Holiday		CH	
August 15	**Assomption**	Assumption Day	F		B
November 1	**Toussaint**	All Saints Day	F		B
November 11	**Armistice**	Armistice Day	F		B
December 25	**Noël**	Christmas	F	CH	B
December 26	**Saint-Etienne**	St Stephen's Day		CH	
Movable dates:					
	Vendredi-Saint	Good Friday	F	CH	
	Lundi de Pâques	Easter Monday	F	CH	B
	Ascension	Ascension	F	CH	B
	Lundi de Pentecôte	Pentecost Monday	F	CH	B

Time Les heures

The official time system uses the 24-hour clock. However, in ordinary conversation, time is generally expressed as shown below, often with the addition of **du matin** (morning), **de l'après-midi** (afternoon) or **du soir** (evening).

Excuse me. Can you tell me the time?	**Pardon. Pouvez-vous me dire l'heure?** *pardawng poovay voo mer deer lurr*
It's …	**Il est …** *eel eh*
five past one	**une heure cinq** *ewn urr sangk*
ten past two	**deux heures dix** *dur zurr deess*
a quarter past three	**trois heures et quart** *trwa zurr ay kar*
twenty past four	**quatre heures vingt** *katr urr vangt*
twenty-five past five	**cinq heures vingt-cinq** *sangk urr vangt sangk*
half past six	**six heures et demie** *see zurr ay dermee*
twenty-five to seven	**sept heures moins vingt-cinq** *set urr mwang vangt sangk*
twenty to eight	**huit heures moins vingt** *weet urr mwang vang*
a quarter to nine	**neuf heures moins le quart** *nurf urr mwang ler kar*
ten to ten	**dix heures moins dix** *dee zurr mwang deess*
five to eleven	**onze heures moins cinq** *awngz urr mwang sangk*
twelve o'clock (noon/midnight)	**midi/minuit** *meedee/meenwee*

at dawn	**à l'aube** *a loab*
in the morning	**le matin** *ler matang*
during the day	**pendant la journée** *pahngdahng la zhoornay*
before lunch	**avant le repas** *avahng ler rerpa*
after lunch	**après le repas** *apreh ler rerpa*
in the afternoon	**dans l'après-midi** *dahng lapreh-meedee*
in the evening	**dans la soirée** *dahng la swaray*
at night	**la nuit** *la nwee*
I'll be ready in five minutes.	**Je serai prêt(e) dans cinq minutes.** *zher serray preh(t) dahng sangk meenewt*
He'll be back in a quarter of an hour.	**Il sera de retour dans un quart d'heure.** *eel serra der rertoor dahng zang kar durr*
She arrived an hour ago.	**Elle est arrivée il y a une heure.** *el eh tareevay eel ee a ewn urr*
The train leaves at …	**Le train part à …** *ler trang par a*
13:04	**treize heures quatre** *trez urr katr*
0:40	**zéro heures quarante** *zayroa urr karahngt*
10 minutes late/early	**dix minutes en retard/en avance** *dee meenewt ahng rertar/ahng navahngss*
5 seconds fast/slow	**cinq secondes d'avance/de retard** *sangk sergawngd davahngss/der rertar*
from 9am to 5pm	**de neuf heures à cinq/dix-sept heures** *der nurf urr a sangk/deesset urr*
between 8am and 2pm	**entre huit heures et deux/quatorze heures** *ahngtr weet urr ay dur/katorz urr*
I'll be leaving by …	**Je partirai avant …** *zher parteeray avahng*
Will you be back before …?	**Est-ce que vous serez revenu(e)/ de retour avant …?** *ess ker voo serray rervernew/der rertoor avahng*
We'll be here until …	**Nous y serons jusqu'à …** *noo zee serrawng zhewska*

United
Kingdom

NORTH
SEA

Netherlands

ENGLISH CHANNEL

Calais

Lille

Belgium

Cherbourg

Le Havre

Luxembourg

PARIS

Orléans

Strasbourg

Nantes

France

BAY OF
BISCAY

Switzerland

Bordeaux

Lyon

Italy

Toulouse

Montpellier

Marseille

Monaco

Spain

MEDITERRANEAN SEA

Corsica

Netherlands
Antwerp
Belgium
BRUSSELS
Germany
Luxembourg
Czech Rep.
France
Zürich
BERN
Liechtenstein
Switzerland
Austria
Genève
Slovenia
Italy
Croatia

Quick reference En un coup d'œil

Good morning.	**Bonjour.** *bawngzhoor*
Good afternoon.	**Bonjour.** *bawngzhoor*
Good evening.	**Bonsoir.** *bawngswar*
Hello.	**Bonjour/Salut. (fam.)** *bawngzhoor/salew*
Good-bye.	**Au revoir.** *oa rervwar*
Excuse me (*getting attention*).	**Excusez-moi.** *exkewzay mwa*
Pardon?	**Pardon?** *pardawng*
Sorry!	**Pardon!** *pardawng*
Please.	**S'il vous plaît.** *seel voo pleh*
Thank you.	**Merci.** *mehrsee*
Do you speak English?	**Est-ce que vous parlez anglais?** *ess ker voo parlay ahngleh*
I don't understand.	**Je ne comprends pas.** *zher ner kawngprahng pa*
Where is ...?	**Où est ...?** *oo eh*
Where are the restrooms?	**Où sont les toilettes?** *oo sawng lay twalet*

Emergency Urgences

Help!	**Au secours!** *oa serkoor*
Go away!	**Allez vous-en!** *alay vooz ahng*
Leave me alone!	**Laissez-moi tranquille!** *layssay mwa trahngkee*
Call the police!	**Appelez la police!** *apperlay la poleess*
Stop thief!	**Au voleur!** *oa volurr*
Get a doctor!	**Allez chercher un médecin!** *alay shehrshay ang maydsang*
Fire!	**Au feu!** *oa fur*
I'm ill.	**Je suis malade.** *zher swee malad*
I'm lost.	**Je suis perdu(e).** *zher swee pehrdew*
Can you help me?	**Est-ce que vous pouvez m'aider?** *ess ker voo poovay mayday*

Emergency ☎	France	Belgium	Switzerland
Fire	**18**	100	*118*
Ambulance	**15**	100	*114 or 117*
Police	**17**	101	*117*
Embassies/Consulates ☎			
UK	**01 42 66 91 42**	287 6211	*031 352 50 21*
U.S.	**01 42 96 12 02**	513 3830	*031 43 70 11*
Canada	**01 44 43 29 00**	735 6040	*031 44 63 81*
Australia	**01 40 59 33 00**	231 0500	*031 43 01 43*